# Service-Learning

# Service-Learning

## A Movement's Pioneers Reflect on Its Origins, Practice, and Future

Timothy K. Stanton

Dwight E. Giles, Jr.

Nadinne I. Cruz

*Foreword by Goodwin Liu*

Jossey-Bass Publishers • San Francisco

Jossey-Bass books and products are available through most bookstores.
To contact Jossey-Bass directly, call (888) 378-2537, fax to (800) 605-2665,
or visit our website at www.josseybass.com.

Substantial discounts on bulk quantities of Jossey-Bass books are available to
corporations, professional associations, and other organizations. For details
and discount information, contact the special sales department at Jossey-Bass.

Manufactured in the United States of America on Lyons Falls Turin Book. This
paper is acid-free and 100 percent totally chlorine-free.

**Library of Congress Cataloging-in-Publication Data**

Stanton, Timothy K.
    Service-learning : a movement's pioneers reflect on its
origins, practice, and future  /  Timothy K. Stanton, Dwight E.
Giles, Jr., Nadinne I. Cruz; foreword by Goodwin Liu—1st ed.
    p.  cm.—(The Jossey-Bass higher and adult education series)
Includes bibliographical references and index.
ISBN 0-7879-4317-7 (cloth)
    1. Student service—United States—History.   2. Education,
Higher—Social aspects—United States—History.   I. Giles, Dwight E., Jr.
II. Cruz, Nadinne I., 1948–   III. Title.   IV. Series.
    LC220.5.S72  1999
    378'.015'0973—dc21                                                98-40252

FIRST EDITION
*PB Printing*                                          10 9 8 7 6 5 4 3 2 1

The Jossey-Bass
Higher and Adult Education Series

# Contents

# Foreword

Almost four years ago, at a national conference hosted by the American Association for Higher Education, I gave a speech hailing service-learning as a revolutionary pedagogy with the potential to transform existing paradigms of educational practice and institutional organization. The conference took place in Washington, D.C., at a high point of interest in the idea of integrating community service with the academic mission of colleges and universities. New programs were being created; old programs were being revitalized. Foundations saw great promise in the concept and put their resources into play. College presidents, federal officials (I was one at the time), and other educational leaders were on the stump across the nation, encouraging institutions to strengthen ties with their local communities and to provide students with opportunities to develop and sustain a life-long ethic of service. In that atmosphere of optimism, heady talk of revolution and paradigm shifts seemed appropriate, and my speech was well received.

Four years later, service-learning remains a vital force for educational change. For many faculty members, it is a creative method for relating the abstractions of disciplinary study to the realities of human need. For community-based organizations, it is an invitation to participate in the process of higher education and a mechanism to enlist the talents of student volunteers. For students, it is an opportunity to integrate the life of the mind with the habits of the heart. In these ways, service-learning offers a fresh response to what Paolo Freire called the "banking method" of education and to the banal stereotypes of young people as self-serving yuppies (the me generation) or apathetic slackers (generation X).

Much of the attention and excitement that service-learning has generated in higher education today is attributable to the sense of newness that its participants and advocates feel. Indeed, innovation and change have tremendous power to motivate. But the rhetoric of revolution, however motivational, rings true only on the surface.

To characterize service-learning as a new development in education is inaccurate at best and presumptuous at worst. The concept (if not the label) has an impressive pedigree that includes the university-based extension programs of the 1860s land grant movement, John Dewey's philosophical pragmatism during the early decades of this century, and the campus- and community-based organizing initiatives in the 1960s civil rights movement. Viewed in this context, the current movement is best understood not as a revolution in educational practice, but as a phase in the evolution of a more general aspiration to bring theory and practice, schools and communities, thought and action closer together. To be sure, there is ample creativity among today's service-learning practitioners, and much of their work will expand our insights into pedagogy and social activism. But it is a mistake to believe that the movement and its core commitments are new in any historical or conceptual sense.

The purpose of this observation is not to tame the hubris of those in the field today, nor is to glorify their predecessors. Rather, the primary purpose is to deepen our understanding of what service-learning is and what it should be, and to provoke inquiry into its potential and limitations. In other words, the history of service-learning provides a lens for evaluating our current practice. Prior movements, no less than the present, sought to address concrete community needs through structured initiatives embedded in a political context, circumscribed by institutional constraints, and shaped by various tensions between local and national leadership. The lessons learned from past attempts to implement related reforms should inform our approach to a set of common and fundamental questions: What theory of knowledge can account for the pedagogical role of community service? Should we aim to assimilate service-learning into the norms of the traditional academy, or should we advocate it as a critique of those basic norms? What does it mean to enlist the community as a true partner in education? Is it possible to build a national movement without unduly compromising local autonomy and self-determination?

There is no need or reason to answer these questions de novo. Rather, we should build on the insights of those who have confronted these challenges before.

A second purpose that is served by placing service-learning within a broader historical context is the cultivation of awareness within the current movement of its own significance as history—that is, its significance as a phenomenon worth recording and explaining so that future generations might learn from it. Today's practitioners are mired in issues of practice—how to sustain relationships with community partners, how to integrate service with disciplinary study, how to institutionalize programs—and this is what one would expect in a robust and evolving field of programming. However, it is important to step back from the day-to-day challenges of practice to examine not only the efficacy of particular programs but also their historic role within their respective institutional settings, as well as the role of the entire movement at this juncture of our nation's social and political life. In addition to thinking about such questions, it is important that we record our thoughts, no matter how tentative or incomplete. The point is not to aggrandize our work or to secure its place in history, but rather to enable future educators and advocates to share in our successes and prevent them from repeating our mistakes.

In the light of these purposes for telling service-learning's history, the principal virtues of this book come into clear focus. *Service-Learning* traces the work of thirty-three advocates, scholars, and practitioners of service-learning throughout the 1960s and beyond. It offers a close look not only at the structure and content of early efforts to combine education with social action, but also at the motivations and personal agendas of the pioneers themselves. The latter insights provide a precious resource for recognizing and reflecting on our own subjectivity. There is no doubt that the draw of service-learning is its normativity, but we are far from fully comprehending, much less agreeing on, exactly what service-learning ought to be or what it ought to do. Although the social context has changed, these fundamental questions remain the same, and from this book we derive both substantive guidance and the comfort of knowing that we are not the first to struggle with these difficult questions.

Rich in detail and deeply attentive to local circumstance, the book also offers a worthy example of how we in the current movement might record our own history. The unmediated voices of the early pioneers speak about their students, communities, and programs just as we might speak about our own. There is no reason, then, why we should not begin to write narratives of our present work. Firsthand accounts of the familiar and even the mundane will have greater importance as history than the most "objective" reconstruction of events by detached observers further down the road.

There is one additional virtue of this book, and that is its capacity to affirm and inspire the work of the current movement. In their storytelling, the early pioneers are careful not to inflate their own personas, but any reader who is even casually acquainted with the field of service-learning will recognize more than a handful of the people in this book and their work. Quite simply, these are the scholars and activists to whom we owe the greatest substantive and spiritual debts, and the most important payment we can offer is our best effort to motivate and teach the next generation just as they have motivated and taught us.

When Tim asked me to write this foreword, I asked him, "Why me?" After all, as a member of the new generation of service-learning advocates, I had a limited temporal perspective and all the biases that come with it. Tim had a simple and ready response. "We want to pass the torch on to you," he said. The comment—along with everything else Tim, Dwight, and Nadinne have said throughout the project—made clear to me that the purpose of this book is not to write heroes into history or to indulge the temptation of nostalgia. Rather, its purpose is to teach, to inspire, and to expand the vision of those of us who, knowingly or not, inherit the achievements of the movement's early pioneers.

Washington, D.C.                                           GOODWIN LIU
November 1998

# Preface

The past decade has been breathtaking for service-learning. A new generation of practitioners has expanded the number and variety of service-learning courses and programs across all sectors of postsecondary education, as well as at the K–12 level. Service-learning pedagogy is now advocated by students, faculty, presidents of colleges and universities, and even by Congress and the president of the United States (Wutzdorff and Giles, 1997).

This is a remarkable change for a pedagogical practice that until the mid-1980s was largely unknown beyond a small, loosely connected circle of practitioners, who in the 1960s began exploring how community action and academic learning could be integrated. In fact, to the three of us, and to many of these practitioners, some of whom lost their jobs as a result of advocating and practicing this pedagogy, this change is astonishing.

Nevertheless, although we are amazed and pleased by this change, we worry. What accounts for service-learning's rapid proliferation in postsecondary education? Have institutions transformed themselves sufficiently so that a once-suspect "radical pedagogy" can be viewed as mainstream? Or has this pedagogy been adapted to survive and expand in the mainstream? When we listen carefully to a new generation of practitioners who lead the field's expansion, we do not find much dialogue on these questions. What we hear instead is discussion of service-learning as "new"—without a past, without roots, without reference to the multiple and sometimes conflicting purposes that animate its history. Indeed it seems often as if service-learning has no history.

In addition, although most institutions and an increasing number of schools support service-learning in some form, the field's literature has only recently begun to draw connections between practice and relevant theoretical work in human development, learning theory and pedagogy, knowledge transformation and epistemology, and social change. Discussion of deep questions related to service-learning's connection to both knowledge and community development, the answers to which can inform and improve practice, is lacking.

In our view, service-learning suffers from "jet lag," or rather "history lag." Due to the field's rapid expansion and perhaps its activist orientation, practitioners appear to operate without a sense of where service-learning came from, why it was developed, and how its varied models and purposes intersect or collide. Assuming that we cannot effectively chart the future unless we understand the past, we worry that this history lag will seriously limit service-learning's potential to develop citizens, build communities, and transform teaching and learning in the academy. This book is our response.

In these pages, some of service-learning's first practitioners reflect on and analyze their work combining service and learning on behalf of students, communities, and postsecondary education institutions. Based on these reflections, they assess existing practice and recommend steps for future policy and practice. Their stories provide a picture of what this field is, where it came from, and what its early practitioners hoped it would be about. In a broader sense, we believe these stories represent a picture of the experience of leaders of any other twentieth-century social movement. Ultimately, our intention is to give this field, which has shaped and supported the three of us so well over many years, a sense of its rich, colorful, diverse, and largely unknown origins. In so doing, we hope to stimulate both individual and collective reflection on this work, and help pass it on to the next generation of practitioners.

Service-learning is at a historic moment. Now that it is in the spotlight, with many new, young staff and faculty involved and many of its early practitioners having retired, passed on, or left the field, there is a need to pass the torch. Through this book, we hope to help these new practitioners, and the broader education community, become aware of service-learning's history, and thereby use its lessons to help the field become more empowered, not as a passing trend but as a critical strategy in the renovation of American education.

## Overview

In the first chapter we describe our approach to developing this story, our strategy to have this field reflect on its past, present, and future. We offer a brief description of service-learning and explain how we identified a small, representative, and influential group of early practitioner storytellers, a group we came to call the service-learning pioneers.

In Chapter Two Seth Pollack offers a conceptual framework for service-learning's beginnings and for introducing the pioneers.

Chapter Three begins the story by drawing on accounts from the pioneers of formative, personal experiences, "seeds of commitment," which they identify as pointing them toward service-learning.

In Chapter Four the pioneers describe their first service-learning roles and contexts, that is, their professional entry into the field. What did they do, how, where, and why?

In Chapter Five, the pioneers tell how and why they targeted postsecondary education as the locus of their commitment to combine service and learning.

Chapters Six and Seven provide a picture of the variety of service-learning practice developed and established by the pioneers. The stories in Chapter Six come from those pioneers who most strongly focused on student development or individual empowerment through service-learning. Those represented in Chapter Seven come from pioneers most strongly motivated to empower and develop communities.

Chapter Eight provides pioneers' stories of their struggles to maintain, sustain, and institutionalize service-learning, often in the face of substantial challenges, in a variety of college and university contexts.

Chapter Nine examines the pioneer experience itself. Here our storytellers identify and assess the outcomes of their work, and the challenges and supports they encountered.

In Chapter Ten the pioneers reflect on their experience in service-learning to share lessons learned and recommendations they have for those concerned with current and future service-learning policy and practice.

The appendixes provide a list of service-learning strands and a historical timeline for service-learning prepared by Robert Sigmon.

## Acknowledgments

We are deeply indebted to the individuals whose stories fill this book. Without them, it would not exist. We especially appreciate their willingness to share and trust us with their stories, and their assistance in weaving them together into a history of service-learning. We feel privileged to be colleagues with them all.

We thank Ellen Porter Honnet, program consultant for The Johnson Foundation, who provided invaluable assistance and support in designing the Wingspread conference where we convened most of the service-learning pioneers to collect and analyze their stories. Ellen's skillful facilitation ensured its success.

Our nominators, J. Herman Blake, Richard Couto, Jane Kendall, and Robert Sigmon, helped select a representative sample of pioneers for both the Wingspread conference and for interviews. Sigmon helped with interviewing and graciously facilitated our use of his service-learning timeline, An Organizational Journey to Service-Learning.

Louis Albert, former vice president of the American Association for Higher Education; Linda Chisholm, vice president of the Partnership for Service-Learning; Fleda Mask Jackson, visiting professor at Emory University; Sally Migliore, executive director of the National Society for Experiential Education; and Nancy Rhodes, former director of Campus Compact, represented their organizations, shared their service-learning stories, and assisted us in analyzing those of the pioneers at the Wingspread conference.

Seth Pollack and Goodwin Liu provided important intellectual assistance by writing discussion papers for the conference. Pollack helped plan the conference and contributed a summary of his paper as Chapter Two. We appreciate Liu's writing the foreword and helping us link the pioneers' stories with new practitioners in the field.

Shellye McKinney served as the Wingspread conference coordinator. Heather Ramírez assisted Pollack with Chapter Two and served as a relentless research and editorial assistant.

Data analysis for this project was made easier by accurate tape transcriptions prepared by JoAnn Johnson. Sharon Powell skillfully and patiently analyzed the small mountain of transcripts into data files and thematic summaries that helped us weave the pioneers' stories into a book.

Gale Erlandson, senior editor for higher and adult education at Jossey-Bass, and her staff provided encouragement, wise advice, and technical support. The book benefited significantly from thoughtful and meticulous reading by and consultation from Anne Colby, Elizabeth Hollander, Cynthia Scheinberg, and Rachel Livsey.

Financial assistance was provided by The Johnson Foundation, Racine, Wisconsin, and an anonymous donor.

Finally, we appreciate the support and patient understanding we received from our families as we carried out conference calls, meetings, travel, and late nights and weekends of writing, which drew us away from normal family life.

Palo Alto, California        TIMOTHY K. STANTON
Nashville, Tennessee        DWIGHT E. GILES, JR.
Palo Alto, California        NADINNE I. CRUZ
November 1998

# The Authors

*Timothy K. Stanton* serves as director of the Haas Center for Public Service and lecturer in American studies, education, and public policy at Stanford University. Prior to joining the Haas Center, Stanton directed and taught courses within the Human Ecology Field Study Program at Cornell University. He also founded and directed a community-based service-learning program for high school and college students in Marin County, California. Stanton is past-president of the National Society for Experiential Education (NSEE). He consults extensively on service-learning program development and assessment for colleges and universities, NSEE, and Campus Compact. He is a member of the Compact's Research Advisory Committee. Stanton's research interests focus on student and faculty development related to service-learning.

*Dwight E. Giles, Jr.,* is professor of the practice of human and organizational development and director of internships at Peabody College of Vanderbilt University. Before coming to Vanderbilt, he was a faculty member and program director of the Human Ecology Field and International Study Program at Cornell University for twelve years, where he taught fieldwork preparation and field study courses and was instrumental in the establishment of the Public Service Center. Giles has served as a national and international consultant in experiential and service-learning for colleges and universities, foundations, and professional societies. He served on the board of the National Society for Experiential Education and chaired the research committee for five years. He is a member of the academic advisory board of the Institute for Experiential Learning in Washington, D.C., and serves as the North American academic consultant for U.K. Centres for Experiential Learning. He co-organized a national Wingspread conference in 1991 to develop a research agenda for service-learning and is currently part of the Campus Compact working group on developing a national strategy for service-learning research.

*Nadinne I. Cruz,* a Filipina American educator, is associate director of the Haas Center for Public Service at Stanford University, where she provides leadership for the center's programming for over forty student and staff-led programs and directs the Public Service Scholars Program, which challenges seniors to shape their honors theses into research as a form of service. Cruz is also a lecturer in urban studies, teaching service-learning courses. She has been executive director of the Higher Education Consortium for Urban Affairs, which develops community-based programs focused on issues of urban inequality in diverse locations. As the Eugene M. Lang Visiting Professor for Social Change at Swarthmore College in 1993, she piloted service-learning for the Political Science Department's Democratic Practice Project. She is a frequent public speaker and workshop presenter on service-learning and issues of diversity and social change.

## Contributors

*Seth S. Pollack* is the director of the Service Learning Institute at California State University (CSU) at Monterey Bay, the newest campus of the CSU system and the only campus to have integrated service-learning as a graduation requirement. Pollack is an organizational sociologist whose research has focused on how organizations influence the way in which society addresses important social policy problems. As a community development worker, Pollack has extensive experience working with participatory development projects in Africa, Asia, and Central America. He is producer of the award-winning PBS documentary film series *The Quiet Revolution,* which captures success stories in sustainable rural development from around the globe.

*Robert L. Sigmon* is president of Learning Design Initiatives, a service-based experiential learning consultation practice, and senior associate with the Council of Independent Colleges. He has been involved with service-based experiential learning since the early

1960s with the American Friends Service Committee, Southern Regional Education Board, State of North Carolina, Public Health School of the University of South Carolina, Wake Area Health Education Center program in North Carolina, and the National Society for Experiential Education.

*To all pioneers of service-learning, known and unknown to us, and especially to Alec Dickson, founder of Community Service Volunteers, whose worldwide efforts to link service and study inspired us to enter this field and whose passing inspired us to write this book.*

# Chapter One

# Helping a "New" Field Discover Its History

*The simplest vehicle of truth, the story, is*
*also said to be . . . "the natural form for revealing life."*
T. MINH-HA TRINH (1989)

The 1960s and early 1970s were times of turbulent upheaval and change in communities and on college campuses. Urban uprisings and the War on Poverty brought attention and resources to the nation's social problems. Loosely coupled student activists and "alternative," "humanistic" educators began chipping away at what they perceived as a monolithic, teacher-centered, alienating, and irrelevant education system that failed to involve and serve an increasingly diverse population of learners.

Within these community- and campus-based movements was a small number of individuals concerned with connecting elements in both movements. They were community activists and educators who found themselves drawn to the idea that action in communities and structured learning could be combined to provide stronger service and leadership in communities and deeper, more relevant education for students. Most of these individuals worked independently and against the grain of what was expected and accepted in communities and the academy. It would take time for them to find each other, conceptualize their work, and begin to institutionalize it as a pedagogy and as a field. Their labors laid the foundation and sowed the seeds for what we now call service-learning, which has proliferated so widely across postsecondary and K–12 education.

This is their story. In the following chapters, thirty-three early practitioners of service-learning describe the trials and tribulations of seeking to develop, establish, and institutionalize postsecondary education courses and programs that combine learning and action in off-campus communities. We have captured these stories and woven them together in a manner that expresses service-learning's interactive, collaborative, participatory, person-centered values. Our goal is to provide a historical consciousness for today's service-learning advocates and practitioners, enabling them to use lessons from the past to strengthen service-learning's future.

## Defining Service-Learning

Service-learning joins two complex concepts: community action, the "service," and efforts to learn from that action and connect what is learned to existing knowledge, the "learning." Although the genealogy of existing practice—what we came to term its DNA—can be traced back to the 1960s, its conceptual antecedents can be found in the philosophy and practice of extension education programs spawned by the land grant movement of the 1860s, in progressive education and settlement house activities early in this century, in work programs of the New Deal, in immigrant education and civil rights organizing efforts (Pollack, 1996). As we shall learn, many early practitioners had experience in the Peace Corps or VISTA.

The earliest definition of service-learning—the accomplishment of tasks that meet genuine human needs in combination with conscious educational growth—can be found in publications of the Southern Regional Education Board (SREB) (1969). In defining and trying to establish service-learning, SREB practitioners were concerned with developing learning opportunities for students that were related to community service, community development, and social change.

Service-learning is not value neutral, or at least it was not in its early expressions. Jane Kendall, former executive director of the National Society for Experiential Education (NSEE), notes that "a good service-learning program helps participants see their [service] questions in the larger context of issues of social justice and social policy—rather than in the context of charity" (1990, p. 20). For example, service-learning programs should not just recruit students to volunteer in soup kitchens. They should also ask them to reflect on why people are hungry. Literacy volunteers should be asked to consider why there are so many illiterate people in an "advanced society."

Service-learning advocates question whether experience alone will yield help for communities and development of civic consciousness in students (Couto, 1982). They call for structured opportunities for critical reflection on service so students "better understand the causes of social injustice . . . [and] take actions to eliminate the causes" (Baker, 1983, p. 10).

In conference presentations and workshops, Michele Whitham, a faculty member in Cornell University's Human Ecology Field Study Program, often described service-learning as on the enabling to empowering end of the service–social change continuum, emphasizing support for people who seek to address their own needs as opposed to a "doing for" kind of service. This articulation is well aligned with "three principles for service-learning" declared by Robert Sigmon (1979), one of the SREB practitioners. The three principles are as follows:

1. Those being served control the services(s) provided.
2. Those being served become better able to serve and be served by their own actions.
3. Those who serve are also learners and have significant control over what is expected to be learned.

Service-learning advocates differentiate their practice from volunteer service by evoking the concept of reciprocity between server and served as well. Such an exchange "avoids the traditionally paternalistic, one-way approach to service in which one group or person has resources which they share 'charitably' or 'voluntarily' with a person or group that lacks resources" (Kendall, 1990, p. 22). In service-learning, those being served control the service (Sigmon, 1979). The needs of the community, rather than of the academy, determine the nature of the service provided.

This view is summarized by the slogan, "I serve you in order that I may learn from you. You accept my service in order that you may teach me" (Stanton, 1992).

Service-learning's early practitioners made their pedagogical home in the field of experiential education. To ensure that service promotes substantive learning, they sought to connect students' experience to reflection and analysis provided in the curriculum (Duley, 1981). They pointed to the importance of contact with complex, contemporary social problems and efforts to solve them as an important element of a complete education. They invoked theories of Bandura (1977), Coleman (1977), Dewey (1963), Freire (1970, 1973), Kolb (1984), Argyris and Schön (1978), Resnick (1987), Schön (1983, 1987), and others to explain the pedagogical foundations of their practice. They saw service-learning, when it combined action with critical reflection, conceptualization, and abstract experimentation with analyses, as standing very much within the liberal arts tradition (Stanton, 1990a).

Morris Keeton, founder in 1974 of the Council for Adult and Experiential Learning (CAEL),[1] viewed this critical reflection approach to service-learning as a direct expression of John Dewey's theories of education: "As Dewey ([1938] 1951) states, this process at least results in a 'reconstruction' of experience (as in the formulation of the Newtonian laws of motion or in Einstein's reformulation), a recodifying of habits (as in overcoming racial bias), and ongoing questioning of old ideas (a habit of learning experientially). Thus, experiential learning so pursued transforms the individual, revises and enlarges knowledge, and alters practice. It affects the aesthetic and ethical commitments of individuals and alters their perceptions and interpretations of the world" (Keeton, 1983, p. 1).

For these experiential educators, community service and academic excellence are "not competitive demands to be balanced through discipline and personal sacrifice [by students], but rather . . . interdependent dimensions of good intellectual work" (Wagner, 1986 p. 17). They see their challenge as "devising ways to connect study and service so that the disciplines illuminate and inform experience, and experience lends meaning and energy to the disciplines" (Eskow, 1980, p. 21).

Service-learning has thus developed a values-oriented philosophy of education. "Rather than a discrete [program] type," writes Stanton (1987, p. 4), "service-learning appears to be an approach to experiential learning, an expression of values—service to others, community development and empowerment, reciprocal learning—which determines the purpose, nature and process of social and educational exchange between learners and the people they serve, and between experiential education programs and the community organizations with which they work."

It is a "pedagogy of learning through service" (Chisholm, 1987, p. 3), using structures such as preservice preparation courses, field seminars, reflection workshops, "critical incident journals" (a structured approach to reflecting on and writing about experience), and other means to encourage and support student learning from experience (Whitham and Stanton, 1979; Permaul, 1981; Duley, 1981; Batchelder, 1977). Its educational goals are articulated in terms strikingly similar to those put forth by liberal arts faculty: "learn how to apply, integrate, and evaluate knowledge or the methodology of a discipline," "develop a first hand understanding of the political and social action skills required for active citizenship" (Duley, 1981), and "develop perspectives and practice analytical skills necessary for understanding the social ecology of organizations engaged in the delivery of goods and services" (Stanton, 1983). There is growing recognition among practitioners that the use of cognitive skills developed in liberal arts education must be stressed in public service in order for these programs to meet the developmental and civic literacy goals they held for students and for the service provided by students to have real impact in the community.

Until the education reform and public service initiatives of the 1980s, service-learning advocates were a small, marginal group within higher education. However, with the boost provided to active learning pedagogies by education reform and to volunteerism by the public service initiative, interest in service-learning began to grow at both the secondary and postsecondary levels. Programs were initiated, and an increased number of practitioners joined NSEE. Campus Compact began to use the term *service-learning* in its publications.[2] The Johnson Foundation convened a

Wingspread conference to articulate and publish principles (Honnett and Poulsen, 1989), which became one of its most requested publications. What was once a marginal, not-well-understood form of alternative education was suddenly on the front burner of numerous higher education organizations and on the minds of a growing number of campus administrators and faculty.

## A Service-Learning Research Design

In his reflections on *Street Corner Society* (1955), William F. Whyte noted that one of the key realizations about his study of this urban neighborhood was that he could not "cover all of Cornerville" (p. 358). One of our key realizations in defining, planning, and carrying out this study was similar: we discovered we could not cover all of service-learning. Like Whyte, whose work has been an inspiration for us over the years, we realized we could not fully describe the history of service-learning in American higher education or even tell the stories of all of the service-learning pioneers. We could only record and retell a few key stories from a limited number of pioneers. As Whyte wrote about Cornerville, "I realized that I could explain Cornerville better through telling the stories of those individuals and groups than I could in any other way" (p. 357). Like Whyte, we realized we could learn and tell the history of service-learning only through the stories of individual pioneers, which reflected their struggles as well as their triumphs.

Our first boundary decision was span of time. This was one of our easier decisions, since the starting point of oral history is living memory. Given the ages of the pioneers we interviewed, this meant that the earliest memories of personal involvement in service spanned from the 1930s to the early 1960s. The time boundary on the other end was more difficult. We settled on 1985 as the latest date that a pioneer could have entered this field and still be considered a pioneer for the purposes of this study. Although this date may seem arbitrary, 1985 represents a critical point in the timeline of service efforts in American higher education. (See the timeline in Appendix B.) It is the year Campus Compact was founded, which reinvigorated public and community service on campuses and began to move service-learning from individual pioneer efforts to a more institutionalized one. We were also thankful for and did not wish to duplicate Goodwin Liu's history (1996) of the community service movement from 1985 to 1995. Although we realize there are pioneers who started their work in this decade, our sample represents the years from 1939 to 1985.

Deciding to take a service-learning approach to capturing service-learning's history led to a complicated, participatory research design. We discovered early on that we had a two-part goal: to develop a history and to use that history to strengthen the field. So although we sought to be rigorous researchers using clear methodology to make a systematic, representative inquiry into the origins and early practice of service-learning, we also viewed ourselves as organizers looking for ways to use the process and outcomes of the inquiry to strengthen service-learning policy and practice.

These seemingly contradictory goals could easily conflict and undermine each other. Mindful of these dangers, we resolved this dilemma by embracing a central value that informs our own practice of service-learning: involve the learners (in this case, the sources) as co-investigators and provide for collective, reflective observation on what we uncover. Therefore, we chose a modified participatory action research design (Whyte, 1991) and focused our attention on individuals and their oral histories. We sought to discover the stories of people who first worked to combine education and social action in varied political, economic, community, and educational contexts. Along the way we invited these people to be sources of oral history and to participate as nominators of other sources, interviewers, and analysts of the stories told.

In this spirit, we designed a two-stage process for collecting the stories. The first was a conference at which a small, representative group of service-learning pioneers convened to tell and analyze stories. This conference, cosponsored by The Johnson Foundation, took place at the Wingspread Center in Racine, Wisconsin, in December 1995. Having developed the foundation for the history at Wingspread and having learned where we needed further inquiry, we then conducted additional interviews and our own collective analysis over the next two years.

Determining who had been a service-learning pioneer and how we would select a representative group to interview was a daunting task. We first set a basic parameter that for this history, we were looking for people who endeavored to combine service with academic study in American postsecondary education. We focused on postsecondary education for a variety of reasons, the chief of which was that we were practitioners in this arena and this work was one of reflecting on the nature, context, and sources of our own practice. But this was not an exclusive focus, because we knew that our practice, and that of other pioneers, began in secondary education or was influenced by K–12 practitioners.

Within these boundaries and parameters, we developed criteria for the people whose stories we wanted to gather. We sought individuals who (1) were pioneers—"ones who go before, preparing the way for others" (Guralnik, 1984, p. 454), (2) used service as a means to strengthen learning, or (3) used learning to enhance service. In applying these criteria, we defined service and learning broadly, seeking to be inclusive of the widest expression of efforts to serve, whether through volunteerism, activism, advocacy, policy work, or research. Similarly we included a wide range of efforts under "learn," whether they were aimed at academic knowledge, skills, civic values, or personal development. Finally, we looked for people who had been practitioners of some duration and would be willing to share their stories of how they became involved in and sought to influence the service-learning movement.

The scholarly nature of our research required that we design a rigorous, fair, and representative nominations process for identifying individuals from whom we would seek information. Based on our knowledge of the field and on numerous calls to others, we generated a list of seventy individuals and twenty-two different strands of effort (see Appendix A) ranging from field study to cooperative education, from community-based participatory action research to policy-focused public service internships.

We handed our list to a panel of nominators with a request to help us identify within and across the strands people who had been pioneers in the effort to link campus and community that is now commonly called service-learning with the criteria identified above.[3] In the first round of this process, the nominators edited the strands list, adding five additional areas of service-learning practice, and identified an additional seventy names. We merged these suggestions with the original list and circulated it a second time, asking the nominators for further modifications and for recommendations of names from the new list to interview or invite to the Wingspread conference, or both.

We articulated criteria for the Wingspread participants. Although we assumed that the stories of each person we interviewed would be important in weaving together the history of service-learning, we wanted to use the conference to stimulate and capture discussion among the most important and representative pioneers. "Important" meant those who have had significant influence on the development of the field. Influence could come about through advocacy, publications, or other means, as well as through example or practice. "Representative" meant that in the aggregate, the conference participants should represent the most important, influential strands of service-learning history (such as experiential education and voluntary student action). These criteria were necessary because of our agenda to identify and explore the common themes and varied journeys that have brought service-learning to its current condition.

## Reflecting on Our Own Experience

We have included ourselves in this study. After worry, debate, and review of literature, we realized that in keeping with the spirit of the project, we were reflecting on our own practice, as well that of our pioneer colleagues. Indeed, many of the people in this book have been mentors, inspiration, and fellow travelers for each of us for many years. Our worries were eased by Rob Rhoads's discussion of "positionality" in his book, *Community Service and Higher Learning: Explorations of the Caring Self* (1997). Borrowing from feminist literature and his own childhood experiences as a needy service recipient, Rhoads helped us remember that we are not disengaged from our scholarship. Inclusion of ourselves in this book reflects our commitment to the scholarship of engagement that service-learning in all of its strands represents. As we ask of our students, such scholarship required us to be conscious of this decision and, as Dewey argued, to "problematize" our relationship to the experience and to what we came to know about it.

## The Pioneer Metaphor

We chose the pioneer metaphor to describe service-learning's early practitioners after much deliberation. The use of this term raises images of land grabs and subjugation of native populations. The "settling," or "civilizing," of "new" land by pioneers may reinforce a very limited, Eurocentric view of American history. However, we failed to identify any other term that adequately captures the independent, entrepreneurial, pathbreaking work of those who explore new approaches in any field, be it geographic, conceptual, or technical. Service-learning's early practitioners were "ones who went before, preparing the way for others."

Like other pioneers, it is possible that those exploring service-learning may have been as blinded by their idealism as nineteenth-century American pioneers were by the doctrine of manifest destiny. This blindness is particularly evident in the difficulty that many service-learning programs have had developing and sustaining truly reciprocal relationships with off-campus communities. Thus, while acknowledging the complex implications of this metaphor, we decided it best expressed both the explorations and quagmires encountered by service-learning's first practitioners.

T. Minh-ha Trinh, a Vietnamese-American filmmaker and writer, says, "The simplest vehicle of truth, the story, is also said to be . . . 'the natural form for revealing life.' Its fascination may be explained by its power both to give a vividly felt insight into the life of other people and to revive or keep alive the forgotten . . . parts of ourselves" (1989, p. 123). This tapestry of service-learning history, woven together from stories these thirty-three individuals told to each other at Wingspread, and to us as researchers, is a tale of lives, moral vision, commitment to a set of values, and pursuit of multiple truths of what education and community development should be in a just, democratic society.

We hope we have built a rigorously assembled archive of service-learning's oral history and shared a collective story that passes the torch from one generation of pioneers to the next. We hope too that by looking backward to service-learning's history through the eyes of these pioneers, we have set a foundation on which the field may build for the future, a collective wisdom on what service-learning has been and what it may yet become.

## Notes

1. Since its founding in 1974 under the auspices of the Educational Testing Service, CAEL has provided individuals, institutions, and organizations with the tools and strategies they need to create practical, effective lifelong learning solutions for their education and training needs. See p. 253 for the history of the organization's name changes.

2. Campus Compact is a coalition of college and university presidents committed to helping students develop the values and skills of citizenship through participation in public and community service. It is the only national higher education organization whose primary purpose is to support campus-based public and community service.

3. In addition to the principal investigators, the nominators were J. Herman Blake, former vice-chancellor of undergraduate education, Indiana University–Purdue University Indianapolis; Richard Couto, professor, Jepson School of Leadership Studies, University of Richmond; Ellen Porter Honnet, program consultant, The Johnson Foundation; Jane C. Kendall, executive director, North Carolina Center for Non-Profit Organizations; and Robert Sigmon, president, Learning Design Initiatives.

# Chapter Two

# Early Connections Between Service and Education

*Seth S. Pollack*

Like beauty, service is a many-splendored thing. Its value is in the eye of the beholder. In this chapter, we examine the varied and conflicting views postsecondary education has of its relationship to service, because these views form the turbulent terrain on which service-learning's pioneers set out. As we shall learn in later chapters, the pioneers also had multiple, and sometimes conflicting, motivations and intentions, which both influenced and mirrored the contexts in which they worked.

## The Meaning of Service in Postsecondary Education

Postsecondary education's relationship to social problems is fraught with conflict over the social function of teaching and research. These debates represent clashes between competing concepts, such as objective science versus social advocacy, classical versus utilitarian education, and critical thinking versus critical action.

In his seminal work on the emergence of the American university, Veysey (1965) recognizes practical public service, or "utility," as one of the three academic aims of the modern university.

Heather Ramírez developed the pioneer profiles for this chapter.

But he also recognizes that the definition of service remains highly disputed: "One could serve society either by offering training for success within the existing order . . . or by agitating for new arrangements. At stake was the definition of the public interest to be served, and this question lurked behind the more general notion of the worth of public service. . . . The mere conception of a useful university offered no answer to this problem, so long as there remained divisions of opinion among Americans over what it meant to be useful. An academic aim had run up squarely against one of its intrinsic limitations" (pp. 74–75).

Two specific examples, one historical and one contemporary, may help clarify this conflict. In 1834, Lane Seminary had an active antislavery society composed of faculty and students. To put their abolitionist views into action, the society organized an educational program for the blacks in their community. But soon after they began, the trustees of the seminary closed the program on the grounds that these activities were "noneducational." The students and their professors eventually left the seminary and transferred to Oberlin College (Ellis and Noyes, 1990). Clearly, the members of the antislavery society and the seminary administration held competing definitions of the term *educational*.

More recently, the social unrest of the 1960s placed demands on universities to be more socially relevant and responsive to the needs of the poor. Nathan Pusey, president of Harvard at that time, spoke of the need for higher education to "reassess, re-examine, and redefine" its central mission (Harvard, 1969). This process of reassessment went on at institutions around the country and produced a variety of programmatic responses intended to reconnect postsecondary education with the needs of the poor. However, this redefinition of higher education's service mission was not universally applauded. This attitude is exemplified in the following passage: "We cannot believe that the mission of the university is to lead mankind to a new Jerusalem. Any attempt to do so would destroy among other things, the university's role to serve as intellectual sanctuary when the winds of popular passion blow. . . . The goal of the university is not the quest for power or virtue, but the quest for significant truth" (Faimen and Olivier, 1972, p. 35). And Charles Muscatine said, "If the road to hell is paved with good intentions in education as elsewhere, then there is nowhere better paving material than in the concept of Public Service. In the sixteen years since I joined this faculty [the University of California] I have heard more bad educational policy justified in the name of Public Service than by any other invocation, human or divine" (quoted in Farmer, Sheates, and Deshler, 1972, p. 65).

Embedded in these responses are strong disagreements over what public service means and how higher education should contribute. Over the years, these debates crystallized into distinct rival positions: "Positions so disparate that on one end of the spectrum are those who see service as the raison d'être of higher education and on the other are those who would reject it altogether as inappropriate or even inimical to the enterprise" (Crosson, 1983, p. 9).

As the stories of the service-learning pioneers in this book make clear, practitioners came to be involved in this turbulent intersection of service and learning from a variety of directions with differing motivations and goals. Before introducing the pioneers, we present two perspectives on the source of the turbulence. First, we look at the differentiated types of institutions in higher education and how each evolved distinct definitions of service. Second, we examine the "contested terms" (Connolly, 1993) at the heart of service-learning, which reveal fundamental social policy debates inherent in postsecondary education's attempt to respond to social problems.

## Diverse Expressions of the Service Mission

Postsecondary education institutions have resolved the "standing antagonisms" or "persistent dilemmas" embodied in their tripartite mission of teaching, research, and service by emphasizing one over the other two. Thus, liberal arts colleges tend to emphasize teaching, professional schools and community colleges emphasize training, and large universities emphasize research (Koepplin and Wilson, 1985; Rudolph, 1962; Bok, 1986).

Amid this differentiation, service has come to be defined through the primary goal of the institution and is expressed in ways consistent with that primary educational mission. As a result, liberal arts colleges, research universities, professional schools, and community colleges have developed varied interpretations of their service missions based on their primary identity as character formers, researchers, teachers of specific skills, or expanders of educational opportunity. Service is subsumed as either "liberal arts education," "research," or "professional education" (Veysey, 1965), or in the case of the community college, making all three perspectives on the social benefits of education available to formerly underserved populations (Crosson, 1983).

## Liberal Arts Colleges

Classical liberal arts colleges have traditionally seen themselves as fulfilling their service mission by emphasizing citizenship training and cultivating higher-order thinking skills necessary for citizen participation in a democratic society (Crosson, 1983; Koepplin and Wilson, 1985). They carry on the tradition of the medieval university, which was disassociated from the quotidian issues of daily life and concerned with more universal quests of ethics, morals, universal laws, and God. In this respect, "education and the pursuit of truth" is seen as service in and of itself. The service function of the liberal arts college is building moral character in students irrespective of its connection to day-to-day concerns (Rudolph, 1962; Crosson, 1983).

## Research Universities

In contrast, research universities have traditionally defined their service mission through their primary role in the creation and application of knowledge. This aspect of the modern American research university evolved from the German model of university-based scientific research (Rudolph, 1962) and led to the development of both pure and applied sciences. The land grant college movement and the development of its agricultural extension service is an example of this applied science definition of service.

## Professional Schools

A third institutional type is the professional school. American higher education in the colonial period, designed to provide the elite with education in the fields of law and religion, was firmly rooted in this model. These "professions" were seen as essential for the elite citizens to fulfill their public service mission. In this era, all other professional training was based on the apprenticeship model and took place in the workplace rather than in institutions of higher learning (Rudolph, 1962). Over time, the training of educators, physicians, nurses, social workers, city planners, architects, and business and public administrators was formalized within the professional school model, incorporating a formalized clinical or internship training component in place of the more informal system of apprenticeship or on-the-job training. Professional schools see the development and application of professional skills (pro bono work by lawyers, medical internships in hospitals) as the basis of their service to the community.

## Community Colleges

The primary mission of the community college, a distinctly American invention of the post–World War II era, is to make higher learning accessible to populations who were formerly excluded from traditional institutions. As a result, it combines all three of the other models, emphasizing to some extent character formation, applied science, and the acquisition of professional skills. The distinguishing factor is that these distinct missions are modified to fit the needs of the local community and its disenfranchised population. For community colleges, filling unmet needs for higher learning and professional training is considered service.

Table 2.1 presents a typology of institutional responses to service that summarizes these positions. The service orientations of universities, liberal arts colleges, professional schools, and community colleges are distinct. Each has developed a definition of service and related organizational capacities that is appropriate to the way in which it has resolved the "persistent dilemma" or "standing antagonism" between developing knowledge (research), passing on knowledge (teaching), and being of benefit to society (service).

## Contested Definitions of Education, Service, and Democracy

Although functional differentiation in response to the competing missions of higher education explains some of the varied perspectives on higher education's service role, there is a deeper level of

**Table 2.1.  A Typology of Institutional Responses to Service.**

| Type | Primary Educational Mission | Definition of Service |
|------|------|------|
| Liberal arts college | Citizenship training for democracy | Engaging with ideas of value |
| | Character formation | Training citizens for public life |
| Research university | Expanding the knowledge base | Applying knowledge to solve social problems |
| Professional school | Teaching applied, concrete skills | Training professionals to perform needed social functions |
| | | Clinical training |
| Community college | Providing access to nontraditional populations | Access to educational opportunity |
| | | Access to employment opportunity |

conflict, rooted in the debate over how education is most beneficial to society. As we have seen, there are distinct rival positions
concerning higher education's service mission. Such rival positions
are viewed by political theorist William Connolly (1993) as expressions of fundamentally "contested terms," or concepts whose "definition is never neutral but always entangled in competing moral
and political commitments." As such, these definitions are subject
to continuous reinterpretation and negotiation in response to
political, socioeconomic, and cultural forces. From this perspective, the degree of tension, debate, and outright conflict around
higher education's service role can be attributed not just to institutional type but also to the fundamentally contested nature of the
concepts of service and education. More important, embedded in
the debates around the social function of education is a third struggle over the definition of democracy itself.

The crux of the debate is whether education should provide
students with the skills and knowledge base necessary to fit into the

existing social structure or prepare them to engage in social transformation. An aspect of this debate is conflict over access to and
ownership of the knowledge base comprising education.

Service is also much contested. Service can be understood as
charity, with the goal of addressing immediate needs, or it can
focus on resolving deeply embedded social problems and bringing
about structural changes in both social and economic relations.

Debates over the concept of democracy can be traced back to
the eighteenth century and the drafting of the Federalist Papers
and the Constitutional Convention. The authors of the Constitution tried to find a balance between the virtues of citizen participation and the anarchic risks posed by a highly mobilized mass
population. These two perspectives represent competing definitions of democracy: the more participatory model of Jeffersonian
democracy and the more elite model of Madisonian democracy
(Boyte, 1989). The fundamental contrast is that more participatory definitions seek to develop full-fledged citizen participants,
active in the process of ruling, while more elite definitions require
knowledgeable, law-following citizens who are justly represented
by an elite group of enlightened, citizen lawmakers.

The way a college or university interprets "education," "service," and "democracy" will have a significant impact on how it
understands its service mission and the types of activities it orga-
nizes to carry it out. There will be differing views as to the purposes
and priorities of education and its relationship to the social, political, and economic order. Those differing views will then determine whether service is an element in the process of social
reproduction or social transformation.

Service-learning efforts, like all other efforts by higher education to address social problems, must, and do, come to terms with
these three contested terms. This reconciliation is depicted in
Figure 2.1. The model links the three contested terms together
in the form of a triangle, emphasizing that struggles over definitions do not occur in isolation. Rather, they mutually influence and
are influenced by each other. The key, then, is the interplay among
the three concepts along the three axes of the triangle, with each
axis associated with a fundamental social policy debate, summarized as follows:

Education ←→ Service: How does education serve society?

Service ←→ Democracy: What is the relationship between service and social change?

Democracy ←→ Education: What is the purpose of education in a democracy?

These debates represent the spectrum of issues that service-learning programs encounter as they attempt to educate students about and in response to suffering and injustice. They represent as well the turbulence that the service-learning pioneers encountered as they designed, established, and sought to institutionalize these programs.

## Paths of the Pioneers

We introduce the service-learning pioneers in the context of these debates, identifying their original motivations for combining community action and structured learning. Some were more focused on educational questions; others on issues of social justice; and still others were most interested in preparing students for effective, democratic engagement (see Figure 2.2). Readers may wish to consult these profiles as a means of connecting the stories that follow with the individuals who tell them.

**Figure 2.1.  Debates Along the Axes.**

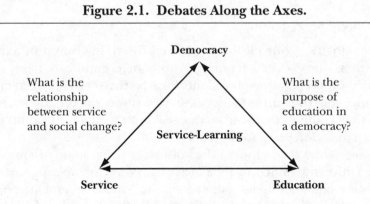

How does education serve society?

## Figure 2.2.  Placing the Pioneers.

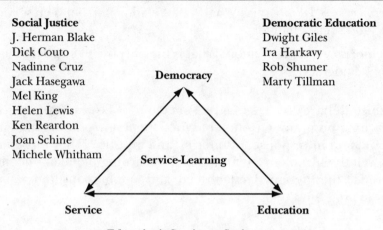

**Social Justice**
J. Herman Blake
Dick Couto
Nadinne Cruz
Jack Hasegawa
Mel King
Helen Lewis
Ken Reardon
Joan Schine
Michele Whitham

**Democratic Education**
Dwight Giles
Ira Harkavy
Rob Shumer
Marty Tillman

**Education's Service to Society**

| | |
|---|---|
| Judy Sorum Brown | Jane Permaul |
| Dick Cone | Bill Ramsay |
| John Duley | Greg Ricks |
| Mary Edens | Gib Robinson |
| Jim Feeney | Nick Royal |
| Michael Goldstein | Sharon Rubin |
| Garry Hesser | Bob Sigmon |
| Jim Keith | Tim Stanton |
| Jane Kendall | Jon Wagner |
| J. Robert Newbrough | Hal Woods |

## Education ←→ Service

The majority of our pioneers entered the field along this axis. Whether they worked from a campus or community base, or focused on preparation of students for effective social engagement or more narrowly on students as service resources for communities, they came to discover service-learning with a motivation to make education serve social needs.

*Judy Sorum Brown* joined the volunteer program at Michigan State University (MSU) in 1968 as assistant director, an assignment that stimulated her lifelong interest in the "capacities and interests of people for high responsibility and leadership." In 1973 she moved from MSU to the University of Maryland, where she became director of community service programs, and then founder and director of the Center for Experiential Learning at the University of Maryland. In 1978 she accepted a White House fellowship, where she stayed for three years. Since then, she has worked as a private consultant in organization behavior and leadership, "seeking to organize a variety of strands of intellectual and artistic work to understand learning broadly and particularly in the workplace." Brown earned her Ph.D. from MSU in comparative literature.

After a stint in the Peace Corps and several years teaching in high schools, *Dick Cone* came to service-learning as a curriculum developer for the University of Southern California's (USC) Joint Education Program (JEP), where he has served as director for over two decades. Through JEP, students engage in academically based service-learning in Los Angeles schools adjacent to the USC campus. He has a doctorate in education from the University of California at Los Angeles (UCLA).

*John Duley*'s first experiences with service-learning came as a college student in a Quaker work camp for conscientious objectors during World War II. This experience led him to Union Theological Seminary and a lifetime of faith-based ministry and service, mostly in higher education. For twenty years he served as chaplain, faculty member at Justin Morrill College, and instructional development consultant in the Office of Learning and Evaluation, all at Michigan State University (MSU). Many service-learning practitioners, noting his work with students and faculty at MSU, his numerous publications, and his national leadership, refer to John as the "grandfather of the field." Duley served on the board of directors and as president of the National Society for Experiential Education (NSEE).

After teaching middle school in the early 1970s, *Mary Edens* moved to MSU, where she pursued doctoral studies in counseling psychology. In 1975 she joined what is now known as the Service-Learning Center at MSU, which she has directed for more than twenty years.

In the 1960s, *Jim Feeney* was teaching sociology and coordinating off-campus learning opportunities at New College, a small liberal arts institution that opened in 1964 in Sarasota, Florida. While searching for and developing relationships with study abroad, field study, and urban internship programs, he discovered that people running these programs were dealing with similar issues, but in isolation. This stimulated him to bring them together in 1971 to form the Society for Field Experience Education (SFEE), one of two organizations that later merged to become the National Society for Experiential Education (NSEE), service-learning practitioners' primary professional support group.

Determined "to bring together the city and its young people," *Michael Goldstein* founded Urban Corps in New York City in 1966. The Urban Corps model of summer internships in municipal departments, compensated with Work-Study funds, spread rapidly across the United States. In 1971 Goldstein accepted a position as associate vice chairman of urban and governmental affairs at the University of Illinois, Chicago, "to link this campus, built after the Chicago riots, with the community." In 1978 he joined a law firm in Washington, D.C., to establish its higher education practice. He continues his involvement in experiential learning as pro bono legal counsel to NSEE, and consultant and trainer in the legal consequences of administering experiential and service-learning programs.

In 1960 *Garry Hesser* and fellow students at Phillips University (Enid, Oklahoma) founded the First Mile Club to volunteer in nursing homes. This action, combined with once-a-week reflection at morning Bible study, formed a model of service-learning that Hesser has followed throughout his career. Hesser's first professional service-learning role came as an assistant professor at the College of Wooster, where he developed, taught, and lived in a community service house in which "everyone initiated a community service project to involve other students, and we all collaborated in the design and execution of a course on community." Since 1977, Hesser has been professor of sociology and urban studies and director of cooperative education at Augsburg College. He has a Ph.D. in sociology from the University of Notre Dame and is a past president of NSEE.

*Jim Keith* identifies his early inspiration for service-learning as coming from "an imaginative, self-taught sociology professor who brought a philosophical and applied approach to the field that would make empiricists' tails curl." In 1967 he embarked on his service-learning career as an instructor at a Georgia community college, determined that his teaching "was not going to be contained solely in the classroom." In 1973 he went to San Francisco to direct Westmont College's off-campus urban program, which "used the city as text." From 1981 to 1991, Keith was an administrator at Guilford College, in charge of career and experiential education. More recently he has developed an ecumenical Servant Leadership School in Greensboro, North Carolina, which links theological reflection with engagement with poor and marginalized persons in the community.

Challenging experiences as a volunteer tutor while an undergraduate at the University of North Carolina in the early 1970s motivated *Jane Kendall* to devote herself to creating programs that would be mutually beneficial for students and communities and to supporting the people who would run them. In 1978 she joined the National Center for Public Service Internships (NCPSI) to develop a Southern Regional Economic Development internship program. That year NCPSI merged with the Society for Field Experience Education (SFEE), which ultimately became NSEE. Kendall's quiet, thoughtful leadership of NSEE as executive director from 1983 to 1990 is viewed by many service-learning pioneers as a critical element in their ability to sustain their work during the field's difficult early years.

*J. Robert Newbrough* came to Peabody College at Vanderbilt University in 1966 to direct the Center of Community Studies, a research service and training enterprise. Prior to his arrival at Peabody, Newbrough completed a postdoctoral program at Harvard and six years' work at the National Institute of Mental Health (NIMH), where he investigated the community's role in mental health, an interest he has sustained throughout his career. Newbrough became a senior faculty member at Peabody in 1980 and added undergraduate service-learning instruction to his participatory action research work with graduate students.

*Jane Permaul* was "attracted to service-learning because its essence is team. It's collaborative as opposed to egocentric and individual." She has expressed these values through thirty years' work at UCLA as a student advisor, dean of experimental programs, director of field studies development, and, since 1990, assistant vice chancellor for student affairs. Permaul describes her interest in service as coming directly from her immigration to the United States from China in 1949, "going from a very privileged, well-provided youngster to being a recipient of service. I felt there were a lot of missing pieces, in both the educational and social service systems, to help people adjust to this country." She provided national leadership to the field through numerous publications, consultation, and as a board member and president of NSEE. Permaul holds an Ed.D. in higher education from UCLA.

In 1955 *Bill Ramsay* joined the Oak Ridge Institute of Nuclear Studies (ORINS) as administrative assistant in the University Relations Division. Ramsay helped coordinate fellowships, internships, and seminars for graduate students and research opportunities for faculty as he looked for ways to involve higher education with the region's social and community problems. In 1966 he recruited service-learning pioneer Bob Sigmon to help administer and expand Manpower for Development, an intern program that required students to publish useful and academically sound research papers on area social and economic problems. They described it as "service-learning," the first articulation of this term. In 1970 Ramsay moved to Berea College in Kentucky, where he served for many years as dean of labor, vice president for labor and student life, and vice president for policy and planning.

*Greg Ricks*'s commitment to education came after his graduate studies in city planning at Massachusetts Institute of Technology (MIT), when he realized that "there won't be any people who can buy housing and begin to control their destiny without jobs and education." His commitment arose from lessons he learned as a Boy Scout in the 1950s and an intense sense of responsibility he feels toward his African American heritage. Ricks has devoted his career to advocating and sparking in students a "loving idealism," as project consultant for the National Center for Service Learning (NCSL); as a student affairs administrator at Northeastern, Dartmouth, and Stanford universities; as vice president and dean of City Year; and as board member and advisor to Campus Outreach Opportunity League (COOL).

As a young assistant professor of English at San Francisco State University (SFSU) in 1970, *Gib Robinson* developed a service-learning approach to the teaching of Shakespeare and two campuswide programs focused on tutoring and community service. His innovative, student-led service-learning programs trained volunteers, who in turn trained other volunteers to work in San

Francisco schools and community organizations. Now as associate director of SFSU's Urban Institute, Robinson focuses on economic development, defense conversion, and employment training. He holds a Ph.D. in English from the University of California, Berkeley.

Prior experience as a volunteer, which included experience in the Peace Corps, influenced *Nick Royal's* pioneering work in international field studies at Merrill College at the University of California at Santa Cruz (UCSC) for more than twenty years. Royal drew on his international experiences to create an innovative, interdisciplinary program that enabled students to prepare for and participate in field studies domestically and overseas. He provided national leadership for international, cross-cultural service-learning through writing, organizing, and presentations on behalf of NSEE.

*Sharon Rubin* developed, coordinated, and instructed service-learning courses and programs as director of experiential learning programs and assistant dean for undergraduate studies at the University of Maryland, as dean of the Charles and Martha Fulton School of Liberal Arts at Salisbury State University, and currently as vice president for academic affairs at Ramapo College of New Jersey. She has served nationally through numerous publications and workshop training, and as a consultant, board member, and president of NSEE. She holds a Ph.D. in American studies from the University of Minnesota.

*Bob Sigmon* describes his service-learning career as an expression of "thinking about what it means to be cared for, what it means to care, and what it means to learn in service settings." This path includes missionary and research experiences in Pakistan and India, graduate study at Union Theological Seminary, and the pioneering service-learning work with Bill Ramsay at ORINS. After his work with Ramsay, Sigmon went on to direct a state internship program and service-learning-oriented health education programs in North and South Carolina. He is a founding father of SFEE and has provided national leadership to the service-learning field through numerous publications, training and consulting, and service on NSEE's board of directors. For the past several years, he has worked in Raleigh, North Carolina, as a consultant to colleges and universities and national education associations.

*Tim Stanton's* service and activism experience in the late 1960s led him to establish in 1971 a youth community action program in Marin County, California, which he directed until 1976. In 1977 he became director of Cornell University's Human Ecology Field Study Program, where he worked with service-learning pioneers Dwight Giles, Ken Reardon, and Michele Whitham to develop a highly structured, interdisciplinary service-based curriculum in human ecology. In 1985 Stanton went to Stanford to help develop the Haas Center for Public Service, which he has directed since 1991. Stanton has been a national leader in service-learning through numerous publications, presentations, and consultation, and as a board member and president of NSEE. He holds a Ph.D. in human and organizational systems from The Fielding Institute.

*Jon Wagner's* interest "in the complexities of service," developed during his undergraduate years in the mid-1960s, led to a concern "of how you could be engaged as an intellectual—how you could be actively involved in society as a complement to your intellectual work, not just as something else you do." Wagner pursued this interest in doctoral studies in sociology at the University of Chicago, in teaching "social problems" and "social action research" at Columbia College, and as director of the field studies program at the University of California at Berkeley from 1978 to 1985. In 1988 Wagner moved to the University of California, Davis, where he served as dean of the Division of Education and helped establish a center for cooperative university-school research, where there is "no service without research and no research without service."

*Hal Woods* attended Northwestern University, where he majored in history and literature of religions. Through his major, he began reading Reinhold Niebuhr, which stimulated him to consider "linking theology to social concerns and action." In 1969 Woods went to the University of Vermont to take a position as fraternity affairs coordinator, where he soon was asked to direct a student-organized volunteer program. Woods directed what became known as the Center for Service-Learning for twenty-one years, doing pioneering work with University Year for Action. He became a trainer for the National Center for Service-Learning (NCSL) and a board member of NSEE. In 1990 Woods returned to the church as rector of All Saint's Episcopal Church in Burlington, Vermont.

## Service ◄──► Democracy

Other pioneers, while certainly concerned with the relationship between education and service, were more directly motivated to enter this field by issues related to the relationship between service and social justice in a democracy.

*J. Herman Blake* founded the Extramural Education and Community Service Program in 1968 at UCSC. Through this program, UCSC students engaged in full-time, residential service-learning assignments in Beaufort and Charleston counties in South Carolina, Tierra Amarillo in northern New Mexico, and in Alameda and Stanislaus counties and Fresno, California. Blake grew up in Mount Vernon, New York, where he was inspired by his mother's resistance to tenant evictions. He earned his Ph.D. in sociology from the University of California at Berkeley. His career is marked by a continuing commitment to grassroots communities expressed through his service-learning work and through research and writing on urban black militants, including a book, *Revolutionary Suicide,* which he coauthored with Huey P. Newton (1973). Blake is currently director of the African American Studies Program at Iowa State University.

*Dick Couto* taught high school in the Bronx and then earned a Ph.D. in political science at the University of Kentucky, where he focused on issues of poverty in Appalachia. In 1975 he became director of the Center for Health Services at Vanderbilt University, where he engaged students with grassroots community leaders who were working on health and environmental issues. In 1991 he moved to the University of Richmond as a founding faculty member of the Jepson School of Leadership, which focuses on leadership, community organizations, and public service.

Student activism in the Philippines in the 1960s swept *Nadinne Cruz* into service and social change. "It was a baptism by fire," she has said, "plunging right into support work for peasant and migrant farmer labor groups and insistence on analyzing the actions that we took in relation to our objective of transforming society." Fleeing martial law, Cruz carried her political activism into higher education in the United States. She earned an M.A. in political science at Marquette University and pursued Ph.D. studies at the University of Minnesota. As director for twelve years of the Twin Cities' Higher Education Consortium for Urban Affairs, Cruz taught for City Arts, a comprehensive semester arts service-learning program, focusing on the role of arts in community development. She also directed community-based learning programs in Latin America, Scandinavia, and the United States, focusing on the multicultural politics of inequality and social change. Cruz is now at Stanford University serving as associate director of the Haas Center for Public Service.

After divinity school in Boston, *Jack Hasegawa* spent ten years in Japan, "half as a missionary working with adults in community organizing projects" and half as a faculty member of Friends World College. In 1980 he became director of Yale University's Dwight Hall, a hundred-year-old center for student volunteerism, where "we spent a lot of time debating the necessary linking of political advocacy, social action, and community service." In 1993 Hasegawa joined the Connecticut State Department of Education to lead statewide planning on "integrated education" and diversity awareness training.

*Mel King* gained his social justice ethic from his father, a leader in a dockworkers' union, and his mother, who led an active life serving her church community. In 1971 he petitioned the president of MIT to devote university resources to community development in its surrounding areas. As a result, King was appointed to MIT's Department of Urban Studies and Planning to develop the Community Fellows Program, an academic service-learning program for community leaders. In addition, from 1973 to 1983, King served as a representative in the Massachusetts state legislature. Membership in both organizations enabled King to connect MIT faculty and students and community-based legal and business professionals to develop and support legislation and programs that promote community development. King retired from MIT in 1996 but remains active in Boston-based community development work.

*Helen Lewis*'s first experience with service-learning took place in 1943 through YWCA-sponsored labor and early civil rights projects. "I fought against segregation. I got arrested in 1948. This changed my life." Lewis continued her activism as an instructor in colleges in the Appalachian region in the 1950s, 1960s, and 1970s, where she involved students "in all the social movements of the region: strip mining, black lung, mine safety, union reform, coal tax, and welfare rights movements." As a result, she lost two jobs for "nurturing radical students." She spent two decades as an administrator and organizer at the Highlander Research and Education Center in Tennessee doing community education, community development, and adult education in rural mountain communities. She currently resides in North Carolina, where she is writing a book on Catholic sisters who are doing extraordinary community development work.

A Catholic priest challenged *Ken Reardon* to tutor at public housing projects in Paterson, New Jersey, and connect that "to what it meant to live a committed life." This high school experience spurred Reardon to organize service-learning programs while studying at Rider College and the University of Massachusetts. In 1984 he joined the Cornell University Human Ecology Field Study Program to teach and manage its New York City program, where he pioneered a participatory action research approach to service-learning. In 1990 he became assistant professor of urban and regional planning at the University of Illinois at Urbana–Champaign, where he coordinates the East Saint Louis Action Research Project. The project integrates participatory action research, community organization, and popular education techniques in order to build the organizational capacity of neighborhood organizations representing the poorest sectors of this distressed urban community. Reardon earned a Ph.D. in city and regional planning at Cornell and was recently promoted to associate professor at the University of Illinois.

*Joan Schine* traces her introduction to service-learning to her school days in 1938, when every student participated in public service activities. Later, as a parent school volunteer, she became deeply involved in issues of poverty and civil rights. In 1967 she joined the National Commission on Resources for Youth to work with retired judge Mary Conway Kohler promoting Youth Participation, an important early service-learning concept. There Schine focused on urban adolescents, which led her to establish in 1982 the Early Adolescent Helper Program as part of the Graduate School and University Center of the City University of New York. In 1991, with fifteen Helper Programs established in New York, the organization expanded its mission and was renamed the National

Center for Service Learning in Early Adolescence to promote service-learning for middle school students nationally.

*Michele Whitham*'s introduction to service-learning came through involvement with the radical religious left in the 1960s. After graduation from Cornell, she and friends remained in Ithaca, New York, and established an alternative middle school and a community-based apprenticeship program. From 1976 through 1988, she taught service-learning courses in Cornell's Field Study Office, building an action-reflection curriculum in human ecology with pioneers Tim Stanton, Dwight Giles, Ken Reardon, and others. "By the mid-1980s, however, my activist soul was languishing. I saw myself as helping students accomplish work in the community that I longed to do. So I went back to school, picked up a J.D., and here I am in Boston as a practicing attorney."

## Democracy ◄—► Education

Finally, a small group of pioneers found themselves most drawn to this field by fundamental questions of democratic participation and the role of education in fostering a more engaged, effective citizenry.

In 1970 *Dwight Giles* was drawn to graduate work at the Union Theological Seminary because it espoused a commitment to "doing theology in the city." During his time in New York, he was inspired by the work of John Dewey and "hired by a group of unrepentant Deweyans to be an adjunct faculty member supervising students' fieldwork in inner-city neighborhoods." In 1980 Giles moved to Cornell's Human Ecology Field Study Program, "the shaping experience of my professional life, to organize community projects that involved students, community partners, and other faculty." Since 1992 Giles has been professor of human and organization development and director of internships at Peabody College, Vanderbilt University, a base from which he has become a leading researcher on student learning outcomes and the practice of reflection. "I span boundaries between universities and communities. I think of myself as a teacher, but also an organizer." Giles earned his Ph.D. in community development from Pennsylvania State University.

*Ira Harkavy* has been "engaged in work with the West Philadel-phia community on a regular basis since the late 1960s, working to change the university's callous and shortsighted policies toward its neighbors" as a University of Pennsylvania undergraduate and graduate student, a community worker, and since 1985 Penn's director of the Center for Community Partnerships and vice pres-ident. Through his efforts to establish and develop the West Philadelphia Improvement Corps, Harkavy has become a nation-ally recognized advocate for what he terms "university-assisted com-munity schools," and for community-university partnerships generally. Creating these community-campus connections honors the civil rights tradition in his family and fuels his conviction to "transform the University of Pennsylvania into an institution that fulfills [Benjamin] Franklin's vision of the cosmopolitan, civic university."

In 1963, as a high school student, *Rob Shumer* discovered that participating in the Key Club helped him "begin to understand that students could begin to take charge of delivering service to the community on our own." His professional and scholarly con-tributions to service-learning have been motivated by a desire to give all students this same sense of effective civic engagement: as a high school teacher, as developer of a community school, as direc-tor of Field Studies Development at UCLA (following pioneer Jane Permaul), and since 1992 as director of a national research center and clearinghouse on service-learning at the University of Min-nesota. Shumer has a Ph.D. in education from UCLA.

In 1974 after several tumultuous years in student affairs and social service work, *Marty Tillman* entered the School for Interna-tional Training in Brattleboro, Vermont, where he engaged in an internship focused on democratic community development and peacemaking with the Gandhi Peace Foundation in New Delhi, India. "Everything flows from that moment in terms of crystalliz-ing my personal and professional ideas," he says. Upon returning to the United States in 1976, Tillman joined the Lisle Fellowship, an intergenerational, cross-cultural, participatory service-learning program established in 1936. He focused on expanding the num-ber of participants, especially from colleges and universities, and the settings in which they would serve, including India. Since his time with Lisle, Tillman has worked on international education issues with the YMCA and the Citizen's Network for Foreign Affairs in Washington, D.C. He helped establish NSEE's special interest group on cross-cultural, international experiential education and served on the board of the Partnership for Service-Learning.

In the next chapter we shall learn more about the service-learning pioneers' early motivations.

# Chapter Three

# Seeds of Commitment

## Personal Accounts of the Pioneers

To understand service-learning's history through its pioneers, we sought to identify the formative, personal experiences that served as sources for their commitments: to service and social change, to a more experiential form of learning, and especially to their decisions to devote large portions of their professional lives to combining the two in postsecondary education. How did the pioneers' family, community, and education experiences spark and nurture an interest in and commitment to service-learning?

### Parental Role Models

> "It seemed as if our family was there to help others when they were in crisis."

> "Give yourself to some movement!"

It should be no surprise that the pioneers identified community roles and activities of their parents as a critical to their development as individuals interested in service and social change.

### Parents as Volunteers

Dwight Giles recalls his mother's service to homeless people in central Pennsylvania in the early 1960s:

One of the things that was expected in terms of my mother's role as a minister's wife was when hobos, as we'd call them in those days, would come to the door. She'd make sandwiches and feed them. When somebody was sick, she'd help them. She helped the other women in the church organize a day care center for migrant kids, and she was the cook. She took food to the migrant camps, and I went with her. So, service—doing for other people, and just doing it because it needed to be done—was part and parcel of everyday life, and it was no big deal. That was what I learned from her.

Mary Edens recalls her parents' contributions: "I'm really proud of my dad's taking time and money to help resettle new immigrants from other areas of the country and get them established. There were lots of times that it seemed as if our family was there to help others when they were in crisis. I recall outreach my parents did, even for farmworkers who worked on our farm picking fruit, to help them out. Those are probably more meaningful experiences to me than any formal activity."

## Parents as Activists

Parents served as well as role models of commitment to social advocacy, both political and faith based.

Herman Blake:

If I could talk about a model of community service, I would use my mother's work in support of the low-income community in Mount Vernon, New York. She fought the authorities, even facing court action, in order to force them to back off their efforts to evict low-income people, and she won. We were on the lead list for eviction, and she refused to allow them to get away with what they were about to pull. They brought court action, and when it came time to go to court, my mother took all of her children. The authorities had this letter, had misrepresented themselves, and had acted in an inappropriate, unethical manner, and the judge ruled in her favor.

That stands in my mind as a classic statement of a person fighting the bureaucracy, winning, and becoming a community hero. She did it primarily for survival purposes, for herself and for her children, but it affected many families in that community. I remember my mother as the community hero, because she wouldn't back off from an oppressive bureaucracy.

Ira Harkavy:

My parents were part of the Jewish secular left, and that's very deeply embedded in my background. My parents were deeply dedicated to issues in civil rights and later in antiwar stuff. I was raised in a house where this was the currency—somewhat too much, I venture to say, as I get older as a parent. But this became the mettle on which you were tested. I was told as a young man that it doesn't matter how much money you make; just don't sell out. That's a tough role for a kid, because you don't know what that even means. But that was the orientation.

Bill Ramsay:

My parents believed in surrendering themselves to a calling. I remember specifically my dad saying, "Give yourself to some movement!" When I was probably six or seven years old [in the 1930s], my dad was the first president of the local union in Bethlehem Steel. He was well respected by everyone, because he was a church man, a Presbyterian of great integrity and ability. Dad went on to become the chief liaison between organized labor and the organized church. He tried to hold the churches to their commitment, and he tried to introduce images of faith into the unions.

　　He was a person of tremendous service. He had access to all these people, who were in our home. I have a receipt signed by Martin Luther King in my office for his expenses to receive the first Economic Justice Award. We were influenced way beyond what normal children are, reading these people's words, hearing them, meeting them.

## School and Community Life

"I came to feel connected and cared for in a contributing role."

Other pioneers were inspired to serve as a result of childhood experiences in school and supportive communities. Joan Schine recalls being sent to volunteer as a student in the 1930s: "My school was a demonstration school for Teacher's College [of Columbia University]. It was made into a school based on John Dewey's philosophy of education,[1] and therefore it was expected that one would participate in service. What was missing was the formal learning component. It was reading to the blind, working in a nursery that became a site for the Early Adolescent Helper Program some forty years later."

Bob Sigmon identifies his "commitment seeds" as being sown through experiences in the rural, family-centered community and school in which he grew up:

> My commitment got started when I was in the second grade
> [1942–1943] in Charlotte, North Carolina. I went to a little six-room school, with six grades. The principal was the first-grade teacher, and she kept back three or four of us second graders to teach the first graders when she was doing her principal work. A seed got set for me there of what it meant to be giving and taking, teaching and learning at a very early age.
>
> I felt as if I was somebody special. You were picked out. You were different. You were seen as somebody with responsibility as a seven year old. At an early age, we want to contribute. This was for me a chance to contribute in a way that I wasn't aware of consciously. But that's the seed I got. It began to get a little mulch, a little water.
>
> I was born in a rural community where I had a grandfather and grandmother, an uncle and aunt, a mother and father in the same house. Living my first two years on that self-sufficient farm had something to do with saying I was a loved child by an extended family. I had six parents who loved me. I came to feel connected and cared for in a contributing role. My parents moved to the city when I was two and half, but I spent all my summers on that farm. I bailed hay. I drove the horses as they put the corn on the wagon to go to the silo. I picked cotton as a little kid, had my little sack at the end of the road to pour my bag out.
>
> I had those experiences growing up in a communal way, which I didn't know was communal. That's just the way things were. People helped one another out. It was natural. You didn't know any different.

## Public Struggles

"When are you going to do something? When are you going to get involved?"

The political turmoil of the 1950s, 1960s, and 1970s had significant impact on the pioneers' development, stimulating and nurturing impulses that would mature into commitments to be engaged in society and seek educational and social change. Bob Sigmon recalls racial issues in North Carolina in the 1950s:

> In the early 1950s, the American Friends Service Committee [AFSC] got together leaders in the high schools in Charlotte: black, white, and the one Catholic high school. At the YWCA once a month for about a year and a half, we would come together, two of us from each school, and have conversation about life, school, whatever. This was 1952–1953. Think about that. Black, white, Catholic together. Where I was raised, Catholic and Jews were more feared and more to be hated than blacks. It was a remarkable setup. It's a theme that led me to what I've worked on all my life.
>
> When I was at Duke, I worked in the cafeteria with law students and other students from North Carolina Central University, a historically black university three to four miles away. They were my friends. They took me in and taught me a lot about discrimination—about my own history and my own separation. I saw institutional racism at Duke in ways that I've never forgotten. It drove another wedge into me to say, "That's something I've got to pay attention to—my own complicity as a white man in that business of cultural segregation, ugliness, and oppression." That's deeply rooted. Those guys taught me a lot just by being with them in the way that they accepted me, loved me and took me to their homes, fed me in their homes, introduced me to their families. That's something white boys in 1954 and 1955 didn't get to do.

For other pioneers, it was civil rights issues in the 1960s.

Tim Stanton:

I trace the roots of my career back to that day in high school in 1964 when one of my teachers grabbed a bunch of us by the collar, and we found ourselves marching down the main drag of Hartford, Connecticut, on behalf of fair housing. We were struck by that day, and by the larger civil rights movement going on. So some friends and I organized a civil rights group in our school.

Ira Harkavy:

In 1963, I was attending a YWHA camp in the Pocono Mountains in Pennsylvania. There were a number of counselors who had been involved in civil rights work, and we would sit and learn from them about their experiences, about what they had meant. Also that summer in 1963, there was a march in Washington, and my father and uncle were there. What was profound was watching it with both fear and a sense of enormous hope, watching to see my father and uncle, and then hearing King's address. That combined experience has profoundly influenced what I've done since.

Michele Whitham:

I was truly a child of the sixties. In high school a bunch of my friends got very involved in the civil rights movement. One of them went South to work as a freedom rider and was horribly injured; he had his pelvis shattered and came home crippled. I can thank him for getting me going, because he threw out a challenge when he got back. He said, "When are you going to do something? When are you going to get involved?" I've never forgotten that. We were both sixteen or seventeen years old. He threw down the gauntlet.

## Questioning Family, Society, and Education

"All of that was leading me increasingly to challenge the education I was getting, questioning its relevance to these monumental events of my day."

Growing up in a turbulent time caused many pioneers to ask serious questions about society and ultimately about their education. For example, as a college student at Harvard in the early 1960s, Gib Robinson found himself going off-campus to seek self-discovery and fulfillment:

Since I came from a very privileged suburban life, what I gravitated to was playing the guitar and going down to Boston and meeting Brownie McGhee, Sonny Terry, and Reverend Gary Davis, playing music, and meeting my first card-carrying communist. I was breaking the mold of being a preppie, of being a suburban kid, and finding that one of my closest friends was a German Jew who got out of Germany in 1938. Understanding that kind of suffering was crucial to my understanding the parts of me that I didn't have a language for when I was growing up.

Jack Hasegawa's experience at the University of the Pacific caused him to question the confining, fragmented nature of his college education as well:

In 1962, I was in my first semester as a fraternity man. There was a discussion group with the chaplain, and every night we would go for evening prayer. The challenge the chaplain would always put to us was, "What did you do today that changes the world?" So we were trying to do things, going out leading demonstrations, and then coming back and reflecting on it. The link of thinking about doing things and then doing something that was political and part of changing the world was very important. But I also remember being at a fraternity dinner and talking about what was happening in the South and having somebody stand up and tell me that it wasn't happening, it wasn't true, that people weren't like that. There were two important learnings from that experience. One was that soon I was no longer a fraternity person. The second was that we needed to have education that wasn't just classroom lectures. People needed to get out and see the world as it really was.

Tim Stanton had a similar experience in the late 1960s at Stanford:

We were moving from civil rights to antiwar work, and I was discovering that I was getting my education on the streets. My friends and I would have these discussions every evening in our living room, talking for hours and hours, analyzing our own experiences and beginning to do an analysis of the university. We asked why there was this huge gulf between who we were, what we were committed to, what we were learning from it, and what we did when we went to school and sat in the classroom. I found my education increasingly alienating. I learned more from the late nights with my friends and my application for conscientious objector status to the war than anything I did that was called academic.

As did Michele Whitham at Cornell:

I had a very strict Catholic upbringing, and part of college for me was breaking away from the institutional church and finding new ways to express my spirituality, my religious commitments. While I was going through all those changes, there was a very large civil rights movement on campus. There was an antiwar movement, and I was involved in it too. But a parallel and equally powerful movement was for equality on campus by blacks who'd been admitted to Cornell. We had some of the more spectacular building takeovers. I was involved with a white radical group and had a lot of involvement with the black activists. All of that was leading me increasingly to challenge the education I was getting, questioning its relevance to these monumental events of my day.

Dwight Giles was one of the few pioneers to find support for his interests from faculty—in this case, in religious studies at Lycoming College:

> We [Giles and other students] were the radicals on campus, and we were trying to do political organizing in the community. We were working with labor unions, neighborhood groups—you name it. I had been struggling to put my academic life and my activist life together. I was interested in questions of social action, and I thought I wanted to be a sociologist, but none of the sociology people got me excited about Max Weber. But the religion department was different. I went to class one day, and the professor wasn't there. It was 1965, and they said, "Oh, he had to go to court today." And I said, "What was it, a traffic ticket?" They said, "No. He got arrested this summer in Selma, and he's down there now as a result." I thought, "This is the major I want. These are the people I want to study with."
>
> I found somebody who let me write a senior thesis on Martin Luther King, which I started before he was killed in 1968. I was interested in the question of how people's ideas and activities play back and forth, particularly on questions of social action and nonviolence.

Nadinne Cruz, feeling betrayed by her education, quit school to learn from the social and political movement of peasants in the Philippines:

> I was a first-year student at the University of the Philippines, in Diliman off Quezon City, near Manila. There was a push by the students to connect the university to the needs of the country, which was extremely poor.
>
> I got curious about student politics, because I had a professor in a course who talked about American imperialism. I raised my hand and said, "Sir, Americans are such nice people." He turned rageful. Politically and ideologically, he was anti-American. I felt offended by the way he screamed back at me. I thought I would prove him wrong, so I started reading everything I could to show that he was wrong. But I discovered, to my amazement, that there was a lot that I didn't know, including American historians talking about the American imperialist period, the emergence of the United States as a country that wished to compete with the great European powers.

The result was that I felt betrayed by my education. How was it possible that for twelve grades I never knew anything about this? Shortly after, I quit school and joined a peasant organization to learn somewhere other than in the classroom. I traveled the length and breadth of the Philippines and got to know the social, economic, and political conditions. We were students doing research, documenting land grabbing, and many other violations of peasants' human and legal rights. That is the source of everything I do. I was about eighteen years old.

The social and political movement in the Philippines was emulating the China model, trying to get away from what they called the "effete intellectual," the bourgeois intellectual, the whole legacy of the Mandarin Confucian scholar, which students saw as parallel with the Western tradition of the effete bourgeois academy. We looked to the Cultural Revolution as a way to return people to useful knowledge. We studied Mao. The main thing I recall is a very self-conscious sense that we wanted to close down the liberal arts institutions, the majors like English literature. This was part of the Chinese revolution applied to the Philippine situation. We wanted to emulate the Chinese experiment by sending the bourgeois to the countryside to unlearn the sins of education, to learn a whole new way of learning from the people.

## Activism and Education

"We were looking at the structural causes of social inequality."

Some pioneers wrestled with the relationship between traditional volunteer service and social change–oriented activism, and sought to build connections between their activism and their education. In their search they experimented, if only as individuals, with forms of service-learning.

Ira Harkavy:

When I arrived at Penn [University of Pennsylvania], there was a tutoring project and a community involvement project. They merged, forming the Community Involvement Council. It became the largest student membership organization by my senior year. Probably because of the times, a lot of antiwar activists were in it and a lot of people very concerned with issues of race and racism.

We were working in liberation schools and freedom schools in West Philadelphia.

Some of us moved away from tutoring to engagement with communities, to dealing more centrally with issues of reducing racism. That became the primary focus. Some of it was very wrong-headed on our part—too strong in our emphasis—but some of it made a great deal of sense.

There was a deep intellectual mode. We were serious. Too much of it became like T-groups and sensitivity training, but there was a powerful political component. We read and we wrote. I remember the autobiography of Malcolm X having a profound impact. We were very sensitive to how to deal with these neighbor-hoods, to the issue of what the role of whites should be in the civil rights movement. A lot of us were impelled by a vision of King, in particular to figure out what it meant.

A friend told me to take this honors history class. I was a sophomore, entirely alienated in college, so I wondered why. I went to the class, and the teacher said, "Study history to understand the world, so you can change it for the better." What he did for me was extraordinary. I was stimulated to study the Gulf of Tonkin Resolution. It was my first experience of combining what I cared about passionately with academic learning. I remember calling him up, because I found that the New York Public Library had the best collection at the time on the Gulf of Tonkin. I'd never been this excited, because this research mattered to me and to society. That was my first taste of service-learning, in the sense that ideas mattered in the world.

Ken Reardon, after seeking to connect student community action with structured reflection and learning in a more struc-tured, programmatic sense at Rider College, found himself drawn to the University of Massachusetts, where there was academic sup-port for examining the structural causes of problems he sought to address through his service:

A group of us students, all of whom had been involved in high school in either antiwar or farmworker support activities, came to Rider College, this small business school, which was located next to a very distressed area of Trenton, New Jersey. We founded a student volunteer program and placed a couple of hundred students the first year with thirty Trenton agencies. But there was no structure for the students to think about their work.

The second year, we realized that was very important. We asked around and found somebody from the Human Relations Council in Trenton who helped us develop a curriculum for students in different kinds of placements. We gave students credit, but the requirement for credit was that they attend a reflective seminar. We called it "The Volunteer Program." We weren't too conscious of exactly what it was we were engaged in.

This was during the Nixon era, and we found the National Student Volunteer Program (NSVP)[2] in ACTION, a federal agency.[3] We got literature from the NSVP in order to figure out how to do this better. We invited colleges from around the mid-Atlantic region; fifteen of them came to a conference on student volunteer programs that combine off-campus service activity with some credited reflection component. This was 1971 and 1972. It was a very interesting meeting, and we learned a lot about how to run our program better. In our second year, we held four seminars. One, for students in education, was on issues of educational reform. The second seminar focused on the penal system for students working with the state prison. We had a third seminar on housing and community development groups and a fourth for students working with folks in social welfare agencies.

After that second year, our faculty advisor told us about funding from the federal government for community affairs programs, so we wrote a proposal to set one up, and it got funded. But it was a one-year grant, and the college refused to pick it up afterward.

Since there was no support from the college, we all ended up leaving. I transferred to one of the schools that had come to that conference on student volunteer service, the University of Massachusetts at Amherst.

At UMass there was a group of students who had criticized faculty for not developing course work that was relevant to community and public issues. They pushed the chancellor to set up a program to deal with this lack of relevance, something called the Center for Outreach, which had two programs. In one you could do a whole-semester internship and get credit for learning and working with a variety of service-based organizations. Or you could do part-time volunteer work for no credit or some credit. I ended up going to UMass to run the part-time internship program as a student. They gave me a scholarship. It paid me a grand total of seventy-five dollars a week, but it allowed me to go away to school.

At Rider we were using service to look at social service systems or educational systems or prison systems. When I went to UMass, I

found students and faculty who were looking at society and
how it produces uneven development. It put service into a
much larger political context. It was much more radical in
terms of the implications of the work. Our placements were
in community action and community organizing projects. We
had a large number of students working with farmworker support
committees, students working with the AFSC in antiwar activities,
anti-imperialism, anticolonial work, as well as more traditional
social service. We were looking at the structural causes of social
inequality.

## Service Experience as a Seed for Service-Learning

"Good intentions were not enough."

"That experience made it important for me to figure out
what this service thing was all about."

Many pioneers had service experiences in their youth that were
puzzling, if not troubling, and that provoked questions that would
motivate them to seek ways to connect action with knowledge
development on the part of both volunteers and those they served.
Mary Edens describes a challenging childhood tutoring experience
that stimulated her thinking about the needs of volunteers:

When I was in high school and tutoring fourth graders, and thinking about a career in teaching, what struck me was how hard it was.
I recall not feeling very comfortable in that setting. It took me a
while before I really became comfortable. What strikes me now was
that there was even that opportunity to volunteer, because there
were not many high schools that offered that kind of secondary-
to-elementary service program. Volunteering was expected.

But because it was expected, there wasn't a lot of support and
teaching involved. Just being there was supposed to be sufficient.
That's probably one of the things that I recalled as I was setting
up education programs years later: the students need orientation
before they go into school settings. They need help from teachers
to feel comfortable as volunteers. In my view, just to be there wasn't
particularly meaningful.

The act of service itself was problematic. Edens recalls her
childhood experience as a service recipient:

I was born during a bombing raid, in a camp for displaced persons in Salzburg, Austria, during World War II. The Red Cross aided us, and we were absolutely at the mercy of these care packages. So from my early years, there was an appreciation by my parents for the Red Cross and the churches that brought us over to the United States. But I also saw the kind of hold and power that people have on you through that service.

There was the Baptist church insisting that my father join when, in fact, he was an Orthodox Jew. I also recall discomfort at the extension agents who told us to spray the fruit on our farm, and even when to spray. We invested a whole year's worth of money in spray rags and poisons to make sure that we could eat our own fruit off our own farm. We were paranoid that the extension agency would come and tell us we were going to lose the farm if we didn't spray. Then there was my grandmother. After she immigrated to this country, the social worker insisted that she go on welfare. That was an affront to my father.

Dick Couto had a puzzling service experience in high school:

It was indicative of the nature of service at the time [1958] that we engaged in a tobacco drive on Thanksgiving. We went to a veterans' hospital to give tobacco to the people in the hospital. I remember one incident; it was the first time I saw people who were close to death. One of the volunteers was bringing us around, and we'd walk up to people who were just beyond help and leave cigarettes. We came to one person, and the volunteer said, "Forget him; he's too far gone," so we didn't leave any tobacco with him, because he was far, far along. That was an experience to see people so close to death. But that experience also made it important for me to figure out what this service thing was all about.

Jon Wagner had a variety of service experiences in college, moving from traditional volunteer helping to what he calls "off-campus field study." As he became more experienced, he began to ask more complex questions about the service in which he was involved.

The Stanford Volunteers program matched student volunteers from the university with community organizations for various kinds of service. I would go a couple of afternoons a week to the alumni house and take calls from students. I had a Rolodex, and I would call up organizations and make matches back and forth.

I did that my first year. In my second year, I got involved
through John Terrell [the assistant chaplain at Stanford]. He
was spending time in San Francisco in the Tenderloin district
with organizations working on drug rehabilitation with a very lively
cast of characters. I got very engaged with these characters.

I remember going up to San Francisco the first time. There
was a concert at Stanford by Jerome Hines, a baritone who was
also an active Christian. I had gone to the concert with Terrell
and a couple of other people. After the concert, Terrell said,
"Let's talk to Jerome Hines." We went to talk to him, and Terrell
said, "Would you like to come over to my house for some juice?"
And Hines said, "Of course." He came over, and we talked until
one or two in the morning, and then we all went to San Francisco.
We spent the night talking with Hell's Angels and drug addicts and
prostitutes and everyone else in a cafe. I remember going back
there several times. There was a service component to this, but it
wasn't organized.

Then there was a course I took in the spring of my sophomore
year in social psychology with William McCord. McCord taught this
course with a broad brush. He brought in community people who
addressed the class, as well as asking students to do a two- or three-
session service activity. He had a whole range of sites.

One of them was at the VA Hospital, where I went and worked
as a teaching aide. Several of us went together. It was the same
time that Ken Kesey was hanging out there writing *One Flew over
the Cuckoo's Nest* [1962]. This was a totally different world. Like
my hanging out in San Francisco, it was a strong sociocultural
contrast from what I was seeing in school. I had some very challenging experiences there, learning something about the complexities of service. I really thought I'd completely failed in
communicating with a group, only to discover that I'd actually
communicated well with some people who were not that active
in the group discussion. In some situations where I thought
I'd really succeeded, I lost the people who were in the greatest
need.

At the Peninsula Children's Center, I remember conversations
where people said, "I got a tremendous breakthrough with Jerry
[a kid at the Children's Center] today. He's never talked to me
before. Today I put my hands over my eyes, and he started talking
to me. He's really coming out of his shell." And I'm thinking, "Is
this a breakthrough for Jerry, or this a breakthrough for Nancy,
who's telling the story?" Jerry might just be going about his life as

he always has, but she has found a way to connect. He may not
have found a way to connect. How do those ambiguities about the
rewards that a person gets from this enterprise match up with
the rewards that the client gets?

It is apparent in Wagner's recollections that it was not just service per se that nourished his service-learning interests. These
experiences were stimulating questions about who was serving
whom when service takes place.

College volunteer work stimulated Sharon Rubin to consider
how service and learning ought to be connected:

In 1963, when I was at the University of Chicago, the Hillel, which
is the Jewish students organization, was running a Big Brother, Big
Sister program for a poor African American community right next
to the university. Somebody I admired invited me to a meeting, and
before I knew it, I was a Big Sister to this young girl. The students
ran this program, and I think they ran it out of very good motivations of an old-fashioned sort. That is, here we were, these privileged University of Chicago students, and there were those poor
black children, and we were going to go save them. I bought into
that because I didn't have much consciousness for anything else
at the time.

I did that for two semesters every other week. I picked the
little girl up, and we would go places, but it was really hard to make
conversation. She said yes to everything I suggested, but she didn't
seem very happy. She wasn't grateful, and I had expected her to
be grateful. This experience made me very unhappy. I felt guilty
because I didn't know what I was doing, and I didn't know how to
get out of it. So I finished out the school year and said I'd call my
tutee in the fall. But we both knew I wasn't going to call her. And
I didn't call her.

It was a painful experience. I don't think I ruined her life or
anything; I wasn't important enough to her. The problem was that
I didn't know enough, I didn't have anybody to talk to, and I didn't
have a professor to help me out. I was just out there on my own in
an environment that was not mine, trying to do things without
some basic understanding of what my purposes were or what I
needed to know about my tutee or her life or her community. We
had good intentions, but they were not enough. I think this was
the beginning of my interest in service-learning, as opposed to just
service. You can still screw things up if you have a great support

system and a wonderful faculty member to talk with, and a set of terrific readings, but you're less apt to if you are focused on what needs to be learned as well as on the service to be provided.

Bob Sigmon began seriously reflecting on the complicated nature of service in his postcollege missionary work:

It was when I left college and went to Pakistan, between 1958 and 1961, that the real seeds were sown for how I got involved. I went as a missionary to "save the heathen." My Eurocentric arrogance was deeper than I ever want to admit. It took me only six to eight weeks to understand that that was not the way it ought to be. The work I had to do there was as a hostel manager for outcast kids who were coming in from villages to a boarding school that had been set up by the Presbyterians and the Methodists. This time of year there would be thirty to thirty-five guys with severe malaria. I had sulfa-quinine and wet towels, and that's about all we could do, and keep them clean. They were serving me in fundamental ways. I started reflecting on that while I was there, reflecting on the mutuality of serving and being served.

There was a small group of Pakistanis and a missionary couple from America. The husband had been raised in India. After the kids went to bed, especially in the winter, we would sit around a fire—there was no electricity—and it would be reflection time. We would talk about these issues, asking, What are we learning? What's going on? When you're dealing with the kind of families we were living with and the kind of environment and persecution that these families were enduring, and the pain every day, without that kind of support I would have never made it. There was a sense of community and sense of reflection from people who had a long history sharing together. I had to talk about what I was doing.

After three years in Pakistan, I went to Bangalore, India, for a year and lived in a south Indian seminary. That was the only time in my life when I haven't had to work. I had a scholarship, so I had nine months to study, and wonder, and do a lot of talking. I did a lot of reflection on the missionary movement.

I then came to New York, to Union Theological Seminary. I spent two years looking at the Isaiah servant songs and the conflicts of that, *diakonia* and *doulos,* the words for servant or slave in the New Testament. I spent two years playing with that theme, trying to make sense of the fact that what I experienced in Pakistan and India had absolutely no connection to the abstract nature of all those fine theologians. Their fine lectures and the books they were asking me to read had no connection. But I knew that somehow the servant thing was important. It was a powerful motivator. That's where another seed for my commitment to connect service and learning came about.

Seeking to resolve "what this service thing is all about" would form the basis of a lifetime commitment for many pioneers.

## Spiritual Seeds

"Talk about a conversion experience. My life was changed."

Finally, some service-learning pioneers came to their activist commitments through more spiritual routes.

Helen Lewis:

One of my most important experiences was when I was a freshman in college. Clarence Jordan, who started Koinonia Farm,[4] came and spoke. He told the story of the Good Samaritan. He did those Cotton Patch Gospels. He rewrote the gospel according to the segregated style of cotton. This man was a Baptist preacher, a country man. He got up there and told a story, and talk about a conversion experience. My life was changed. I was never able to go back.

From then on I fought against segregation. I was involved in all sorts of student things in the 1940s in Georgia, which people don't believe could have happened, but they did. I got arrested in 1948 with a group of YMCA students. It was an integrated group in Atlanta, and it was before the lunch counter. It was on the front page of the *Atlanta Constitution,* and we were charged with disorderly conduct. They didn't want to charge us with breaking the segregation laws, because we would have taken that to court. So our names were in the paper as being in a mixed dance. Most of the young women had just graduated from college and had jobs in Atlanta. They lost their jobs, they lost their housing, and their parents disowned them. It was incredible the things that happened to people.

John Duley:

I attended a conference of the World Council of Churches on the theme of "The Ministry of the Laity in the World." This was a revelatory experience for me. A light went off in my head that is still there. It shaped my whole sense of who I am professionally and what my role should be. The central theological concept was that the ministry (read "service") of the church belongs not to the clergy, of which I was one, but to members of the church. They are already in the world where the church's ministries are meant to be carried out, and they have been entrusted with that ministry and commissioned to carry it out by their baptism. My job as a clergyman was not to be the church and do its work, but to nurture and equip the laity (Greek, meaning the "People of God") for their service in the world.

I was fortunate during that period to become a member of the Iona Community.[5] It is an international community dedicated to the renewal of the church. During that year, I developed a strong theological basis for what I came to know later as experiential learning. It was developed through my attempt, in the light of this new emphasis on the ministry of the laity of the world, to understand my role as a minister. I discovered in my own tradition an emphasis on the minister's role as a "teaching elder," one who leads among the people, is one elder among many, and whose primary responsibility is the support and equipping of the laity for their ministries in the world of work and society. The main thrust of the lay ministries, from my point of view, was service: concrete expression of love and justice in the world, and witness. Witness to me meant showing forth the sovereignty of God in the affairs of men by working for peace and justice, and manifesting the Lordship of Jesus Christ in the world of work through personal relationships and ethics.

The early lives of these service-learning pioneers were diverse in terms of the times and places in which they grew up, their family situations, and their school and college experiences. Nevertheless, three general characteristics are already apparent in most of them.

One is a drive to be of service, whether that service meant helping those in need or changing society, which was nurtured by parental and community role models, challenging friends and mentors, and a turbulent society struggling with the demons of war, racism, and poverty. The second is a critical, questioning stance toward life, society, and its institutions, a stance nurtured as well by the social, spiritual, and political movements of the time. The third is an impulse to connect thinking with action, or vice versa— to bring about "useful" education or more thoughtful service.

In most cases, this impulse appears to be internal to the pioneers, a personal and sometimes political response to the fragmentation they experienced between school and society as students. The seeds of this third characteristic were planted early but nurtured for different pioneers at different stages of their growing up by varied people and events. The "blooming" of these seeds would await the pioneers' first attempts to engage as service-learning practitioners, and their finding each other as a community of education and social change agents.

**Notes**
1. John Dewey advocated that a school in a democratic society should itself be a democratic institution and therefore closely connected to the community. Accordingly, a school should be a place where service and participatory citizenship are the norm.
2. According to Hal Woods, "Jim Tanck, one of the originators of the student volunteer program at Michigan State University, went to Washington in the late 1960s to set up the National Student Volunteer Program. NSVP was the group that got me going in 1971. They were holding workshops around the country. One was in Vermont, where I met people like Bob Sigmon and many others. Many of us were invited to participate as trainers in those events and to write for NSVP's national publication, *Synergist*. NSVP contributed important concepts around the theme of partnership between educational institutions and communities that were especially helpful. This partnership notion was a prelude to the reciprocity and empowerment concepts, which came later. In addition, we learned to make the link between student volunteering and the curriculum. NSVP was a part of the ACTION agency, and several of us were advocates before Congress in those years to change NSVP's name to the National Center for Service Learning. NCSL then continued its mission to foster the development of service-learning. This was the first national entity to promote this concept. The agency operated through the 1970s until it was closed by the Reagan administration."
3. ACTION was formed in 1971 to bring together such programs as the Peace Corps, VISTA (Volunteers in Service to America), RSVP (Retired Senior Volunteer Program), SCORE (Service Corps of Retired Executives), and NSVP.
4. According to Helen Lewis, "Koinonia is a communal, integrated farm located near Americus, Georgia, that was started in the early 1940s by Clarence Jordan, his family, and friends, based on primitive Christian ideas of communal ownership and social justice. Jordan and his col-

leagues were leaders of the early Civil Rights movement, and many leaders and social programs developed at Koinonia, including Habitat for Humanity. Jordan wrote the Cotton Patch Gospels—translating the gospels into modern Southern language and the context of segregation, discrimination, and economic injustice. He was a great influence on 1940s and 1950s college students."

5. The Reverend George MacLead founded the Iona Community in 1938 in an effort to make the church more relevant to life in the world. Comprising laypersons and clergy, this community had a common set of five disciplines: (1) daily prayer and Bible readings, (2) sharing and accounting for the use of money, (3) sharing and accounting for the use of time, (4) action for justice and peace in society, and (5) meeting with and accounting to each other.

# Chapter Four

# First Professional Steps

## A Journey into Uncharted Territory

Like those who explored the American West, the service-learning pioneers made their way into what we now call service-learning through multiple and widely varying paths. They had at least one thing in common, however: they had no road maps. In different settings and in varied roles, they found themselves groping for programmatic and pedagogical means for connecting community experience with academic learning, linking social action with critical reflection. Like true pioneers, they made their road by walking.[1]

Twenty-five of the pioneers began their explorations as educators: fourteen as instructors and ten as administrators. A significant number, however, were not focused on postsecondary education. Couto, Edens, Schine, Shumer, Stanton, and Whitham first worked with high school or middle school youth, and Sigmon and Tillman with adults.

Eight of the pioneers began their professional work in community-based or government organizations. Sigmon was a missionary in Pakistan. Hasegawa and Reardon found themselves supervising college student volunteers on behalf of urban community-based organizations, and Stanton established a community-based youth volunteer center. Tillman was attracted to the Lisle Fellowship, an independent, international service organization, after doing social service work in New York City. Goldstein worked for the mayor of New York, and Kendall joined a North Carolina statewide internship program. Ramsay initiated a manpower development program in Appalachia.

As is evident in their seeds of commitment, most pioneers were involved in or at least touched by the progressive social movements of their youth, among them civil rights, the antiwar movement, and anticolonialism. As they made their way into the work world, their developing interests in student empowerment, experiential learning, education reform, and social justice became common bonds and foundations of what would become known as the service-learning field.

Even in these early days, the pioneers' primary professional motivations tended to coalesce around one of the three axes of the service-learning triangle: connecting education with service, moving from service to social justice, and using experience in communities to prepare an effective citizenry. Although most pioneers possessed some combination of these motivations, their primary motivation caused them to focus on either community or student empowerment, or on service as opposed to learning. These two pulls, and the related tensions and conflicts over purpose, policy, and practice that result from them, were established early on and still animate the field today.

## Empowering Students to Learn and Change the World

> "What we were really interested in was empowering people, and service-learning does that."

The majority of pioneers were attracted to the pole of student development and education change. They describe their early, primary motivations to practice service-learning pedagogy as efforts to empower students, improve curriculum and pedagogy, and change education. Those focused on student empowerment describe many, varied expressions of that goal. For example, Joan Schine began her explorations of service-learning in 1967 with the National Commission on Resources for Youth, with a clear goal of youth development eventually focused on early adolescents:

> My passion at that time was largely combating racism: to convince minority youngsters who were poor and disenfranchised that they

could act as citizens and take some control of their lives. My work began with the National Commission on Resources for Youth [NCRY]. NCRY stood for youth participation. And Mary Kohler, the founding director, was very clear in defining it. Programs had to give youth a real role in the community. The youth had to work equally with peers and adults. There must be an opportunity for preparation and reflection. And whatever their activity was, it had to have a real impact on others. Youth need to be responsible for the results of their actions. That was her whole definition. You don't need much more.

The preparation and the reflection components, rather than just getting out and doing good, were extremely important. You'll remember that was the era of youth alienation. That was one of the buzzwords. Mary had an absolute conviction that alienated youth would not be alienated if we didn't tell them that they weren't very useful.

By the time I entered the commission's work, it was clear that younger adolescents were having the same kinds of alienating experiences that their older brothers and sisters had had five or ten years earlier. We thought, Why haven't we tried youth participation at an earlier age? One of the things that we learned early on in working with these youngsters was that many of them had never received credit before for making a positive contribution. That was a very powerful thing. What we were really interested in was empowering people, and service-learning does that.

As an undergraduate at Cornell in the 1960s, Michele Whitham was deeply involved in campus activism. Upon graduation, she began to focus on education as a means to develop and empower young people to make change. Like Schine, she focused on early adolescents.

Some of the people I was involved with in college, in particular Dan Berrigan, said to a group of us—white radical student activists who hadn't really found a niche—"You know, the most important thing is the transformation of people's consciousness. Why don't you start a school?" I said, "Yeah, why don't I?" My father was a professor at a university. He was in agricultural extension, and I had learned a lot about empowerment from watching his work, so these notions were familiar.

I got together with a group of other students who were in a similar position. We got a house and set up an urban collective.

We went to the local school district and asked them, Didn't they think the time was right for an alternative school? We laid out the language of the day—the stuff Jonathan Kozol [1968] was pioneering, along with Postman and Weingartner [1969, 1971] and all the other people who were talking about educational reform. We said we could bring all that to Ithaca, New York, for a very small amount of money, because we'd work for free. We were going to be graduate students, and we would get credit. They would get a bargain, and they'd have this wonderful school that would solve all of their educational problems.

The guy who was the superintendent at the time, a wonderful man, bought it. I guess it struck some chord in him. He gave us the money, and we set up a little school for sixty kids called Markles Flats Junior High School. The curriculum was to be a Foxfire [Wigginton, 1985] type.[2] We were going to get the students involved in community projects and community activities. They would learn experientially.

We did crazy things. The math course was building a building, so the students had to learn how to measure and work with fractions. I was the English teacher and was particularly concerned about the nonreaders, the blue-collar kids for the most part, who for whatever reason were failing in traditional education and couldn't read.

By this time I was aware of Freire's work [1970, 1973],[3] and I thought "naming" was potentially one of the most powerful forces on the face of the planet. I was very concerned about people who were cut off from naming, because they were cut off from literacy, so I started to work with those kids and designed a funny little program, the kind of thing that eventually the experts told us was the right thing to do. We got students to work with their reading problems by having them tutor nonreaders in elementary schools. They became the teachers. They had to learn the alphabet to teach the alphabet. They had to learn words to teach words. It was a wonderful program. I made it up as I went along.

By then I was also involved with Illich [1972].[4] I liked the notion of "deschooling," particularly after I had done that teaching, because I saw the ways in which kids were wounded by schools. Their imaginations were just completely suffocated by shoving them into these institutional boxes, even an alternative one, so I wanted to try my hand at developing deschooling. I founded with a man, who eventually became my husband, a program called the Learning Web, borrowed right from Illich. We talked to Illich about it, and he blessed it. I think he was touched that someone took it seriously.

From 1972 to 1976 we placed kids in internships in the community. One of the boys who went through the program early on today owns the business in which he interned. I remember one of the boys who wanted to intern as a chef; he had a dream about cooking. So we got him a job at a restaurant, helping the chef in the kitchen. But the poor kid lived in a trailer in the country, and they didn't have water. We had to work with him to help him think how he was going to address that problem, which was really to teach him about what the rest of the world expected. He had to work with us to figure out where he could put clean clothes and where he could shower and do all the things he needed to do to work in a food establishment.

During this same period, Garry Hesser was a young assistant professor at the College of Wooster. As he tells it, he was set on a path to service-learning as a result of calls for support from student activists at this rural college, which resonated with his long commitment and involvement in faith-based social action:

I had a seminary education; I had been a local pastor. I had gone back to graduate school to get a handle on as well as a set of credentials to deal with what was pretty critical to me and to lots of other people in the 1960s: civil rights and the war in Vietnam. Teaching was something I thought would be a way to get a hold of things.

When I arrived at the College of Wooster, almost immediately the first group of students I encountered, or rather they encountered me because I had been hired to do urban studies, were folks coming back from the Great Lakes Colleges Association Urban Quarter—students who'd been in internships and field study programs in Detroit, Portland, San Diego, Cleveland. These students approached me and said, "We're back in this little town of Wooster, but things have fundamentally changed for us from this experience we've had on the Urban Quarter. What can we do to keep that happening?" The group of us organized a house in which we had twenty students; almost every one of them had been an alum of one of the Urban Quarter experiences. My family and I lived in residence with these twenty students, and every student was expected to design a community service engagement and recruit students from the house and from the rest of the college to be involved in

carrying it out. Then all of us together designed a course on community to reflect on and study our community together as a group.

I remember one of our students who had come to Wooster to
play basketball. He came to me when he came back from one of
these urban experiences for his junior year and said, "You know, for
the first time in my life, people look at me, and I look at myself, as
something other than a basketball player. For the first time in my
life out of the Urban Quarter experience, other professionals and
other people look at me, David, and say, 'Hey, you can do something. You're valuable.'" He was a transformed person. He decided
to quit playing basketball and affirm other ways for his sense of
identity. It was this sort of personal transforming experience that
I saw happen to students that reconnected me to why I went into
higher education. I began to see students taking charge of their
own education. These students challenged me and gave me an
instant opportunity. That work became the center of what I did
at Wooster.

## Changing Education to Change the World

"I was an educator who had training in literature and was very
interested in how people learn. What should we be teaching them?"

While clearly committed to student development and empowerment, several other pioneers focused most closely on design and
establishment of an experiential pedagogy that linked service and
learning in diverse efforts to transform education. Like many
young faculty members today, Gib Robinson, a young assistant professor at San Francisco State College in 1971, found himself in
need of a new, more vibrant way to teach:

I had a clear sense that what was most compelling to me about my
graduate education was what I did with fellow students. I had
learned the mechanics of being an English professor, but what
compelled and excited me had much more to do with my work
with a group of colleagues and companions who were students with
me. It was a group, actually a men's group, that included people
from different disciplines, who were focused on educating themselves and were very drawn to alternative styles of education.

That group gave me an experience of watching students take
over their lives and become very active in the service of something

they believed in, which was not, obviously, in the classroom. It was morally compelling and politically very exciting and very successful.

When I got to San Francisco State, I wanted to get students actively involved in work they really cared about. I did two things. First, I found somebody who'd done volunteer work in VISTA and was now supervising reading tutors, and we set up a reading tutoring program. I took work I had done in graduate school at Berkeley using small group processes as a cornerstone of educational, personal, and social change. We used small groups as a cornerstone to the tutoring program. We took the first group of tutors and trained them to supervise other groups of tutors. The idea was to get students very active and engaged in taking care of, training, and supervising the students who tutor. The Center for Reading Improvement had a very good first four years. We trained about two hundred students each semester who tutored at elementary and secondary schools.

The other strand that was important to me was a Shakespeare course. I asked the students to create things that could be taken into the schools and into various kinds of public settings, working with senior centers, halfway houses of one kind or another, and a lot of high schools and elementary schools. We took a Shakespeare fair out there that included puppetry and representations of key scenes in Shakespeare plays. We had people doing costumes. We all wore costumes. We did some singing of Renaissance songs. We brought some food. We got engaged by feeding the audience and having them participate in various parts of the activity.

For me, there was again this sense that the students had a lot of organizing energy and a lot of capacity to design and build structures that they used to provide their service.

At that time I was not someone who was most interested in the service-learning, but I was an educator who had training in literature and was very interested in how people learn. What should we be teaching them? At the end of the Renaissance, John Milton said that the end of education is to repair the ruin of our first parents. Now, we don't think of education as that closely tied to the kind of basic restructuring of a human life, which was what Milton was talking about. But the fact is, the Renaissance has this very profound sense.

The best schoolteacher in the Renaissance, the most important to me, is Prospero, from Shakespeare's *Tempest*. He has an island, and he's doing experiential education with everybody who comes there. His goals are healing, that is, healing himself: understanding himself and educating everybody on the island to the extent that they are educable. Some of them are marginally educable, and some, like Alonso, are profoundly changed by the experience.

The Renaissance was so profoundly committed to education and change, to service-learning, that it combined personal transformation and service. Prospero's renovation of Alonso is the renovation of a king who will then serve his people in a way that is wiser and obviously less destructive.

That sense in me about being an educator came before service-learning. What I was looking for was to create an educational environment where people are open, alive, actively engaged, and joyful about learning. I didn't care what it was. It was just that service-learning brought out more of those qualities than any other format I had—certainly more than I could generate in the classroom.

At about the same time, Judy Sorum Brown, assistant director of volunteer programs at Michigan State University, was also thinking about the relationship of learning, leadership development, and the training needs of student volunteers. Like Robinson, she found guidance in the humanities:

We did a lot of leadership training of students. That launched me into my life work, which is leadership training for organizations, because we'd put the students out in the community, and the organizations would just misuse the students or underuse them. I thought that we needed to see what was going on. It must be that they didn't know how to use volunteers. Well, the irony was that they didn't know how to use anybody, forget volunteers. The leadership and managers of these organizations were struggling with those issues. I began doing staff training, ostensibly on how to manage student volunteers, but it was really about how to work with people.

What was driving me were developmental questions about what helps people become whole people. I got my degree in humanities, and went on for a master's and what would eventually be a Ph.D. in comparative literature. I was interested in various cultures and traditions and, because of my student leadership experience, in the capacities of people for high responsibility and leadership.

Like Robinson, Brown found roots for her service-learning interests in Renaissance literature:

I was doing my dissertation on the worldviews of Shakespeare and Molière, and the way in which a society that is unhealthy in Shakespearean comedies is healed by a process of everybody ending up in a kind of retreat setting in the woods with characters of various kinds with whom they wouldn't usually talk or rub elbows with. There's something that happens in those plays that is not linear and logical. It's a kind of transformation that comes out of being exposed to people you wouldn't otherwise listen to. There are mistaken identities, and roles get all mixed up. There are usually clowns, and the clowns speak both truth and nonsense. There are low-level kinds of characters like shepherdesses you wouldn't usually talk to. Somehow, out of all this confusion of being thrown into a completely different setting, the society breaks itself; in some way it heals itself and comes back into some new equilibrium. That's what I was doing intellectually at the time I was working with student volunteers.

There's some link between serving and learning that has to do with what happens when we co-create with a group of people a bounded experience in deep learning. We come in often thinking that we're teachers, just as we did, I think, with service-learning—coming in often thinking that we are serving. But we are being served through our learning rather than through just serving and teaching.

## Questioning the Relationship of the Knower to the Known

> "You have to show them how you can use sociology to understand something about the world and use that as a template for altering it."

Stimulated in his undergraduate years at Stanford to engage the world as a scholar, Jon Wagner continued to wrestle with the relationship of scholars to the society they were investigating as a graduate student, and then in his first teaching assignments. These issues influenced his approach to combining service and learning and have formed the basis of his research and teaching since:

> At Stanford, people were posing the question of how you could be engaged as an intellectual. It was part of my undergraduate life. There was never a service-learning model per se. There was not an exemplary sort of program, but you were looking for ways to answer that question: how you could be actively involved as a complement to your intellectual work, not just that you do your

intellectual work over here and then you do something else over there.

I went to graduate school in Chicago and dropped out at the end of my first year. I remember studying for my comprehensive exams. I was reading a book by Peter Blau [*The Dynamics of Bureaucracy*, 1955]. I thought all he's doing is to see whether his theory about a bureaucracy is correct. That's just not good enough to stay with a project: to see whether something's correct.

When I dropped out, I started working for an experimental school—a combination school-community organizing effort out the West Side of Chicago. It was a job, but it was very much a service reform job. I felt we were working with a community in a struggle to change by teaching kids to read. The school was relatively successful in the sense that it took high school dropouts and got them their high school diplomas, and some of them went on to college.

The other thing that happened for me—the other lens that started forming, through which I've understood most of the service-learning that I've done—has been the lens of social science field research. My graduate program was in sociology, and I enjoyed reading fieldwork and ethnographic studies. I remember reading *Street Corner Society* [Whyte, 1955] and thinking, "Gee, this is really good stuff!" and reading *Talley's Corner* [Liebow, 1967] and Irving Goffman's *Asylums* [1961]. The whole process is one of how people can be engaged in an unfamiliar setting, trying to make sense out of it and making sense of it to people who are completely outside the setting. You're trying to understand the world of mental patients and communicate it to other researchers, or trying to understand the world in books like *Street Corner Society* and communicate that to other social reformers and researchers. That's the challenge that's stayed with me.

I next started teaching at Columbia College. The first course I taught was called Social Problems. It had always been taught as a book course in the past. On the first day of class, in addition to doing all sorts of naive and crazy things to interrupt the classroom process, we had a two-hour discussion on what a social problem was. I said, "I don't think we can investigate this any further without identifying a social problem and trying to solve it." So then the whole class was focused on the problem we were going to take on and how we would try to solve it. The problem that the class took on was air pollution.

A second problem they took on was getting more donors for an eye bank. These were all student-initiated proposals. The class was organized on how to do that. On air pollution, the students had a guerrilla theater group, called the Air Pollution Rescue Squad, and would stage people collapsing with respiratory failure around the city and loading them into a van and handing out leaflets. With the eye bank, there was lots of community organizing. The eye bank was short of donors, and students were out trying to build a community base for recruiting them.

Shortly after that class, there was a social action research initiative. That was where we looked at a range of social issues—housing, transportation, air quality, education—and a range of disciplinary and media ways of responding to them, some of which included photography, creative writing, and social science research itself. The students would sign up for an issue and sign up for a section in a project. The assumption was to take these undergraduate students and teach them sociology, photography, and so on by having them engaged in these social issues and doing these collaborative community projects.

I don't think we were smart about how to do it. There was just this notion that you can't keep treating the social sciences for undergraduates as vocational preparation for graduate school. You've got to find a way to engage students as undergraduates for social sciences in ways that they can make a real impact in the world. You have to show them how you can use sociology to understand something about the world and use that as a template for altering it. You need to think through the relationship between your work and its impact on the social order. It's a responsibility to sort that out.

## Service-Learning to Strengthen Communities and Change Society

"It had to be real service—not academics, not made up, not superficial, not tangential, but real—and that's why it had to be agency based."

While fewer in number than those who used service-learning to reform education and scholarship, the pioneers who most focused on community service and social change had goals and motivations that were equally varied. Edens and Woods, based on university campuses, sought to support and strengthen the work of student volunteers and, through them, the communities they served. Hasegawa and Reardon worked in community-based organizations seeking to make effective use of student volunteers, as did Giles after he left his first teaching job in New York City.

In 1965 Bill Ramsay and Bob Sigmon established the first program to be labeled "service-learning." Unlike many of their fellow pioneers, they worked from a community base, which was, surprisingly, the Oak Ridge Institute of Nuclear Studies in Tennessee (ORINS). While very much committed to the learning and development of the students they worked with, they had an explicit, primary goal of community development. In fact, their program was first called "Manpower for Development." Their story exemplifies the community development approach to service-learning. Ramsay tells it:

> In 1965, I was employed by the Oak Ridge Institute of Nuclear Studies as a manager in the University Relations Division. ORINS was a corporation of southern universities and colleges, essentially all the major institutions of the South, formed to be the liaison between higher education and the atomic energy program.
>
> ORINS was concerned about the region as well as with its science. It was the mood then: we need to pay attention to developing our institutions and our people, and provide greater opportunities. Of course, the whole civil rights thing was coming along about that time. We were involved in that on the local level. It was a time of ferment, of social change, and we began to look for ways to assist that through involving higher education in dealing with these social and community problems.
>
> Wanda Russell, my colleague at Oak Ridge, and I were active in the Tributary Development Program in our community, which we called the Clinch-Powell Rivers Development Agency. We did research and reports that showed what we had in the way of natural, physical, and human resources. In that process, we realized how much information was needed and that information gathering is difficult. We arranged with the Tennessee Valley Authority (TVA) to carry out four pieces of research on development in our area. To carry out the research, we established four internships through the University of Tennessee. We developed this pattern of having somebody from the TVA, which was the technical agency, somebody from the local community, and somebody from the university work

as a committee to help each intern—not to supervise so much as to give points of contact and access to resources.

In each case, the intern's task was developed to meet a need of the agency. That took some doing, because some agencies weren't very sophisticated. For example, in Campbell County, the intern had the assignment of trying to sort out for the school superintendent what kinds of programs were available to him for development from federal agencies. It was a very poor county. The intern found over a hundred different programs that were available to the school system, most of which the school didn't know about.

He published a report, which was another feature of the internship. The interns actually had to come up with something publishable: useful but also academically respectable, properly documented, footnoted, and expressed. So, it had to meet both disciplines: usefulness to the community and academic integrity. That intern's report became very popular in Washington, because no one had catalogued these things before. It led to later catalogues like the *Yellow Pages of Federal Programs*. Several things sprung from this little intern's work down in a rural county in Tennessee.

We had another intern, in Union County, whose experience showed what happens to a student and, through the student, to faculty members. He was doing a study on serving the health needs in Union County. The health department had closed down, because there was a feud between two factions in the county. The intern went over there to see what he could find out about how to restore services to the county and came back saying that he'd discovered the problem. The problem was that this faction of people wanted the health department located in the building that they owned, so they could get the rent. He was outraged that this could happen.

We said to him, "You need to go talk to the other side. You just talked to one side." So he went back and talked to the folks who were on the other side, and, of course, they had a totally different story to tell. The problem was some doctor who was politically in with the other group, but he wanted the consulting contract or something like that. I remember the intern saying, "I thought it was a case of good guys versus bad guys, but it's not. It's a case of bad guys versus bad guys." That was one of the lessons he learned. His professor got involved and began to think of how he taught local government and how he might change the way he taught because of these experiences.

At the same time, we were looking at other devices to relate education and experience. We recognized that in Oak Ridge, we had the finest technology that could be found anywhere, so we put together a proposal to link a vocational training program with the fabrication plant to see if we could give access to this high technology and technical knowledge to people who didn't have it.

We brought together education, the Union Carbide Company, which ran the facility, the Atomic Energy Commission, the Department of Labor, and labor unions. Everyone had to be involved; we wanted support not only for the experience in the workplace but for trade-related instruction, the mathematics, and the English that you simply didn't have in the plant.

It was a tremendous success. We took people who were either in dead-end jobs or had no jobs, but they had to have shown some ability to learn. They worked side by side with the workmen in the plant in such areas as machining and nondestructive testing, even glass blowing and, at one point, welding. This was not machine shop welding; this was welding to nuclear specifications—space age stuff. They had to go to work on the same schedule as the workers did, live by the same safety rules and same standards, but their assignments were based not on production needs but on training needs. It was a hybrid of on-the-job training. When we graduated the first group out of this program, they went from either no job or jobs paying minimum wage to jobs paying at that time $6,000 to $7,000 a year, which was tremendous.

We recognized that we had something that was working in both the tech training program and the internships. We wrote a report, *Manpower for Development,* for the Department of Labor, which identified some of the programs we thought could be used to help develop the kind of manpower needed for the development of our community. That report included proposals for expanded internships, the technology training program, and other programs having to do with seminars and conferences. We found a ready ear in Washington, and we suddenly had funds from both the Labor and Commerce departments. In 1966 I hired Bob Sigmon, and we began to expand the program.

Now this caused a ripple in ORINS. When presented with these growing programs outside nuclear science, the board was supportive and said, "Yes, you may proceed down this direction." But keep in mind that these board members were university presidents and deans, people who had a broad picture, whereas the representatives from the universities who worked at ORINS tended to be heads of physics departments, chemistry departments, biology departments—people who were not in a position to have as broad a view. Some of them got very concerned that we were going to dilute the scientific emphasis.

It was a big question, and there was enough opposition to it that the board decided that it would be better to move the programs that could be moved. The technology program couldn't be moved because it was technical; it fit within the framework. But these intern programs, these social things, they were just too, too far afield. The board decided they should be moved to the Southern Regional Education Board in Atlanta. We were caught up in the excitement of our new work and didn't have a hard time deciding that we would take the risks and go to Atlanta.

It was in Atlanta in the late 1960s that Ramsay and Sigmon began to conceptualize their service-learning approach to the internship program. Bill Ramsay continues:

I remember specifically deciding that we had to give this program a handle; we had to give it a name. These were not interns like medical interns, although there were some similarities. They were not practice teaching. We were trying to find a phrase that would describe the program, and we tried all kinds of things: *experiential learning, experience learning, work learning, action learning.*

We decided to call it service-learning, because *service* implied a value consideration that none of the other words we came up with did. In my mind, it was never intended to restrict us to those things that can be put in a box called service. It was more of an attitude, more of an approach to be of service. It's not just any experience that's important for the kind of education we were talking about. It's experience with a value judgment involved. You could have experience with the mafia, and it would be tremendous learning perhaps, but it's not the kind of thing we were talking about. We were looking for something with a value connotation that would link action with a value of reflection on that action—a disciplined reflection. That was the model. It had to be real service—not academics, not made up, not superficial, not tangential, but real—and that's why it had to be agency based. It also had to be something that involved disciplined learning, not just casual learning.

Helen Lewis brought a strong community development focus to her work in Appalachia in the 1960s as well. In her case, her students, from families employed by the coal mines, represented the community she sought to serve. This made her goals and motivations clear and simple: educating and organizing community folks so they could take control of and improve their communities. Experience-based learning was her method:

> It was getting students involved with what was going on in the community—the social movements that were happening in the mountains. I was teaching at a branch college of the University of Virginia—Clinch Valley College in Wise, Virginia, which is in central Appalachia in the middle of the coal fields. I'd gone there in 1955, and this was in the 1960s, when things began to boom, things began to happen.
>
> The area had become a poverty pocket of the United States, because of mechanization in the coal mines. There was a loss of coal miners, with refugees going into the city. VISTA volunteers were coming in. Office of Equal Opportunity [OEO] programs were getting started.[5] It was also the beginning of a lot of strip mining. So there were a number of things that were of concern to the students where I was teaching, because most of my students were from coal mining families.
>
> I developed something called Appalachian studies. It's a big field now. Almost every university in the South has an Appalachian Center. But this was actually the first class, the first one of that sort. We had seminars every Wednesday night that would be open to the public and would focus on an issue or a problem that was important.
>
> Students helped plan those programs each time. They had to do research on the community and bring people in from the community to help do those programs. When we had a program on strip mining, we had a strip miner and people who were fighting against the strip miners.
>
> I remember one class we had in which I invited speakers from West Virginia: two doctors who had started the black lung movement. They came to class, and we invited miners and their families to come. We had 450 people show up for our class and had to move it to the gymnasium. In the process, the students got out a list and asked people to join the Black Lung Association. They formed the Black Lung Association of Virginia at that time.
>
> We began to get involved in various issues of the day. I started assigning tasks for the students, such as developing histories of the declining coal camps, developing information on land use and taxes of the coal companies, trying to understand what the root

causes were of some of the poverty. I began a social work program, placing students with emerging community action groups that were being formed through OEO and the War on Poverty.

The other class I did was called Community. Every weekend we would travel to a different community and learn from them, and then we might bring them to the college to talk to other people.

We also had a January term, where I taught a course in urban sociology, so we would go to urban centers. We went to New York City and visited with the Black Panthers. We visited with the Young Lords, who had just taken over a church in East Harlem. We had been in this church, and the leader of the Young Lords was talking to the students and saying, "You know, everybody who's tried to make change in the society has been assassinated." He went through the list—Robert Kennedy, John F. Kennedy. Afterward, we were down at Times Square, and we looked up and the news tape said "Yablonski and Wife Killed," and it hit the students; they had been working with Yablonski on his campaign.[6] The students said, "Remember what he [the Young Lord] said. Remember what he said."

When I wrote up the rationale for both the Appalachian studies and for the rural social work programs, I used Freire's pedagogy. That was the inspiration for it and for the style of teaching I insisted on. You had to learn through experience with the communities and with the people. If you used the region of the community as a lab, the people there had to be involved too and had to be teachers. *They were the teachers.*

Like Lewis, Mel King's focus in going to MIT in 1971 was community development and how the university could facilitate that. He came from a community base, working at the Urban League, and his students were not typical in terms of age or background. In establishing the Community Fellows Program, he sought to provide service-learning for activists in the Boston community:

The question for me has always been, What are the resources that are available? and How do they get shared? The university is a resource. How do we share it?

The story goes like this. I had been very concerned about two things. The first is that a lot of the people who were working in the civil rights movement had a lot of burnout, and with the burnout some family disruption. They needed to have time out; they needed to get off the firing line. I kept thinking about what it would take to do that. The second thing is that as I was doing work in New Hampshire, I used to go up the "electronic beltway" [several electronics companies were located along Route 128 outside Boston], and one of the things I was struck by in terms of meeting with people was the number who had been at MIT, who had used their time there to develop some new thing that they put together and marketed with some of these big companies. I just kept being struck by that, and I also thought about the fact that a number of us had some ideas, but we had no way to think about them.

One day I got on an airplane from Washington to Boston, and I went through the first-class curtain, and there, sitting in the first row with an empty seat beside him, was the president of MIT. I sat next to him and told him about what I thought was an important role for MIT to play in providing community people with an opportunity to do some research and think about issues in their community. When we got off the plane, he gave me the name of a professor and said he would call him. He did, and we got the Community Fellows program going.

## Urban Corps: An Involved Citizenry for Cities

"The model was that students could go out and make a difference. They could perform service to the city, the community, and it could be meaningful service."

Mike Goldstein's establishment of the New York City Urban Corps represents a third, distinct path to service-learning as a form of community development. While Ramsay and Sigmon focused on community development–focused internships, and Lewis and King developed curriculum-based experiential learning and structured reflection for community members, Goldstein's goal was to unite students and city government to give students paid opportunities to serve and learn about the city and provide the city with needed assistance. A longer-term goal was to build a more involved citizenry for the city.

Like many other service-learning pioneers, Goldstein was called on to take this role. The invitation resonated strongly with values and commitments he had developed in college:

In college I had been involved in the radio station as news director and program director. I was first a stringer for United Press and then worked at a newspaper on fellowship, and then independently worked as a reporter and editor for United Press in New York. I had experience out in the real world, seeing the value of doing things and how different that was from the classroom.

I was working in the mayoral campaign of John Lindsay in 1965 simply by having known a professor at New York University in the business school, Timothy W. Costello, who was running for city council president as one of Lindsay's running mates. Because I had experience as a reporter, I became the deputy press secretary of the campaign, which gives you some notion of the high level of sophistication back then. One of my jobs was to be a speech writer.

Costello, being a college professor, was given the job of drumming up support for the Lindsay ticket on college campuses. I wrote a speech for him to be delivered at Columbia. The speech talked about how the city and its young people were becoming strangers to each other, how this was bad for the future of the city, and how this alienation was something that needed to be affirmatively dealt with. In the speech, Costello said, "I propose an Urban Corps to bring together the city and its young people." The speech was well received. Lindsay was well received and won the election. My candidate, unfortunately, went down to a somewhat crushing defeat and returned to New York University as a business professor. I returned to NYU as a second-year law student.

Shortly after Lindsay was inaugurated, he appointed Costello as deputy city administrator. Almost immediately he said to Costello, "I really like the Urban Corps idea. I'd like to do it." Costello proceeded to call me up and, after I congratulated him on his appointment, told me how excited the mayor was about the Urban Corps idea. Then he said, "Mike, what's an Urban Corps?" I said that I hadn't the vaguest idea, but he replied, "You put it in the speech. Get down here and make it happen."

That's how I was very carefully and thoughtfully recruited to public service in New York City. A graduate student who was doing a fellowship in the mayor's office, Andrew Glassberg, now a professor of political science, and I were given the assignment of figuring out how to create a large-scale, urban internship program that would bring the city and its young people together. By the way, we had no money. Lindsay indicated that they had absolutely no resources to put into this program.

We discovered the College Work-Study Program, which appeared to us to be an obvious source of revenue for running this kind of operation.[7] We also discovered that the local office of what was then the U.S. Office of Education viewed Work-Study as something to be used purely on campus. The notion of using it off campus was something very foreign. We further discovered that the financial aid offices at each campus, which administered these funds, viewed them as intended to support the operations of the campus. The purpose was to have students shelve books, carry trays in the cafeteria, or rake leaves on campus and be paid minimum wage, and in that way have 90 percent of those costs absorbed by the federal government. They viewed any of those dollars going off campus as a raid on the institutions' treasury.

So, on one hand, we clearly had a significant source of funds, and on the other, we had two major constituencies: the government agency administering the program and the campus officials controlling the dollars, who were not particularly enamored with our idea. Glassberg and I, both being young and lacking in the knowledge of things one shouldn't do, decided to convince the mayor, which we did through Dr. Costello, to convene the presidents of the fifty-two colleges in and around New York City—invite them to a meeting in city hall. We had both New York senators; we had the deputy commissioner of education from the U.S. Department of Education; we had several members of Congress; we also had the director of the College Work-Study Program in Washington, whom we had gone down to talk to. When we talked to him, his reaction had been, "Well, no one's done it. But, damn . . . "—and this is a direct quote—"It really sounds like what Congress intended in the first place." So we had a bureaucrat who had an affirmative sense that a government grant was being used one way, when in fact the money could be used another way that's really much closer to what Congress intended the program to be.

So these college and university presidents came to city hall excited, because John Lindsay was a very Kennedyesque figure, who was going to transform our city as Kennedy sought to transform the nation. The mayor addressed the group and talked about his Urban Corps and how important this was. The senators and congressmen and the Department of Education official spoke.

Then we handed out a description of the program and what each campus had to do to sign on. The presidents went back to their campuses and told their vice presidents in charge of student affairs that they were going to do this program. That message ultimately worked its way down to the student aid administrators, who at that point realized that they had just been mugged. But they were in no position to tell the president, "No, sir, I'm not going to allow you to use this money which you have now committed to the mayor." This was in March 1966.

By June we had a thousand students at work in city agencies as a result of political interest in a concept of the city and its students needing to come together, a political commitment on the part of a mayor who thought that it was actually important and not merely a matter of rhetoric, and the commitment of a very senior political official, Tim Costello, saying what needs to be done and then giving two twenty-two-year-old graduate students the latitude to figure out a way to do it and support us in doing it. Those were the critical ingredients.

When Costello asked me what an Urban Corps was, my answer, "I have no idea," was very honest. I knew ultimately what the grand notion was: give students and the city a chance to interact with each other without firmly defining that involvement. But in the fine iteration of it, it was a concept that had no particular root. The domestic Peace Corps concept was on our minds. The model was that students could go out and make a difference. They could perform service to the city, the community, and it could be meaningful service.

## Pioneering Characteristics

These stories illustrate the multiple roles, goals, and motivations the pioneers brought to their explorations. They display as well interesting and perhaps critical characteristics of these pioneers, and perhaps of pioneers generally: characteristics in both the individual pioneers and in their social contexts that appear to be necessary ingredients for catalyzing bold, creative steps into unknown territories of educational and community development practice.

One characteristic that jumps out of the pioneers' stories is a strong sense of self and one's ability to have an impact. For example, Schine commented that in her growing up, she had never been "defined by her deficits." Duley noted that he "never learned to ask myself the question, 'Am I competent to do this?'" Blake spoke of a strong spirit of independence, which he learned from his activist mother: "First of all, I've little worried about authority. I couldn't care less and have never been reluctant to articulate myself in the face of authority, even to the people to whom I directly report. I've always had to be independent. I simply cannot work in a situation where I have to be a sycophant for somebody else."

Numerous pioneers carried strong religious, ethical, or spiritual motivations that were formed at an early age. Six attended seminary, with four of them (Duley, Giles, Hesser, Sigmon) going to Union Theological Seminary, before setting off into this work. Jack Hasegawa offers a description of his early motivation, which is exemplary of this group:

> I remember thinking this really early: that if I was going to be a Christian, I wanted to be the kind of Christian who makes a difference. So my models were people like Dr. King and Andrew Young. That's why I went to divinity school: because all these divinity school guys were doing all this important work. My religious motivation led directly to involvement in the civil rights movement, because I felt a literal Christian vocation to be there.
>
> One of my heroes, interestingly, was Harvey Cox, who was my advisor.[8] He is an example of a hypereducated, white, middle-class guy who literally spent every other weekend in Mississippi, at his own expense, working with freedom schools and preaching in local churches and doing whatever he could. He was a tremendously inspirational speaker. He was a deep thinker. He had a knack for translating complicated theological thinking into things that people would then act on.

As exemplified by Hasegawa, numerous pioneers had well-developed political convictions, whether spiritually based or not, that formed the core of what their work was about. Some of these convictions were instilled in home and family life, as with Herman Blake:

> My origins and my roots are in grassroots communities. In all of my work, I have tried to bring that perspective to the universities. So to the extent that I would characterize my work, it's that of merging the bottom with what you might consider to be some of the most elite educational institutions—the University of California and Swarthmore College. That was my intention, my goal, right from the start.

Other pioneers found their social and political commitments nurtured by the times and places in which they came of age, especially by the civil rights, antiwar, and anticolonial movements: Lewis and Sigmon in the 1950s and 1960s South; Cruz, Giles, Hasegawa,

Reardon, Robinson, Stanton, Wagner, and Whitham on college campuses in the 1960s and 1970s. Not only were the pioneers outraged by poverty, injustice, and war, however. They also learned from and were inspired by heroes of these times who took action against these problems. As we have seen, this combined sense of being moved by social problems and inspired by individuals taking heroic actions to right the wrongs played a critical role in what the pioneers chose to do as professionals and how they chose to go about it. Dick Couto articulates the influence of this social context:

> I saw my work as an extension of social movements of the 1960s, and I saw myself aligning with poor people's groups and organizing, being at least one avenue between those groups and movements and resources of more affluent communities. My motivation was political change. It was the 1960s, when things were possible. It was intolerable to be part of a society in which there were gross inequalities. Everyone has to do something about it. The Peace Corps addressed some of those issues in other nations. Then we had VISTA.
>
> My response was part of responding to domestic issues of poverty and inequality, to move students to address these issues. The motivation was also spiritual in the sense of my being tied to the problem. As part of a society, it was my problem, even though I might not have the negative consequences of that problem. It was mine to do something about. I had a responsibility for it.
>
> It made me feel part of a progressive movement, especially in western Tennessee, which was predominantly African American. It became very apparent that the work we were doing was connected with people who were very active in the civil rights movement. That area of Tennessee had the earliest voter registration drives in the rural South, locally led. This is where the Student Non-Violent Coordinating Committee [SNCC] gained its lessons—not where SNCC led, but where SNCC followed and learned. There was an incredible energy of feeling a part of a progression of social change that was going on. That fed me intellectually. It was rich to discover this history and to get insight into this social change.

## Finding "True North"

These pioneers are individuals who share compasses pointed at a broad set of internal social and political values, which were stimulated and nurtured by the times and places in which they came of age. This combination of internal values and external support greatly influenced the professional directions they took. But this can be said to be true of many, maybe most accomplished people.

There is another ingredient to the early experience of these pioneers, both internal and external to each of them, that appears to have been the catalyst for their taking on the pioneer role and that helped them find a "true North" toward service-learning specifically. This ingredient is a sense of being called to the work philosophically and even literally. Like Goldstein, more than half of the pioneers report that they were literally invited to step into roles that catalyzed their development as service-learning pioneers.

Recall Stanton's teacher's invitation to participate in a civil rights march while still in high school. He was later picked out and invited to establish a youth community service program in California, where he developed his commitment to service-learning. Whitham was challenged to think about starting a school by Dan Berrigan. Sigmon was invited to develop the first program described as service-learning by Ramsay. Students at Wooster College asked Hesser to support their experiential learning in an urban semester.

Just as Lewis and Clark were recruited and appointed by President Thomas Jefferson to explore the American West, most of the service-learning pioneers describe one or more instances where they were invited and encouraged to take their first exploratory steps as pioneers. This interpersonal dynamic in the early stages of pioneering work suggests that the pioneer experience, at least in relation to service-learning, is not only an assertive, individual act. It depends on context, both the time and place, and on canny individuals who have an eye for setting the stage for pioneering work. Each pioneer had a compass set to "true North," but as with all other compasses, they could not function without the appropriate magnetic pull.

## More Than Noblesse Oblige

A final characteristic of these pioneers relates to their understanding of and feelings about the act of service itself. Although many of them worked out of traditional service contexts (Brown, Edens, and Woods at university offices of volunteer services; Stanton at a community volunteer center; Giles at a mental health agency; Sigmon as a missionary), none of them viewed service alone as an acceptable response either to providing substantive experiential learning or effective community development. In fact, as their stories unfold, it will be evident that the pioneering nature of the work of these individuals resulted from their commitment to overcome deficits they perceived in voluntary service as traditionally defined and practiced on behalf of communities, and in experience-based learning as it was defined and practiced in the academy. In many respects, the history of service-learning is one of pioneering efforts not only to formulate the relationship between service and learning, but also to reformulate the concepts of service and learning themselves. "True North" for these pioneers, as Ken Reardon remarked, is the development of thinking people committed to and able to act on behalf of community development and social justice.

## Notes

1. To "make the road by walking" is a phrase articulated by Myles Horton, a pioneer adult educator and community organizer often cited by service-learning pioneers. Horton founded the Highlander Research and Education Center in 1932 as a training institution for union labor leaders and later for civil rights leaders in the 1950s and 1960s. First located in Monteagle, Tennessee, Highlander has become a leading adult education center focused on enabling Appalachian poor people to use their experience and knowledge to solve social, economic, and political problems.

2. "Foxfire education" refers to a teaching method developed by Eliot Wigginton in Rabun County, Georgia, where he assisted tenth-grade students in collecting and publishing oral histories from native Appalachian culture. This "cultural journalism" resulted in a magazine, a nonprofit education fund, and numerous similar projects nationwide and throughout the world.

3. Freire argues that oppressed people revolt by engaging in a dialogue by which they "name" the world by speaking of its conflicts. This naming begins problem solving, leading to equal participation and ultimately the end of oppression.

4. In his controversial book *Deschooling Society,* Ivan Illich advocates the total disestablishment of educational systems, because they are designed

to reproduce the existing social order. In place of schools he envisions participatory, decentralized, and liberating learning technologies and activities that radically transform social relations between youth and adults, and learners and teachers.

5. Established in 1964, the Office of Equal Opportunity was created as the official federal office implementing President Lyndon B. Johnson's War on Poverty programs. In a period of five years, spanning 1964 to 1969, it was responsible for starting Head Start, the Neighborhood Youth Corps, and the Teacher Corps.

6. Joseph A. Yablonski, unsuccessful reform candidate to unseat Tony Boyle as president of the United Mine Workers, was murdered with his wife and daughter on January 5, 1970, by assassins linked to Boyle, who was later convicted of conspiracy.

7. The federal College Work-Study Program, authorized under the Higher Education Act, provides jobs for undergraduate and graduate students with financial need, allowing them to earn money to help pay education expenses.

8. Harvey Cox, a Harvard Divinity School professor, argued in his book *The Secular City: Secularization and Urbanization in Theological Perspective* (1966) that God's work should be carried out through social action in response to the problems of a society.

*Chapter Five*

# Which Side Were They On?

## The Pioneers Target Higher Education

In many ways, this is a history of choosing sides. Not only did the pioneers find themselves drawn toward student empowerment and social change. They had to determine whether paths to reach these goals could most effectively be taken from inside or outside the walls of academe. These choices, not always conscious, were animated by their understanding of how and why they sought to join service and learning, and ultimately on their theories of how they could most effectively bring about social change.

Twelve pioneers took what we would consider traditional paths into higher education: undergraduate study, occasionally punctuated with stop-outs, followed closely by graduate work, which was closely, if not immediately, followed by campus-based employment as a faculty member or administrator. Like most other campus-based colleagues, they were drawn to postsecondary education by desires to teach students, engage in research, or participate in an intellectual community. However, of these twelve pioneers, four would eventually leave the academy, voluntarily or under duress.

Eighteen pioneers crossed the moat from community to campus, taking less traditional paths. Fifteen in this group would remain in academia; the other three chose to recross the moat, to work the community side of service-learning development: Sigmon quickly and permanently, Hasegawa eventually, and Ricks after several moat crossings in both directions. Three pioneers—Goldstein, Schine, and Tillman—are "outsiders" who, while often affiliated with post-secondary education institutions, explored service-learning from outside the campus walls.

## The Academy as Organizing Base

Whether they came to postsecondary education through traditional paths or crossed the moat after work in the community, most service-learning pioneers sought to make change from inside the academy. Several of the cross-over pioneers moved to the academy with explicit community development goals. Herman Blake wanted to "merge the bottom with the top, bringing the community to the university and educating students nobody wants to educate and moving them to high levels of achievement." Throughout his career, he has used service-learning both to expose university students to the knowledge and wisdom of low-income, disadvantaged communities and to interest and recruit youth of these communities to make effective use of the university.

Ken Reardon describes his move from the community to the academy, only slightly tongue in cheek, as a "low road to morality":

> I had worked as a community organizer full time for six years and worked as the trainer or support person from a campus with community-based organizations for a longer period of time than that. Why move to the university? I got sick and tired of raising money as a director of a community organizing project. How many times can you go plead to the Catholic bishop or Episcopal vicar that you are coming short of your payroll? Some of it was just fatigue.
>
> But some of it was because that's where a lot of resources could be mobilized to support the efforts I was interested in. It's sort of like Willie Sutton, who robbed banks because that's where the money was. In a sense, universities have some of the most important resources for revitalizing communities. Ideas are given credence or not based to an extent on how universities present them. Often students, future professionals, come to view their roles through lenses that the university helps provide. That's important. We have to change people's minds and hearts about what they're going to be about as members of society. Universities have received extraordinary amounts of support, and those resources should be made available and should serve the needs of people who pay their

taxes, who do hard work every day, who don't see much from those institutions.

Dick Couto and Jack Hasegawa originally worked their institutional bases to gain access to resources on behalf of communities. Couto, who started out as a schoolteacher, describes his role as director of health services at Vanderbilt University as "an element of redistributive justice":

> Here I was within a university with a lot of resources, and I was one avenue, a broker, between students, faculty, and services at a university and community needs. I was in a position to support outstanding community leaders who could invoke the Vanderbilt name, and that gave them credibility. We could deliver a number of resources to them, which gave them credibility as well. They could make other people believers that things could happen in their community by saying we're going to organize a health fair, and all of a sudden twenty students showed up. It reversed the tide of resources in a lot of those communities, where people had seen things leaving all the time. All of a sudden, something was coming in, and that provided leaders more credibility.
>
> I never thought of myself as a community organizer. I got very clear on that, because I don't think you can organize from a university that has insufficient accountability to local people. A community organizer needs to be around to take the consequences of actions that he encourages others to take. I really saw myself as an educator who stood at the edge of the university, so I could raise a window and hand out some machinery that the university wasn't using and find places for students to get out of the curriculum that they didn't find satisfying and get into learning experiences that they did. First and foremost, I saw myself as an educator, a member of a university, and an agent of change, trying to push the boundaries of the institution further towards the community.

Jack Hasegawa uses the open window analogy as well in describing his role at Yale University's Dwight Hall:[1]

> My earliest motivation came from my involvement in the civil rights movement. I was acting inside the institution, opening the window and handing stuff out to help Dwight Hall identify itself as a community organization that happened to be on the Yale campus and had access to Yale's resources. I was rejecting the attempt to

become a part of Yale or to hook up to Yale's educational mission.

The important thing was to get students to provide service, because the growth and leadership that they would get from that would be more meaningful to them in the long run. On the other side of that, what the community needed from us was not a bunch of undergraduates making decisions about what happened in the community, but for the community to have real ways to use students to get access to Yale in a wide variety of ways, from obtaining nonprofit sponsorship of community organizations to enable them to collect money, to accessing Yale's space without having to pay the $600 insurance fee, to being able to grab a group of undergraduates to provide tutoring or mentoring or survey work.

The most important teaching we did was to place students constantly in uncomfortable settings, in which they were forced to see community people as their bosses. I must have said that a thousand times in thirteen years: *The community is the boss.* You can go there, you can start stuff in Dwight Hall, but if it doesn't have a community board and community director within two years, then we're not going to continue to help. I was less interested in defending Yale students and their rights to make their own decisions than I was in making sure that people in the community, who had a need or desire to work with Yale students, could do that on their own terms.

The fact that few service and service-learning programs in postsecondary education today exemplify Hasegawa's emphasis on community control in either structure or practice suggests that focus on community development as a prime motivation to engage in this work may have eroded as the work has proliferated and moved toward the academic mainstream. As we shall learn in later chapters, this consequence of successful institutionalization of service-learning raises serious questions for many pioneers.

Ira Harkavy returned to the University of Pennsylvania to obtain a Ph.D. in history after several years of community work in Philadelphia. He did not feel effective serving urban youth. Like Reardon, Couto, and Hasegawa, he was deeply concerned with how the university could assist the Philadelphia communities in which he had been involved. He had an additional motivation for using the academy as his base. West Philadelphia could not change, in his view, unless there was fundamental change in the University of Pennsylvania. And the route to change at the university was connected to having it come to see its institutional destiny as tied directly to that of its neighbors. In Ira's view, the university could discover and develop this relationship through service-learning:

I had a lot of sobering experiences that led me back to the university to get a history Ph.D. I'll give you a quick story. I had this white kid from Sacred Heart Elementary School whom I was crazy about. He was a really good student. I said to him, "What did you learn from this program?" We were sitting around, I guess reflecting, and he said, "I learned a lot of history. I learned that the niggers had it as bad as we did." I realized I wasn't getting too far.

Sobering experiences like that made me realize my theory was wrong and my practice, too, no matter how good it was. I was excited, and I had good relationships, but I wasn't getting far. I had a sense that I had to go back to graduate school to study the world to change it.

I did my dissertation on reference group theory, group conflict, and cohesion of capitalist society, focusing on workers, Jews, and Presbyterians. I clearly was being socialized to become an academic. I became very concerned with status anxieties and other things. However, in 1981, my colleague, Lee Benson, gave a paper, a keynote address, in which he connected poverty with the state of American historiography, and he blamed American historians. He said the talk was a howling success, because everyone howled at him. He called for the creation of a national academic-practitioners alliance—a progressive alliance, which actually was formed with progressive unions, civil rights organizers, and academics. We then worked to do it locally.

We turned it toward West Philadelphia, to the neighborhood, on schooling issues. There the notion of academically based community service started to develop out of a participatory action research mode, asking the question of how universities can change the world.

The big change for me was realizing something I knew that I had gotten steered away from: you understand the world if you change it. I got back to that as I did this project. The learnings I've had since have been enormous.

I always felt that higher education had to play a role. The idea was, How do you make things better? How do you transform the University of Pennsylvania as an institution into fulfilling Benjamin Franklin's vision of the cosmopolitan civic university, which I don't think any university has achieved? That is my primary mission.

Like Harkavy, Nadinne Cruz sought ways to use the university as a base to further her activist goals and commitments. Finding a niche in which to do this work was a struggle, but one that eventually led her to the urban studies internship program at the University of Minnesota:

> I spent a lot of years as a political activist. I left the Philippines because Marcos was close to declaring martial law, and it had become quite dangerous for people like me, who worked with peasants and migrant labor workers.
>
> I went to graduate school. Fresh off the field, my questions were about how to close the gap between the haves and have-nots and how to deal with several hundred years' history of foreign domination of countries like the Philippines. I got to the political science department, and it seemed that they mostly wanted to do regression analysis or choice theory—mathematical modeling. The elegance of that was the name of the game. I remember some faculty saying to me that I should go to the math department and get some tutoring, because I needed to know some systems theory. What they meant by systems theory was engineering theory. But I wanted to study social change and development theory.
>
> So, finding no place for me in the purely academic setting, which I never felt comfortable with anyway, and seeing no home for the questions I had, I returned to being a political activist. I remained in the department, but I reconnected with people here in the United States who were working for social change in the Philippines. I got involved with the Alliance for Philippine Concerns, made up of the same activists from the Philippines who were coming out of the same intellectual mode of looking at the China model and having a very rigorous, disciplined way of connecting acting and thinking.
>
> It was very self-conscious, and we called it "practice of social investigation." For example, one of the skills of an activist was to read social settings, like field research. How to enter a community. How to read the social text of the community. How to enter and belong and be able to do things well, because you know the community well and know how to work in it. At the same time, I became more and more estranged from political science. I didn't feel at home there.
>
> About 1977, I was hired to run the internship program for all urban studies majors. Although I didn't have any background in

experiential education, I found myself coordinating internships, doing placements, and running seminars for interns. I was following the philosophy of the university, which said there was to be no credit for experience alone, so the seminar that I taught was to be the credited part of the program. That was my first connection to streams of practice in experiential education.

Consistently from then until now, I have seen myself mostly as a political activist whose paid job happens to be by choice in the academy. I see myself as having figured out a niche in academic spaces in order to continue work I started in 1963 as a student volunteer caught up in social change. I see the academy as an organizing base from which to do social change work.

## Changing Society by Changing Students

Although the role and development of students through community service was important to Couto, Hasegawa, Harkavy, and Cruz, they were clearly more focused on community development and institutional change. Other pioneers saw the route to community development and institutional change happening primarily through student empowerment and development. These pioneers crossed the moat into postsecondary education, because that is where students were. They wanted to encourage students' idealism, support it, and make it long-lasting and effective. Students would become the change agents.

Greg Ricks crossed the moat between campus and community many times. Whether working from campus or community bases, he always focused on using service-learning to inspire students to their highest ideals. For him and other pioneers of this stripe, service-learning was a means to student development, and students were the route to social change:

> My work has been around optimism and idealism over cynicism, about trying to inspire and give people the courage to be idealistic and to use that as a motivating source. My work has been about loving idealism.
>
> Service is synonymous with community. The more service you do, the more exposure you're going to have to your community, the more questions that are going to come up in your mind, and you'll become more curious. From that curiosity, you'll become a

much better student. A stream in my life is to maximize the potential for success on the part of college students through service.

I came out of undergraduate school thinking that housing was so important. Then I got into how people were educated and got hooked up with housing education. I was coming out of city planning and finding that almost all the policies were formed and controlled by developers. It was just building malls and that kind of stuff—the move toward the suburbs. There were so few efforts that looked as if they had any possibility of exciting me.

I started to move toward education, saying that there won't be any people who can buy housing and begin to control their destiny without jobs and education. You had to get education to get jobs, so that's why I decided to move into education.

I ran a program at Northeastern for minority youngsters who were coming to the university to take English, history, math, and writing to get ready for college. We had a phenomenal summer. We lost only one or two of the kids, and they all did very well, passing their two courses for credit. And the president said to me after all this, "I believe you can be a dean. I believe with your energy and enthusiasm, you're ready to be a dean right now." So here I was, twenty-three years old, and appointed the youngest dean in Northeastern's history. I was made a dean that day. That's how my career started.

The other thing for me is the sense of responsibility I feel to black people. I have to live a life that I owe to my grandparents, to my elders. I'll give you a classic example. When I was a student at MIT, I didn't go to graduation. It was back in the 1970s. Who wants to go to graduation? Who needs that bullshit? That was the cool thing to do. About three years later, I was talking to my aunt, and she was crying a little bit, saying, "Greg, I got to tell you this. I was so proud when you got into MIT. I was so proud. I can't begin to tell you how important your graduation was. I did day work for the chairman of your department for ten years. I raised his kids, and I saw him one day in Harvard Square, and he didn't recognize me. He walked right by me in the store, and I had tears in my eyes. He didn't even recognize me. I raised his kids! Now you were at MIT."

She gave me nickels, dimes, and dollars, and stuff to get through school, cooked dinners for me on Sunday, made me care baskets, and sewed my pants and all that kind of stuff. So my graduation was for her a "get-even" day. When I would have walked off that stage, she was going to walk right up to my chairman and say, "That is my nephew!" But I was too stupid to stand on that stage.

The next year I was invited to speak at this MIT alumni thing, and I brought my aunt. I said to that department chairman, "Do you know who this woman is?" He looks at her and is squinting his eyes, and my aunt says, "I'm Millie, I'm Millie." That's all she could say. After that, I told every kid of color: "You go to graduation. You go for the maids and the custodians, because they're counting. You go, because that's critically important."

Hal Woods crossed the moat after preparation and practice as a pastor. His commitment to service-learning developed from spiritual routes. Service-learning came to be a means for ministering to students: helping them develop values and effectiveness in community service:

> After seminary, I went to Madison, Wisconsin, to Grace Church, where I was responsible for developing a ministry for students in a project called Hayes House—a coffee house with student-faculty dialogue events and theater events. We started a school called Student Directions, with courses taught by students. Of course, the Vietnam War was going on, and there was a lot of dialogue about that. There was conflict between kids and their parents. That's where my interest with working with students developed and my interest in service.
>
> I worked with the students as they worked out their commitments and thought about the roles they were creating, and it got me thinking about my own role. There were the riots in Newark; the country was floating. Robert Kennedy was assassinated, and Martin Luther King before him. Those were very profound moments.
>
> I just started doing what I could where I was to help students increase their awareness of the world they were living in. We didn't have a volunteer program at that point, but they were starting to do that on their own. So we engaged them in discussion of issues of what could be done. It was ministry—in this case, in the context of church. I was working with students to engage them in serious issues of their time.
>
> A friend was at the University of Vermont and told me about a job there working with fraternities. That didn't appeal to me particularly, but it was a way to get into higher education. I went there in 1969, and there was an event called the "Kake Walk," which was from the nineteenth century. It had been a tradition for eighty years, and it was very racist. Fraternity teams would walk in pairs

in blackface, walking for this prize, which was a cake. It was televised all over the state. It was a major institution.

There was a movement from the minority students and the people of conscience on campus to get rid of the Kake Walk. We did in the fall of 1969. We replaced it with a film festival of student-created films the next year. A couple of our students created a film about volunteering that won first prize and helped get the service-learning ball rolling.

I was assigned to work with the student volunteers, because the fraternities would not have much to do with me because of my role in helping to get rid of Kake Walk. We had a community-faculty-student-administrative team study what could be developed. We began in the fall of 1970 and called ourselves the Office of Volunteer Programs.

That was a motivator: the events of that moment and the motivation of students to do something positive in the wake of that terrible historical artifact at the University of Vermont. I felt that student awareness, skill development, career aspirations, and ethical judgment could take place through service. It would just be enormous.

After a long stint in the Peace Corps and years as a classroom teacher, Dick Cone returned to graduate school at UCLA. While completing his doctoral studies, he was invited to work at an emerging university-community partnership, the Joint Education Project (JEP), at the University of Southern California. What started as a temporary assignment has lasted more than twenty-five years.

It was 1972, and there was a woman who saw a university in an inner-city community that could really make use of its resources, so she decided to create this Joint Education Project. She was a person with a lot of energy and vision. She designed it and came up with principles. We're still with those principles today. We take students in a course like geology, and they go out into schools in teams and teach it.

I was brought in to do curriculum development. I had spent ten years teaching, so I was hired to put together lesson plans. I remember my first reaction was, "This doesn't make sense. Why would a professor give credit to students going out into the community to teach?" I had problems with that conceptually. Only after I'd been around for a couple of years and started playing with the model myself did it start to make more sense. I'm still there, still trying to make sense of it.

My view of my role in changing society is to change it through students. I don't think we're going to change it through service. There are some programs in the country that have that possibility, where students do research and get information back to communities. The service our students render is easy in the sense of their impact on the lives of the [younger] students in the community. But the notion that somehow we're going to change this community by the service we do—I don't see that, even if we were to do this for a hundred years. Our students are essentially service providers in the form of tutorial help, mentoring, teaching reading, and offering mini-courses. But they're not able to have any real impact on why these schools are the way they are or why there's poverty in the community or why there's transience.

The only way we change the world is by changing the students we send out to do direct service—changing them so that when they become corporate lawyers, maybe they will be a different kind of corporate lawyer or a different kind of doctor. We have the potential of putting students out in an environment that will shake some of their fundamental beliefs and some of what they thought they knew about life.

## "True North" Is a Campus Home

Although many of the pioneers' paths into the academy were traditional, and many more made conscious choices to seek institutional bases for their work, only a few had typical academic assignments of regular classroom teaching, traditional scholarship, or conventional program administration once they got there.

Bob Newbrough is one of those few pioneers who found it relatively easy to find a campus home after a brief and frustrating sojourn in professional work. Although he describes his return to academia as "accidental," the ease with which he settled into Peabody College may have been due to the compatibility he found there between his commitment to community psychology and Peabody's history and applied mission:

When I finished my Ph.D., I didn't have any particular aspirations to work at a university. In fact, I expected to be a clinical psychologist in a mental health center or a veterans' hospital. It was one of those accidents of history that got me into this.

During the last year I was in graduate school, two of my friends, both of whom were at Harvard doing post-docs, came back to a Christmas party and said, "This is really a neat post-doc. You ought to apply." So I said, "I don't know what I want to do, so I might as well." I did and was accepted. It was that accidental move that sent me to both the Harvard School of Public Health and the National Institute of Mental Health [NIMH].

I figured I would stay at NIMH, but I became very demoralized about the kind of civil service mentality that existed—a sense that you worked by the rules and didn't do any more. By about 1965, I needed out. In fact, I said that if I ever start worrying about my pension, that's my signal to leave. I found myself worrying about my pension.

Within a short time I got a phone call from Nick Hobbs inviting me to come to Peabody for an interview. Initially, Peabody was very involved in Peace Corps and antipoverty work. He had been very much a part of getting the Peace Corps started and identified with what was happening. Peabody was probably one of the best examples of Lewinian action research of the day [Lewin, 1997]. [2] It had a community psychology program that Bill Rhodes had started. He left by the time I came, so I was seen as his successor. But when I came to interview for the job, I found that almost everyone on campus had a community orientation.

I stayed at Peabody because I liked it. I had good colleagues; I had good students. I was able to do the work that I wanted to do, and I was able, for a long time, to attract money to do it with. It has been an environment that has been very supportive of my work. Hobbs's public service ideology, which was there even before him, was one I liked and that has continued.

Several other pioneers found safe and relatively comfortable campus niches. Jane Permaul, Gib Robinson, and Sharon Rubin, for example, have sustained long careers on their respective campuses and were able to focus attention on developing service-learning as a response to their desires to enliven their teaching and make it respond more effectively to the needs of their students. Robinson's story of his work at San Francisco State University in the previous chapter exemplifies this response.

## "True North" Is an Off-Campus Home

In the previous chapter Jon Wagner, one of the traditional path pioneers, described his struggle to find a home for engaged instruction and scholarship in sociology—an intense personal effort to align his personal values and social commitments with a scholarly career. Jim Keith had to look hard to find an academic niche in which to pioneer community-based teaching and learning as well:

> My undergraduate training was at Wheaton College in Illinois. I was fortunate to have had a sociology instructor who emphasized the community base of sociology. I was carrying part of that vision with me—the vision of using the environment as text for students rather than the traditional textbook orientation.
>
> I began teaching in this two-year college and was given an education course. I designed that around student participation in nearby elementary classrooms, working with teachers. I did that more for the education of my students. It was only later that I began to realize the high value of this for communities.
>
> I left that job for several reasons. One was that I'd been teaching introductory courses four times a quarter for seven years, and I was beginning to burn out. But when the head of the college blew the whistle on what I was doing, because he didn't think it was appropriate for students that age to be involved in schools, that was a major disenchantment.
>
> Coupled with that was a call in 1973 from a dean from Westmont College in Santa Barbara, California, who had known me when I was teaching at my undergraduate institution in Illinois and had caught up with me, realizing I had a background in student development as well as academic sociology. He explained that Westmont had started an off-campus program in San Francisco—a combination of eclectic, independent urban studies and internships. That tapped into exactly where I was. I was tenured at the Georgia school; I was due a leave, so I went to San Francisco for a year, and I knew that, like Tom Wolfe, I couldn't go home again. I cut the ties with that institution and was in San Francisco for eight years.

Keith's difficult experience of trying to find a home on campus is more typical of this pioneer group than Newbrough's. For example, both Couto and Hasegawa eventually discovered that

Vanderbilt and Yale, respectively, would seek to lower their windows to the community, if not close them altogether. Both left their posts under pressure. A strong, explicit focus on accessing institutional resources on behalf of communities was difficult to sustain.

Indeed, most of the campus-based pioneers searched, found, and often lost institutional toeholds from which to explore service-learning. Of the thirty-three individuals represented in this history, sixteen were pressured out of their jobs or saw their programs closed down at least once in their careers.

Helen Lewis, whose pioneering instruction was introduced in the previous chapter, is exemplary of this group. She made her way into the academy along a traditional path. However, as her service-learning teaching came to be viewed as straying from the purposes and traditional practices in postsecondary education, it led to her being bounced out:

> My students got involved in the anti–strip mining movement and developed the Virginia Citizens for Better Reclamation. Some were involved in United Mine Workers elections at the time Yablonski was running for office. They monitored union elections and helped study land use. These things resulted finally in the programs' being stopped. I was fired. The students were in trouble too. It was tremendous. It taught me the very great power of that kind of learning and that kind of education. But it can be very dangerous work. Some of the students were threatened. People tried to run them off the roads. They said they were going to burn their houses down. According to the former chancellor of the college, the coal companies offered $7 million to get rid of the program. They said, "Get Helen Lewis and the students back in the classroom where they belong."
>
> I was a tenured full professor by the time I lost my job. If they want to get rid of you, they can. They did away with the whole program and put me in an untenable situation, where I would have had to completely change the way I teach. I could no longer take students out of the school. I could not bring outside people in, such as welfare rights people or union people, to talk to the students. I had no budget for telephone, no budget for film. I was placed in a business and public administration department.
>
> Myles Horton used to say, "You stay in the institution, and you try to change it as far as you can go. When you get to the place

where you're batting your head against a stone wall, then you go."
So I said, "It's time to go." I wrote a note and said, "Farewell, I
would rather raise turnip greens on my farm than do this."

A few pioneers never found home within the academy.
Instead they chose to work from community bases, seeking access
to the resources of higher education, primarily students, on
behalf of communities. As we learned in Chapter Four, Goldstein
targeted students and institutions' College Work-Study funds in
establishing the New York City Urban Corps. Ramsay and Sigmon
recruited students into service-learning internships on behalf of
southern community development needs. Schine established and
developed the Adolescent Helpers Program, which focused on
service-learning by middle school youngsters. Tillman recruited
student participants for the Lisle Fellowship, an independent,
intensive, intergenerational, international service-learning program. While response to "dis-ease" with postsecondary education
animated the work of these outside pioneers, it was not their
primary motivator. They were more focused on the community's
role in service-learning and service-learning's impact in communities.

The pioneers' commitment to social change, and their operating theories for how to bring that about, guided their choice
making related to where to establish their bases. These choices
were intimately intertwined with their goals and motivations for
combining service and learning. As we shall see in the next chapters, the motivation animating these choices found expression in
the program models the pioneers established and in their efforts
to sustain and institutionalize them in postsecondary education.

### Notes

1. Founded in 1886 as the Yale University Christian Association, Dwight
Hall was incorporated twelve years later as an independent, nonprofit
educational and religious organization. Undergraduate student service
groups are involved in a wide spectrum of activities in New Haven.
Although Dwight Hall often works in close cooperation with Yale, it
remains an independent organization, with budget and officers determined by undergraduates and alumni.

2. Kurt Lewin's field theory applied the principles of Gestalt perceptual theory to social, personality, and organizational psychology. Lewin and his students were pioneers of experimental social psychology and produced studies of cognitive dissonance, leadership, group cooperation and competition, conflict resolution, and group dynamics.

# Chapter Six

# Strategy and Practice

## Empowering Students to Serve Communities

One criterion for identifying the pioneers was that their work represent the widest spectrum of service-learning expressions. We identified twenty-seven strands in the field (see Appendix A) and selected individuals whose pioneering work strongly influenced or expressed most of these strands. Edens and Shumer placed strong emphasis on service-learning as a means to career education and civic engagement of students. Hesser and Permaul fused service-learning with cooperative education.[1] Cruz, Duley, Hasegawa, Royal, and Tillman focused on international and cross-cultural service-learning. Blake, Giles, Reardon, Stanton, Permaul, Wagner, and Whitham took an intensive field studies approach. Hesser and Keith focused on service-learning-based urban studies, and Edens and Sorum Brown on student leadership development. Couto, Lewis, Harkavy, Newbrough, Reardon, and others used participatory action research methods to develop community-based research as service-learning.

As we shall see in the pioneers' accounts of how they designed their service-learning practice, their choices of which way to turn were driven by institutional contexts, roles, and locality in terms of geography, demographics, social problems, and community leadership at hand. Thus, pioneers working in research universities tended to focus more on rigorous, structured learning strategies and/or research as service-learning, as opposed to those working in liberal arts or state colleges, who often placed more emphasis on leadership and career development. Pioneers with teaching appointments tended to focus on the process of experiential learning through service, while those who were administrators more often focused on program development and community impact. Those pioneers working in urban settings tended to focus the content and activities of their programs on urban issues in adjacent neighborhoods, while those in suburban and rural institutions tended to send their students into diverse and distant settings. Finally, those working outside the walls of the academy focused on the development of a specific region, community, or program in which they had a role.

The choices the pioneers made on how to design and establish service-learning pedagogy varied in a pattern similar to that we observed in their first professional steps and in their motivations to locate themselves in or around postsecondary education. Early service experience, values, and politics strongly influenced the goals they set and the strategies they took to establish their practice.

Although they broke new ground on such discrete routes, the pioneers shared a common commitment to integrating service experience and learning on behalf of "true North" goals of student and community empowerment, educational change, and social justice. While holding these broad, common objectives, some emphasized student development as the primary path, and others focused on community needs and outcomes.

We shall examine the pioneers' descriptions of their strategies and practice along this student-community development continuum. This chapter focuses on those pioneers whose primary focus was on developing and empowering students through service to communities. Chapter Seven looks at those whose primary emphasis was to strengthen and empower communities through student service.

## From Student Leadership to Career Development

> "We began to move from community service to service-learning in a career development model."

In 1975 Mary Edens joined Michigan State University's (MSU) Office of Volunteer Programs. Ten years old at the time, this office was perhaps the first university-administered volunteer program in the United States.[2] Prior to returning to graduate school, Edens had been a schoolteacher who used MSU students as volunteers in her classroom. From this experience, she developed ideas as to how the university could improve its support of student volunteers so they could be more useful in schools. Working in the volunteer office gave her the opportunity to apply these ideas.

Edens was not aware of the term *service-learning* or its concept at the time. But her urge to strengthen the partnership between the program and schools as a means to improve the experience and impact of student volunteers was the catalyst for turning the goals of this program from community service to service-based learning:

> Volunteer programs at Michigan State started in 1962 with a student leadership model. A professor initiated what was called the Student Education Corps: students going out to Flint. Within two years, there were six hundred students involved in a variety of educational projects. By 1965, there were approximately fifty student leaders, who were working with community agencies and organizing a wide variety of programs. Significantly, well over a majority of the volunteers were African American. They were taking leadership roles and working with the community, particularly in organizing new Head Start programs.
>
> It was Jim Tanck and Maxie Jackson, both African Americans, who wrote the proposal to the board of trustees for the program. That's unique for what is essentially a white majority university at that point in history. Maxie's dissertation was about volunteerism—I think it was the first dissertation [1972] on the African American community and forms of volunteerism. It summarized the non-formal ways that African Americans participate that tend not to be noticed in more formal surveys, such as those conducted by INDEPENDENT SECTOR.
>
> There were new forms of volunteering that students created in those days. Students at MSU were the first to organize volunteer income tax assistance for senior citizens in housing projects in Lansing. Adopt a Grandparent was founded at MSU. Each fall students organized their own leadership camp, trained each other, and provided a sense of continuity to the student-led service efforts. Service-Learning pioneer Judy Sorum Brown was one of the early assistant directors.

In 1975 Jane Smith came to head the office because university administrators wanted a change. According to some reports, during the time when many students were protesting the Vietnam War, MSU had milked the publicity it got from students' doing good in the community. This was tremendous for the administration and for institutionalization of the office. MSU got a lot of mileage out of the volunteers.

But in 1975, the war was over. There was frustration among students who wanted more money for the program. There was a sense on campus that student leaders had gained more authority than they needed. Community members were saying that students were trying to move programs along too fast. So Jane Smith was brought in to reorganize the program from a community agency perspective. She brought with her the concept of volunteer management.

She was a mentor to me. We organized a course on volunteerism through the urban affairs program, and we created a library that would be useful for communities. Ivan Shire and Marlene Wilson, leaders in the field of volunteer management, are two names that I learned a great deal about from Jane.

We were privy to related research in social work and other disciplines, and we tried to integrate the new concepts of volunteer management. Jane made a strong case that as a land grant institution, we should serve the people of Michigan and that the volunteer effort was a very important aspect of teaching community leadership. But it was still a time when if we didn't begin to integrate what we did more fully with mainstream university educational programs, then I don't think we would have survived.

Jane wanted a graduate assistant who had experience in education, and that's how I got there. Within a year I was made assistant director. It seemed overwhelming. Two-thirds of the volunteer programs at MSU—approximately twenty-five—were involved in educational settings, almost all working with young people or kids in some way, through the courts or through the schools. The programs were run by student organizations and student leaders, and it took a tremendous effort to work with them.

Edens's assessment of MSU's student leadership model and her response should be both familiar to and informative for today's practitioners:

It had tremendous strengths but also drawbacks. The strengths were that the programs were dependent on and responsive to student leadership, but the drawback was that student leaders varied sometimes, semester to semester. We couldn't provide consistency across programs, so we began to think about how we might better train student leaders or reorganize some of the programs for some consistency in the kind of training the volunteers were given and the way that students were placed and oriented.

We involved more of the teachers and counselors at the school sites, so we weren't just providing a service that was an add-on. For example, when I was a teacher and had volunteers working with my kids, I filled them in on what I thought might be helpful. No one from the university had asked me to; you didn't feel as if you were in partnership with the university in any way. My goal now that I was in that office was to create more of a partnership and involve the professionals more with the students.

The second thing was to get the schools to develop position descriptions so we could know what was needed. I worked closely with them to develop volunteer position descriptions.

The third thing was recruitment. It wasn't related to a student's career or major interests. The challenge was to tap the university better in the way it was organized to provide linkage to majors, programs, and student needs. We were getting students coming in saying, "I really want to volunteer for this," and then finding out that the reason they were doing so was in part because they wanted to explore special education or a career option. But that had to be a hidden motive, because there was such a strong community service or volunteer ethic in the office. We had at that time a department of special education that required ninety hours of volunteer work prior to admission into the major. But even those students were reluctant to admit that the reason they were volunteering was for credentials and admission into a program.

I thought, "Why don't we work on making volunteer service okay as part of a major?" The idea was to integrate volunteer programs with MSU's professionally based curriculum in a way that ensured that both student and community needs were met. We organized this model with three phases. First, students would research service opportunities with descriptions, categorized by department and colleges, that had been written by community professionals. The second step was for students to go out to the sites or to an orientation meeting and hear more about the placement. Then the student would use a decision-making model in selecting a site for volunteer work based on a combination of his or her interest in community issues and what that person hoped to learn, matched with what he or she had to offer: skills, research ability, writing. I thought this was especially important at MSU, where so many students were extremely career oriented, and parents, faculty, and students themselves expected that a career should be selected by junior year.

Finally, we made evaluation formative, given to students at a midpoint, so they could know how they were doing. Somebody was assessing their experiences and not assuming that whatever they did was okay. In this way, we began to move from community service to service-learning in a career development model. By 1979 we had three thousand students involved serving over a hundred agencies.

## Service-Learning for Civic Engagement

"By definition, civic engagement is a voluntary act, with people living in a culture where they have a say about what's going on. Learning how to do that is the power of service in experiential learning."

Rob Shumer built his service-learning practice off a career development model as well, one called Experience-Based Career Education (EBCE).[3] His early work took place as a high school teacher working with, as he states it, "students who hated school," exploring ways to make their education fun and therefore attractive and motivating. But he also realized quickly that students needed to feel important and effective in both school and in their communities in order to become successful. Experience-based service-learning became his method to reach this goal with both high school students and at the University of California at Los Angeles (UCLA), where he followed pioneer Jane Permaul as director of the Field Studies Development Program.

In 1969 I was a reading specialist, in my first year of teaching. I had a group of high school students who pretty much hated school. I was also taking courses and had learned about language experience stories, which were a nice way of teaching reading skills.

There was an elementary school right around the corner from our school. I was looking for a way for my students to do some reading, do something that was constructive, and try out this language experience activity. So every week my students and I went to the elementary school and worked with the first-grade class. My students would listen to stories from the elementary students and then take the stories back to the high school and write them out on large print paper. They had to make sure that they spelled the words correctly. The first graders did artwork for the stories, and we produced books.

We didn't call it service-learning, but it was integrated into what we did. It became a mechanism to give students an opportunity to assume important roles. I still remember one student who was involved in gang activity; he was a real hellion. He was leading a bunch of first graders who weren't paying much attention. I remember he said, "Rob, am I like this?" And I replied, "You bet." It was a transformational experience, because he never realized he was such a pain in the neck to teachers.

That experience propelled me in 1972 to teach a class called Urban Workshop, which was a social studies elective. Students did service in the community. We met with them twice a week, and they would reflect on their experience and what they were learning about community problem-solving skills. And that experience propelled me to develop an alternative school for kids who hated school. While developing the program, I heard about the EBCE movement. Far West Lab in San Francisco was involved in developing curriculum, and I had an opportunity to go to San Francisco and learn about it.

I came back and refined some of my projects and started the program in September 1976. My students spent 70 percent of their time in the community and earned all of their academic credit in community experiences. A few of them took traditional classes, at the high school or in adult education programs. We basically asked, What are you interested in learning? Then we constructed an entire curriculum based on that. If a kid was interested in sailing as a hobby, then he or she would do the American history activity through sailing the waterways in American history.

When I went to UCLA to work on my doctorate, I never expected to finish. But I wanted to know more about this kind of active learning, because it seemed so effective. There I had an opportunity through my chair to work in the Watts district of Los Angeles. The Charles Drew Medical School was developing a high school for health sciences and wanted to have some kind of community involvement. A doctor called and asked if I would talk with them about developing it. To make a long story short, I took the job about three weeks before I took my prelims. It was an opportunity to spend several years developing a magnet high school in South-Central Los Angeles.

The original notion was to have doctors and nurses come to the school every couple of weeks to do presentations. The students would occasionally do a field trip to the medical center. But I said, "No, that's not the way to do it. Kids ought to be in the facility every week as part of their English class, their math class, and their science classes." So they allowed me to develop sites in the hospital. I spent a few years finding what students could learn there and developing curriculum packages. I did my dissertation [Shumer, 1987] studying how learning took place in those field sites.

My other motivation is a deeply felt belief in democratic values, that somehow education is key to promoting these values. I studied theories of democracy from Dewey to Marx. The more I read, the more I believed that education is related to democratic values and civic participation. We needed to have more effective education-community connections. Part of my goal became to develop programs that engaged students in public dialogue and get them concerned about their own issues. Here's an example.

One of the students I had in the high school program had been kicked out of school for drinking, but he was a really bright kid. His social studies project was to work on his street. There had been two people killed in automobile accidents, and he felt the street was unsafe. He went through a whole year's investigation, learning about state, federal, and local guidelines for safe streets. He actually got the city to put in one of those electronic counters that checks the frequency of traffic. He held public meetings to try to get the public in this community to support him. It was a real-life story, because he lost. He never got the stop light put in where he wanted it. But it was such an engaging learning experience for him. I don't think he was ever going to go back to being a passive citizen. After that experience I think I could never go back to any other way of teaching.

Some students at the LA high school were studying health. They took on the school district because they were learning in a health class about hypertension. We had primarily an African American student body, and these students had learned that African Americans have a higher incidence of hypertension. They were realizing that the school district was feeding them high-fat, high-salt diets, which are not good for hypertension. So they said, "If you care about us, don't feed us this food." They actually got the school district to change the food. That was another example of this philosophy. I want to see students take action and win, change something. Students are the center of learning, and through learning they can improve things on their own.

The word *service* confuses people, as does *volunteerism*. I prefer the term *civic engagement*. By definition, civic engagement is a voluntary act, with people living in a culture where they have a say about what's going on. Learning how to do that is the power of service in experiential learning.

## International Field Studies

"I always had terrible culture shock when I went abroad for lengths of time. . . . I wanted to help students deal with that."

Nick Royal and Marty Tillman explored the use of service-learning pedagogy as international and cross-cultural learning. As with all of their pioneer colleagues, they were concerned with service itself, with improving the lives of others, and with social justice. Their route toward these goals was combining service and learning to educate students about other cultures, especially about how to interact ethically and effectively with people of diverse cultures and nations.

Royal came to the University of California at Santa Cruz (UCSC) in 1969 to direct the Merrill College Field Program. UCSC was a new, alternative institution in the University of California system. Merrill focused on community issues from multiple social science perspectives. To enable students to learn directly about these issues, the college required them to engage in field study away from campus, and it established the field program to coordinate and support these field studies.

Royal's approach to service-learning was drawn from what he had gained from, or felt was lacking in, his own experience as a YMCA volunteer in Venezuela after graduation from college and as a Peace Corps volunteer in the Philippines. His reflections on the contrast between these experiences formed the foundation of his work with UCSC students:

I always had terrible culture shock when I went abroad for lengths of time—to Venezuela with the International YMCA, and to the Philippines through Peace Corps. And I learned from UCSC students about reentry shock. I wanted to help students deal with that.

When I went into the Peace Corps, we got our training in Manila and then had a couple days to kill. Our trainer, David Szanton, said, "I know an artist and the cabinet member for education, the Rojar brothers," so we went and met Rojar, the artist, and later we met his brother. We met intellectual people in Manila, and that set a tone. We would meet with people who wrote short stories—a lot of great writers—who helped us think about where we were. I never had that in Venezuela, because the guy who was in charge of the Y had a very Protestant work ethic. He worked very hard, nose to the ground, but he wasn't particularly interested in the arts or anything. Szanton set the tone in the Peace Corps. He got us thinking in ways where we were always raising questions. There was a real academic tone, a learning tone, in the Peace Corps as opposed to when I was in Venezuela, where it was a work tone.

There were two aspects to the Merrill program. One was that we did local, part-time field studies in the public sector. It could be women's crisis or legal aid. A lot of placements were in the schools. The local placements could be ways of getting experience before students went abroad on a full-time placement. If you're going to work with children in Mexico, work here before.

We did full-time international placements. With these placements and Volunteers in Asia, we sent out maybe twelve people a year.[4] Students saw these as more exotic. But to me, both were important. Even when somebody came back from six months in Mexico, they might say, "I've got these Spanish skills now. Can I use them here?"

One of the things I would tell students was that you have to be an actor. You can't sit back. You can go into a big biology class and snooze, but in the field you have to be actively involved. It doesn't always work out well, but you get through it, and it gives you a sense of achievement.

When students did their field studies, they were asked to keep a journal. They were asked to write letters, and unlike the teachers who never wrote back very much because they were so busy, I would write back to them within two days. Some of the letters I used in a reader, but I'd give the letters back. Then they had to write a final paper, so there was quite a bit of reflection. There was one woman who was from Taiwan and lived here. She wrote a paper entitled, "Am I Chinese-American, or American-Chinese?" The papers varied a lot. A student who went to Peru kept an eighty-page journal.

Many, many students would come back and do more field studies. I remember one time, when I taught a course for many years, Social Change in the Third World, when the Sandinistas were in power in Nicaragua. A student said, "How can I go there?" I said, "Well, you have to take the prep class, and you have to do some Spanish work, and then you can go." She took the prep class in the winter and Spanish during winter and spring, and in the fall she went to Nicaragua for six months. Then she went back again as a senior sociology student and spent a year there. To me, that was what was exciting: to see that sort of continuity, that students used it that way.

Royal's preparation course was one of his major innovations. The Merrill program assumed that students needed to prepare themselves, in terms of both knowledge and skills, before undertaking cross-cultural field studies. Recalling his own lack of preparation for dealing with culture shock, Royal drew on diverse resources as he developed this aspect of the program. His method in this campus-based course was to give students experience of other cultures through readings, films, first-person stories, and cross-cultural training exercises. Through reflection on these experiences, Royal sought to have his students consider cultures on their own terms and how they should interact with them through their service-based field studies.

In 1978, I audited a course by Nancy Tanner in the anthropology department called Anthropology As Experience. We read *Blackberry Winter* [Mead, 1972], the experiential writings of students who had done fieldwork, and Malinowski [1967]—a lot of interesting stuff. I give credit to Nancy, because I was sitting in her class and realized what I was doing. It was philosophically parallel to training anthropology students to go into the field. The difference was that my students were doing projects that were appropriate for undergraduate, cross-cultural learning—living with a family, maybe doing simple research or language study—while an anthropology graduate student was doing something that would result in a book.

I also started reading field accounts. I read Hortense Powdermaker's *Stranger and Friend* [1966] and Rosalie Wax's wonderful book, *Doing Fieldwork: Warnings and Advice* [1971]. I put together bibliographies and got to know fieldwork methods in a way that worked well for the field program.

The other area that I got interested in was first-person accounts of going abroad. I call that "creative nonfiction." I used films to help students experience other cultures, I used Bafá Bafá.[5] I used novels or short stories from Third World countries. So we had writing that we were doing and writing from other places. For example, I used a wonderful novel from Peru and brought in an Argentinean woman to talk about it. We would read it and understand as best we could, and then she'd come in and expand on it.

I had a whole file of papers. If somebody was going to live with a family in Latin America, I'd say, "Here, look at this paper." I had a bibliography of books about India, novels and first-person accounts that I could share with students, and a lot of students' papers on their field study experiences. So papers were coming and going. Finally, I almost always used the students themselves after they were back from the field. These were some really great students.

## Cross-Cultural Experiential Learning

"My goal was to reengage undergraduates with Lisle's philosophy and methods of experiential education and cross-cultural learning."

Marty Tillman developed his practice from experience as well. In his case, the experience came from an internship he undertook in India as part of graduate study at the School for International Training (SIT). Tillman used what he learned in India to involve and support college students in the Lisle Fellowship, a small, intense, cross-cultural service-learning program, which was established in the 1930s and designed to build bonds across race, cultures, generations, and nations.

SIT grew out of work that the Experiment in International Living did training Peace Corps volunteers, and it gained a national reputation for that work. Jack Wallace, who came out of a rigorous academic background, was at the Experiment and became the first director. It was his vision. He wanted to develop an academic arm for the Experiment. He wanted to institutionalize the capacity of many people who had become affiliated with the Experiment and had international experience and put it inside a more disciplined, focused training program. He also had a vision that this would be a training program specifically for individuals who wanted to do their work within the nonprofit sector. It was, and I believe still is, the only academic degree that you can get that explicitly targets careers working with the international development community, say, with U.N. agencies and the like, or to be a campus foreign student advisor, or study-abroad advisor. Through SIT, I could connect my interest in student affairs and my desire to get out into the world.

I was the first American intern at the Gandhi Peace Foundation in New Delhi. It was a foundation that had been established with a trust fund after Mahatma Gandhi was assassinated. It was the linchpin administratively in India for the Sarvodaya movement. *Sarvodaya* means "for the betterment of all." The Gandhian network became the vehicle for my understanding what being a social change agent was all about: how to build a community to support social change. None of this I clearly knew before I got there.

I entered SIT in September of 1974, and in spring of 1975 I got off the plane in Bombay. I traveled by train to New Delhi. And everything flows from that moment in terms of crystallizing personal and professional ideas I've developed since.

I threw myself unwittingly into a highly political environment. The leadership of the Gandhi Peace Foundation was in opposition to Indira Gandhi. In June 1975, a "National Emergency" had been declared in India for the first time since independence. I was this nice little Jewish boy from Brooklyn who found himself in this incredibly volatile political climate. I became known as a CIA agent who had infiltrated the workings of the Sarvodaya movement, someone to be watched over very carefully. It was a wild time, a very unanchored moment.

The head of the Peace Foundation and some of the other men and women I met, who were elders in the movement, were wonderful folks to meet and become involved with. These were people who when they were my age, had already spent years in jail working for Indian independence. This "emergency" was small potatoes for them. I was incredulous at how calm they were at that moment in India's history.

I learned an enormous amount from them about what it meant to be a social change agent, what it meant to be engaged and committed. And I learned both through my own research and oral interviews a lot about Gandhi and his life and times that I had not been aware of at all. I learned how he was a teacher and educator. I learned that he had actually evolved a pedagogy for teaching teachers, who had themselves become change agents, leading to independence. Not many people realize that Gandhi was more than just a political activist. He had a larger vision. The ashram communities he set up were communities of change committed to building individuals who could manage change in postindependence times. They were communities geared toward training teachers who could work in the villages and help people understand how they could become economically self-sufficient.

Later in 1976, after I returned to New York, I attended a meeting where by accident I met DeWitt Baldwin. I came into this big hotel lunchroom and sat next to him. DeWitt and I started talking, as one does in strange environments, and he learned about my having come back from India. I learned from him about the Lisle Fellowship. He was the founder. DeWitt was seventy-eight and I was twenty-six or twenty-seven. I had never before met a man that age who was so engaged, active, and alive. We connected immediately, because I had just returned from India and he had been a Methodist missionary there in the 1920s and 1930s and had been influenced by Gandhi.

In 1976 DeWitt asked me to lead a Lisle Fellowship cultural group in Washington, D.C. I did that for eight summers. It was the first place where I could organize my interests and focus my work on cross-cultural learning with an international educational organization. My goal was to reengage undergraduates with Lisle's philosophy and methods of experiential education and cross-cultural learning.

The Lisle program that evolved in the 1930s was a very structured field experience learning program. It was one of the first, if not the first, program that talked about group dynamics long before NTL [National Training Lab] was established, before one could ever talk about sensitivity training or interpersonal dynamics.[6] They were ahead of their time in terms of what it meant to build small teams.

Some of the language used to interpret this secular philosophy was rooted in their student work in the 1930s and 1940s with the Methodist church, and it was really old-fashioned. Undergraduates didn't know what it meant and how to make sense of it. I thought the program was a wonderful idea, and I wanted to make sense of it in the current context. That's what led me to attach myself with the Lisle people I was meeting.

I became fully committed to Lisle and earned $7,000 the first year, because that's all DeWitt could pull out of a very measly budget. I was given the title national field representative. What that meant was that I was paid to network for Lisle on college campuses and with organizations in the international education community. DeWitt introduced me to virtually all the key leaders in the international education community because he was involved in the founding of every major international educational organization that existed in the United States. I was very young, but with DeWitt writing letters and making phone calls, it was a great door-opening experience. I traveled throughout the country for two years, doing that on two hundred campuses.

All of my work focused on undergraduates, but Lisle had always been committed philosophically to intergenerational learning in groups with undergraduates, graduates, and adults. Lisle was a mini–learning community for six weeks each summer. When it started in the 1930s, it was unique on two levels. One was diversity. It was interfaith and interracial at a time when no one was doing that. Also, it was extracurricular. Lisle was saying, "Do something with your free time in the summer." There were very few experiences like this offered after the school year ended in the 1930s and 1940s.

Lisle was about service in the context of an educational experience. In the middle of it all, the larger group—say twenty—would be broken up into five groups of four. The four on a team would be mixed: men, women, black, white, from different states—whatever it might be. These small teams would go out for a week or two at a time within a reasonable distance from the base community where everyone was living. They would basically be four short, very intense service experiences with a community agency or an institution. When the small groups came back to the main community, we would mix them up—change the teams. Then they would have a second or a third experience, depending on how well connected we were in the community.

When everybody came back, we would share the experiences and process the information. We tried to figure out what we learned about the dynamics of the community we were living in. That microlearning experience was incredibly rich for everyone.

The thing to remember is that this action-reflection process had been happening with both American and foreign students inside the United States and abroad since the 1950s. From 1952 to this moment, it has been all over the world. Lisle was always processing information in different cultures, from host national students and other students from abroad as well.

What you gained from that were the unique "why questions" from foreign students. Why is this happening? Why are you doing it? The whys were all over the place, because there were no assumptions that you could take for granted, if the people you were side by side with were not from within your own culture.

## Reflective Pedagogies

The reflective, questioning pedagogies Royal and Tillman developed for students doing service in cross-cultural and international settings are hallmarks of the approach to practice expressed by pioneers devoted to student development. Service was important, but the primary goal was to have students learn knowledge, skills, and self-awareness through structured reflection, so they would be more effective in their service while in these programs and throughout their lives.

## Popular, Artistic Approaches to Reflection

"I tried to get away from mostly using analytical modes of the academy. This is closer to how communities deal with their experiences."

Nadinne Cruz was fiercely committed to a social justice orientation to service. Her growing up in the Philippines imprinted on her the need to have community impact. However, having situated herself in an academic environment, at the University of Minnesota and then for many years at the Higher Education Consortium for Urban Affairs (HECUA), Cruz began to tinker with her understanding of popular education and progressive politics to develop a service-based pedagogy that used the arts as a means to help students understand urban contexts and their role as allies with those seeking to make change.

I went to HECUA in 1981 as assistant and then associate director, and finally as executive director, and was there for twelve or thirteen years. I mostly did administrative work and developed curricular materials for the faculty we hired. I didn't teach until later.

HECUA operated full-time residential internship programs in many cities. We served eighteen colleges, like Macalester, Hamline, and Carleton. They sent their students to our programs, which had course descriptions in their catalogues. The only public institution of the eighteen was the University of Minnesota.

We had a program in Bogotá, Colombia. The students studied the relationship between urbanization and economic development there and in other cities. Essentially the focus was on urban inequality and its impact, and what could be done. I had a hand in developing a program called Community Internships in Latin America; students did service, but also a lot of reflection connecting theories to what they were doing.

I helped develop and eventually taught the City Arts program. City Arts was about the multicultural politics of arts in relation to community development and social change. I connected the program to artists and community-based arts organizations and focused on how they defined their work as change agents, community developers, development organizers, and sustainers of change. I placed my students with these artists and community-based arts organizations. I understood the work that I was doing as connecting students to people who call themselves cultural workers. It included artists of color, who identified their work in terms of race or ethnicity, like Native American artists, as well as artists who were self-consciously European American, Italian, or Irish. I was very conscious about that, especially on issues of class.

I tried to get away from mostly using analytical modes of the academy by collaborating with artists to develop reflection activities. We would do rituals or ceremonies that artists could set up. We worked with music, or we would actually do arts activities together, sometimes in silence as a mode of or preamble to articulated reflection. I found that this is closer to how communities deal with their experiences. Their articulation is often not necessarily talking. I had seminars and reflections that went from 6 p.m. to past midnight, because of the students' involvement and commitment. The HECUA programs were comprehensive and semester long. We had a full monopoly of the students' attention for an entire semester. We had the luxury of using pedagogical approaches that took a lot of time.

## Cornell Field Studies: The Critical Questioning Model

"It was compulsively structured."

"Like Cinderella, even when you shove the foot into the glass slipper, something miraculous happens."

While Cruz was tinkering with reflective pedagogy in her urban studies program, Giles, Stanton, Reardon, Whitham, and others

combined their efforts at Cornell University to design and establish an experience-based, interdisciplinary curriculum in human
ecology. These pioneers were committed to working sensitively with
communities. However, because of their institutional context—an
Ivy League research university—and their desire to develop and
empower students with both a critical consciousness of the ways
society functions and a life-long commitment to social change, they
focused their attention on design and establishment of a highly
structured pedagogy of praxis. What resulted was a field study curriculum of prefield preparation, fieldwork analysis, project-based
community data gathering, and distance service-learning, which
effectively integrated theories of human, organization, and community development with related practice in diverse organizational
and geographical settings.

Whitham begins the story:

> I was at Cornell from 1976 until 1988 designing a large-scale field
> study program. We worked particularly on developing the action-
> reflection practice, because of where we were in a big, formal Ivy
> League institution. We had to justify the community involvement
> piece by wrapping around it a very structured reflective piece. We
> were designing formal courses, and the students had serious reflec-
> tive requirements. We were pushing the critical questioning model
> that I had learned from Freire[7] into a somewhat structured academ-
> ic mold in order to make it palatable to the academic institution.

As with Nick Royal at UCSC, part of the seriousness with which
these pioneers went about their work was reflected in the program's prefield preparation course. They felt that students needed
skills to function effectively in the field as experiential learners and
an orientation to the interdisciplinary human ecology curriculum,
which would be used to analyze and learn from their experiences.
Dwight Giles describes the prefield course:

> This course was developed by Michele Whitham. I'd read an article
> she wrote on it with Tim Stanton [1979]. It was a project-based
> course where she got teams of students together to take on commu-
> nity projects with the assistance of faculty to solve community prob-
> lems using a knowledge approach. I think it was one of only four or
> five preparation courses in the country at the time. It was the most
> academic—four credits—and it was required of all students want-
> ing to do fieldwork.

The first six or seven weeks of the course focused on building field skills: how to learn from experience, how to observe and interview, how to enter communities. The second half of the course took on a case study project in which students would apply these skills while trying to understand and contribute to the solution of a community problem.

When I came, I needed to develop a new case study project. Since I was new to the community, I started reading the newspaper to find out what was hot, calling people on the telephone and asking if they would like to do a project. I started developing one focused on a recently closed elementary school. The question was, What would the community do with this building? I designed the project and had it ready to go by the end of August. Then the parents decided to sue the school board for closing the school, so the project was put on hold. I had about five days to develop a new project!

One of the perennial problems in Ithaca was that Cornell housed only 40 percent of its undergraduates and dumped the rest of them into the local housing market. This created enormous problems for people in the neighborhoods. We tackled this situation by looking at different perspectives on it. Community people were the sponsors, and they guided the work. At the end of the semester, the students made presentations of their understanding of the issues to the community. Usually, because these were controversial issues, they were public events, sometimes covered by the press. Sometimes they were David and Goliath projects, where Cornell was always Goliath.

Once the students completed the prep course, they could choose to undertake field studies through one of three program options: a full-semester residential program in New York City, part-time field study in the Ithaca area, or independent field study in locations determined by the students, who were connected to the home campus and to each other through a correspondence curriculum modeled on that developed for the New York and Ithaca area courses.

The curriculum of these courses contained a three-pronged approach to connecting students' field experience with substantive reflection and analysis. One part was a focus on self-directed learning. Building on the work of Malcolm Knowles [1975], students were asked to articulate learning and accomplishing goals for the field semester and negotiate these with their field site supervisors. These goals were monitored by students, instructors, and placement supervisors during the term and assessed at the end of the semester. A second part of the curriculum supported that monitoring and assessment process through critical incident journal [Stanton, 1994] writing and intensive self-evaluations. The third part of the curriculum, labeled fieldwork analysis, provided a structured process for enabling students to analyze their field settings and host organizations through a hybridized social ecology framework, to gain an in-depth understanding of the conditions, systems, and politics at work in urban (New York) or rural (Ithaca) areas.

Tim Stanton describes the program's approach to this pedagogy:

It was 1977. The program had been given a mission by the College of Human Ecology to do two things: develop a curriculum of human ecology, and nobody knew what that was, and make it experiential. So, Michele and I, and then Dwight and Mady Holzer— Ken Reardon came a bunch of years later—crafted this curriculum. It's where I got this notion that experiential learning pedagogy was not just combining education and action. There had to be praxis, integration of the two.

I had been to the People's Republic of China in 1977 to look at what they called open door learning. There were many things we loved about what we saw, but open door learning was basically a political work program added onto a European education model. There wasn't, after all the Maoist rhetoric, any kind of engaged reflection for the students, any connection, much less integration, between the students' work and academic learning. So what we worked on at Cornell was a reflective curriculum, which enabled students to unite intellectual ideas with action in a systematic way.

We were developing it among ourselves. We were stimulated by this stuff. There was a lot of cooking that went on among us. The key to it all was student empowerment. Students who went through this program came out the other side more powerful.

We got to know the students. We were always trying to figure out what would stretch them in the direction we wanted to take them with the right level of intensity, but not at the cost of the community. Since I came from the community side, that was always important to me. The two poles of service-learning were always there.

I got letters from students after they graduated saying they were applying the curriculum in their work lives. What we were trying to do was develop people who could connect their thinking to their doing and could do things very well and be articulate about what and why they were doing it. It is our curriculum that would be the best description of what we did. It was compulsively structured.

Ken Reardon describes what he found and built on when he joined the program in 1984:

I saw a weird ad for something called "experiential education in New York City" with the Human Ecology Field Study Program at Cornell. That's when I met Tim, Michele, and Dwight, who became my colleagues in what was very explicitly an experiential education program with a commitment to service-learning.

I ran the New York City field study office. During my first year, I learned the ropes of how one functions as an experiential educator, which is a harrowing experience of going in and dealing in a much more interactive way with students than one is trained to do as a faculty member. In New York, we required that, in addition to the internships and the all-day seminar, students do a group community service project. It wasn't voluntary. We would work together in a low-income neighborhood with a community-based organization as client.

The students did some very good action-oriented policy research for community groups. In some cases, we got New York City to change a major decision that became very public. Our students were involved in that kind of activity. When we first instituted it, students were very angry that they had to leave an internship at, say, Merrill Lynch to go hang out on the Lower East Side. But evaluations every semester showed that the thing the students valued the most about their field study experience was the service-learning.

Dwight Giles describes the roots of the Cornell approach and the two basic pedagogical models that evolved:

We didn't use the "I" [for internship] word much at Cornell. I always thought of my work as community research or action research. At least that's the way I learned community development. It always had a participatory research component. Field study essentially is the academic idea from sociology and anthropology that you go into the field to study what's there. What we were trying to do at Cornell when we talked about it was use ethnography as a place to draw from. We were under pressure to draw a rationale for what we were doing, so it wasn't just skill and method. We began to talk about things like applied ethnography and community-based research. I wrote in my syllabus that we were doing community research with an ethnographic approach. In one of the last articles I wrote at Cornell, I talked about using community action research as a form of community development and experiential education.

There were two traditions, or models, that evolved. One of our former students was asked to explain the Cornell model, and it resulted in some discussions and then a paper [Giles and Freed, 1985]. That was based on earlier work that Michele and I had done but never published on the difference between a project approach and a placement approach. The project approach is usually community research and community development. For example, if a local hospital wants to set up a project for sick-child day care and wants to understand the feasibility of the market and how it would fit with other day care providers in the community, that would be a project. That would be community research, action research. The placement approach might be a student's going to the battered women's shelter. She may or may not have done a project, although we tried to make that distinction disappear by building in individual projects. That's what I do now at Vanderbilt, where even though you have a placement, you do a project.

In the New York City program, students spent three days a week in a placement and a day working on the project. Sometimes they were related; sometimes they were not. The rationale was that if you are going to see New York, you need to see not only your placement but see, experience, be immersed in, and learn from community issues addressed by your project. Some courses stayed more placement oriented, and some more project oriented. That was by design to give students a menu to choose from.

Finally, Whitham sums up her sense of the Cornell program from her perspective as an attorney several years later:

We developed a model of real community involvement and participation in building things. We would go into the community and say, "Tell us what you need, and we will try to marshal resources from the university to help make that happen." So our students became their employees in a sense. If the community organizations said they needed X, that's what the students would undertake with those people in the community. I was a project manager, helping to make these things happen.

When I think about the students and what they took from it
and what they went on to do, I have to say that, like Cinderella,
even when you shove the foot into the glass slipper, something
miraculous happens, because some of these people really got it.
They went on in their own lives to do amazing things. I would hope
that any of them who went through that program at Cornell came
away from it able to ask hard questions about their own lives and
what they were doing in society. Some of them went on to have very
illustrious careers trying to make social change, but that wasn't
necessarily the goal. It was more that old notion of good citizens
in a democracy. We wanted people of conscience, who were paying
attention, understood that they had personal responsibility, and
who would express that in whatever place they ended up finding
themselves over the years.

## Intensive, Year-Long Service-Learning: University Year for Action

"It's empowering the organization as well as individuals."

A related but different approach to intensive service-learning pedagogy from that which developed at HECUA and at Cornell was
pioneered by Hal Woods at the University of Vermont. Unlike the
pioneers we have heard from so far in this chapter who developed
and instructed their own programs, Woods worked more as an
organizer, brokering community needs, student volunteer interests, and faculty support.

Woods was assigned to work with student volunteers as a consequence of his role in ending the racist Kake Walk ritual. In this
new role, he was looking for ways to institutionalize and intensify
students' service experiences so they would have a stronger impact
on both the students and the communities in which they served.
He found financial and programmatic means for doing so through
the federally supported University Year for Action (UYA), which
was funded through ACTION in Washington, D.C.[8] Since his office
was not an academic program, he had to involve faculty in spon-
soring and facilitating students' learning and academic credit.
While Woods's pedagogy was not as structured and intense as that
of Cruz and the Cornell pioneers, his work well expresses service-
learning's value of mutual benefit for students and communities.

The Office of Volunteer Programs had established connections between the community and the university and had a mechanism to sustain student involvement. This enabled the faculty to focus on the intellectual side of students' work without having to get into management of the internships and connections with community agencies. It enabled us to have a consulting relationship with students, helping them find a path of service that was crucial for their own development and growth.

In the summer of 1971, I heard about UYA and saw it as a means of sustaining the energy of students by giving them the opportunity to work, in depth and full time, with a project or community organization. I felt real growth was possible in terms of student awareness, skill development and career aspirations, and ethical judgment in that year-long opportunity. It would be enormous.

The students went to the faculty and said, "Could we have this new kind of learning? Can we be freed up from ordinary courses to participate in this year-long UYA program, and can we create a course seminar for the program, so that we can be together reflecting on the issues that are coming up for us in the community?"

We were able to institute that course, and the deans and faculty supported it. It was very participatory. Fine things happened in the community in terms of the kinds of projects the students carried out. There was a mobile classroom in Winooski. Students worked with teachers out of a storefront school situation. There was a mobile medical van working with people in the rural areas of Vermont. Students would go out and interact with community members and make appointments and help them to get health examinations. There was a mobile dental van that went around the state, and students worked with it in a similar way. There was a tap-water project, with students doing sewage and water repairs for homes. The projects were very, very meaningful.

Students worked in these projects on a year-long basis. They came back to us every other week in seminar and shared their stories, talking about their victories and failures, their anxieties, how it related to why they were in college, and how it related to the world they were trying to change.

Our office also supported part-time volunteers, who would usually come up with an idea and create a project. But with UYA students, we had staff who could go out and speak to community leaders in a variety of social settings and ask questions about what was needed. Then we identified students who were willing to work on those needs. That's the difference that having resources can make. The UYA model enabled us to have enough administrative support, so we could work with the community to identify real needs and have students work on those instead of creating their own projects.

There was a process for this need finding designed by ACTION. There was a format for identifying the need, saying statistically what represents that need and what action is necessary to address that need, and what resources are necessary to support that action, and so on. We had a two-month planning process that first round and identified fifteen or so organizations that needed support. Then we identified a group of thirty students to start the first round. It was a lot of telephone calls, meetings, talking through the process, proposals, work plans formally written up so they were clear.

What emerged was the term *empowerment*, because what we were doing in those early days was working with student energy and student concerns to structure a process that would enable those students to follow their vision, follow their dreams, and make something happen in the community, whatever their interest was. We tried to design it so those dreams could be carried out to the greatest possible extent, and also have a reflective component for feedback and community building for the students who were working together.

It's not only empowering the individual, but empowering the community organization around its purpose and vision. So in many cases, as in the group of students who wanted to start a rescue squad, they did. We bought an ambulance, and that is still going on. A group started the King Street Youth Center; working with community people, they established it and bought a building, and that organization is still going. There's a new building, a gym. But it basically started with our students being involved with community people back in the early 1970s. It's empowering the organization as well as individuals.

Of all the examples of service-learning practice described by pioneers in this chapter, Woods's approach was perhaps the most balanced between, or integrative of, the twin goals of student and community development. He was able to achieve this outcome not because he was more committed than the other pioneers. Rather, this outcome appears to have resulted from the ability and staff resources UYA gave Woods to support long-term, full-time commitments of student volunteers and to stay connected with community organizations over several years. It resulted as well from his campus context. Woods was not responsible for the academic sponsorship and legitimacy of the program. As broker and organizer, as opposed to academic instructor, he was able to oversee and make sure that community and student learning needs were both met and well aligned.

In asserting this analysis, we do not seek, nor do we have enough data, to make an evaluative comparison of the pioneers' work. We do, however, wish to highlight the role that the pioneers' prior experience, values, politics, and institutional context played in what they chose to emphasize in their service-learning practice. For example, while the Cornell program was fiercely committed to the development of community groups and organizations with which its students worked, its pioneers, who functioned as faculty in a research university, placed most of their attention on design of a structured praxis curriculum focused on student empowerment. As we will see in the next chapter, other pioneers placed less emphasis on curriculum and structured reflection, because they were focused foremost on strengthening the communities with which they worked or found themselves in. Woods's "balanced" story serves as a fitting transition between the two.

## Notes

1. Cooperative education is a program in high schools and higher education institutions in the United States and worldwide through which employer-paid work experience enables students to combine course work with career development.

2. Programs such as Philips Brooks House (Harvard), Dwight Hall (Yale), and Stiles Hall (University of California at Berkeley) were established much earlier, but as separate nonprofit organizations, they were not administered or substantially funded by their host institutions.

3. Experience-Based Career Education is a high school program using experiential learning integrated with career exploration through which students conduct a major portion of their class work with career resource people in the community. The purpose of the out-of-school component is to help students understand the utility of what they study through projects relating high school subjects to careers.

4. Volunteers in Asia was established in 1963 at Stanford University by the dean of freshmen, Dwight Clark, to foster cross-cultural understand-

ing between the United States and Asian countries. This student volunteer program provides opportunities for undergraduate and graduate students in the United States to live in Asian countries and teach English. The program has expanded to offer trans-Pacific exchange, bringing Asian students to study at universities in the United States as well.

5. Bafá Bafá is a cross-cultural simulation exercise created by R. Garry Shirts in 1977. It is available through Simulation Training Systems at www.stsintl.com or (619) 792-9743.

6. Founded in 1947, the National Training Lab (NTL) works with individuals from private, nonprofit, and multinational organizations to improve personal and professional effectiveness. NTL's approach stresses the importance of self as a central agent of change. NTL programs are designed and led by a network of four hundred professionals with significant experience in organization development and change, leadership, team building, training, and related fields.

7. Brazilian educator Paulo Freire initiated a literacy program for slum dwellers and peasants in Brazil in the 1950s that used pictures and words designed to challenge students to think critically about their lives. Dialogue among the students about what these pictures and words represented was aimed at developing understanding of the root causes of problems and how students could effect change.

8. ACTION initiated University Year for Action (UYA) to link universities and communities through student volunteer work in connection with their academic goals. The University of Vermont program was funded as a pilot to link part-time volunteer activities with UYA's year-long structure.

# Chapter Seven

# Strategy and Practice

## Empowering Communities Through Student Service

The stories comprising this chapter reveal a bias toward the community in purpose and practice. In some cases this is because the pioneers themselves were from or often based in the communities they sought to strengthen. In other cases, these pioneers saw themselves as community allies extending the academy's resources—students, research capacity, and even prestige and legitimacy—to people and organizations.

### Urban Corps Internships

> "Urban Corps was simply a transferring of students from one setting where they got money, but not learning, to another setting where they were getting it all—the learning and service combined."

In Chapter Four Mike Goldstein described how he was called on by New York City's mayor, John Lindsay, to make good on an idea he had written into a campaign speech. Goldstein sought to bridge the gap between college students and cities, to provide cities with youthful energy and commitment and provide students with internships that would support them financially and enable them to learn how cities functioned. Working from a community rather than campus base, he had a primary goal of providing city agencies with capable and committed interns. He had a conviction and youthful idealism, verging on arrogance, that is evocative of that displayed in more recent years by the youthful leaders of the Campus Outreach Opportunity League,[1] without which perhaps he never could have envisioned, much less brought about, the establishment of the first national urban internship program. Goldstein was focused not only on enabling cities to gain from service of college interns, but also on using College Work-Study funds to ensure that all students could serve regardless of their financial condition.

> There were many people in the civil service bureaucracy who were firmly convinced that students couldn't be trusted to do anything but file papers and empty wastebaskets. We knew better, but I'm not sure why. It was partly instinctive and partly listening to people like President Kennedy and Mayor Lindsay say that not only can you go out and do these things; you *have* to go out and do these things.
>
> We used the term *internship*. It was called an Urban Corps internship. We didn't use *service-learning*, because it wasn't the term that people were using. On reflection, given the way we conceived Urban Corps as very much in service to the city, it was clearly a service-learning program—much more so than a work program. But we didn't conceptualize it that way, because we didn't have the language. We made a point of trying to say, "It's whatever you want to call it." We took co-op students. We took experiential education students. We took field experience students.
>
> After the first year in New York, we had 104 schools involved. The second year we had almost 200 schools. The third year, students came from as far away as California, with over three thousand students involved. We had one paid staff member, myself, who for at least the first year and a half of the program was still a law student. All the rest of the staff were college students supported through Work-Study. But we were not academics. We were really on the other side. We were essentially the recipients—the lunatics running the asylum, if you will, for students.
>
> What we also saw, at first anecdotally and then in a study, was that there was significant change in attitude among students. Their concept of the role and responsibilities of government changed.

Second, their attitudes toward themselves changed in terms of what they thought they could and would do. Third, the faith-in-people scale—their attitude toward people—changed as a result of the experience. Taking into account the infirmities of that kind of research, that's what we were seeing—and seeing in terms of students coming back for a second and third year, students joining city government. At least at some level, we were changing the students to go to work for the community development agency or the Department of Parks, or whatever, and changing them in terms of simply going back to campus and talking more intelligently about what happens in an urban setting.

One of the other things that was an article of faith for us was the concept of why we went after Work-Study funds in the first place. The easy answer for Urban Corps would have been to set up a volunteer program. We rejected that immediately because we felt that what we had seen in volunteer programs in our college experience was a very narrow sliver of students participating. The students who were excluded were the less affluent ones, particularly minority students—not because they were not interested but because they couldn't afford it. They couldn't take the summer to do this because they had to work at McDonald's to earn the money to go to college. They weren't excluded intentionally, because I think the people running the volunteer programs were of enormous goodwill and would have been horrified at the thought that they were being discriminatory. But they were being economically discriminatory, simply because a class of students couldn't participate.

By using Work-Study, which essentially was designed to support students who had financial need to start with, we were inverting the process. We were saying, "Here's an opportunity if you have financial need. It's available only to those who have to work in order to go to college." So, again, when we did socioeconomic studies of our students, it was dramatically different from the models that one would get in volunteer programs. We had a very substantial number of students who were low income. A substantial proportion of these students were ones who would otherwise have been doing jobs on campus in the library. They had to work; it was part of their financial aid package. Urban Corps was simply a transferring of students from one setting where they got money, but not learning, to another setting where they were getting it all—the learning and service combined.

## Research and Teaching for Community Development

"The best learning is that which involves persons doing mutual exploration, learning together, rather than the 'banking' type of learning, which Freire describes as giving something to somebody else."

As we learned in Chapter Five, Bob Newbrough moved to the academy from a community base. Unlike the activist Goldstein, Newbrough was a researcher who brought a very different approach to service-learning. Rather than involving his graduate students as interns to serve and learn about community settings, Newbrough wanted to train students in what became a service-learning approach to community psychology research—research that would be conducted in partnership with community members and contribute directly to community information needs.

I identified very much with the people on the margins. I was interested in their reality, and did what has been called helping people give voice to their reality. I was very moved by Martin Luther King's talk at the American Psychological Association in 1966, when he said, "You, as professionals, have a position of privilege in society, and part of your responsibility is to tell the story of people who don't have the ability to tell their story. When you do your research in poor communities, it's not sufficient to just report it out in journals. You have a responsibility to get it out to the general public."

Having that interest brought me to work in Latin America, into liberation theology: the assertion of Vatican II that reality and the source of all good is to be found with the poor and in the margins, that the center parts of cultures tend to be exclusionary and forget what's going on around them; they become inhumane. Those guiding principles have kept me going.

I set up the Center for Community Studies as a research and training enterprise, as both a community service and an extension service, and to involve graduate students in that process. We initially took on some work with Meharry Medical College to help them plan for a neighborhood health center. I began working up a survey questionnaire that we did out in the low-income area and involved students with that as we got going. That led to a series of projects. The community development ones, which tended to be out in the rural areas, were funded by the Tennessee Valley

Authority. During that period they had money for community development activities. I recall several projects that we did that were community self-studies of needs of teenagers.

I took the approach that students were colleagues. I told them that they were to introduce themselves not as students but as psychologists in graduate training. We presented ourselves as an action research team. Professionally, I set it up so we split the consultation fee equally. I felt that was symbolically an important move.

In 1980 Newbrough brought his community development focus to curriculum development and teaching:

They wanted me to teach a grant writing course. For a semester, I sat in on the course, just as an observer, to observe how it was done. Then I became one of the co-instructors the second year. At that time, the course was split in half: half a group dynamics course and half a grant writing course. We'd take half the students through grant writing, and then we'd switch—kind of a simulation exercise.

I had trouble with that, so I moved it into real grant writing, where we found a client organization in the community and wrote grants for them. More and more it grew into the students' preparing grant proposals. We would use National Institutes of Health forms and format. We worked with the Council of Community Services, with AIDS, the Nashville Cares group, which was planning a public education project in three counties. We worked at the Neighborhood Health Center. We worked with an antismoking group to do an antismoking campaign. Twice we worked with the Alternative Spring Break group here on campus.[2]

In some respects, the person in the environment is the core idea that I used. Then I brought in the Deweyan notion of transaction or mutual exchange between persons and the environment. The best learning is that which involves persons doing mutual exploration, learning together, rather than the "banking" type of learning, which Freire describes as giving something to somebody else. If you're going to work effectively, you've got to have at least two major theories. You've got to have a theory of the person, and you've got to have a theory of the community. And you've got to figure out how to make those work in some congruence with each other.

## Academic Field Studies and Community Control

"There is a lot of wisdom in the community. It might not be articulated in the way that you would articulate it, but if you learned how
to listen eloquently, you'd hear it."

At the University of California at Santa Cruz (UCSC), Herman Blake
developed a service-learning approach to field studies that differed
from that of the Cornell pioneers and from his UCSC colleague, Nick
Royal. He did not see himself as his students' instructor. That role he
assigned to the community people with whom he placed his students.
He did not take the researcher role, partnering with students and
community groups on behalf of community information needs,
as did Newbrough. He wanted his students to be immersed in the
life of communities in which they served, but their learning and their
service was to be controlled and directed by those communities.

Blake's students left UCSC for a full academic quarter. They
traveled to distant U.S. communities that he identified as distinctly
different from that on campus. He wanted his students to serve
these communities through the work they would do there, but also
through learning the wisdom and knowledge of their hosts—
wisdom and knowledge that was not normally accessible on a university campus. In learning to appreciate this community-based
knowledge, and thereby legitimize it in the eyes of their hosts,
Blake hoped his field studies students would empower the host
communities, so that their sons and daughters might eventually
come to the academy as college students.

Myles Horton taught me that there is a lot of wisdom in the
community. It might not be articulated in the way that you would
articulate it, but if you learned how to listen eloquently, you'd hear
it. I remember sitting with him in 1967 at a community meeting
somewhere, and a lady kept talking to him and said, "I keep asking
you questions, and you keep not telling me any answers." And
Myles's response was, "Ma'am, if you keep on talking, you'll tell me
the answer." What I got from that is that people have a quality of
wisdom that doesn't necessarily say, "This is the solution," but it
does give them ownership and some control.

Septima Clark[3] taught me in a different way that if you have an
idea you want to get accomplished, you don't develop the idea and
then go out and tell people, "Fit in." The best way to accomplish

it—and Myles was along this same point of view—is to go and find people who are doing what you want done and you try to help them. So you have people who already have a vested interest in the project and the idea. Septima also taught me, and so did Myles, that if you listen to the people, you will find the tools to resolve the challenges facing you.

When Page Smith wanted to start a program at UCSC of sending students into these communities, I stood against it. We had huge debates. I was in favor of students serving, but he was saying, "We'll go down there and study the people and write essays, and the students will learn." I kept saying, "Well, what does the community get out of it?"

I was struck by this a little bit earlier when some of the students began to protest as a result of the Vietnam situation. They went on strike. Some students went into the community to do some organizing. I remember one young lady who was trying to organize a buying club on a block. She came to talk to me about her frustration, because it was taking so long to get this club off the ground. I was pointing out, "You know, you just don't go out there and start a buying club." And she says, "Yeah, but the semester's coming to an end, and I have to go home for the summer." It was like the community wasn't operating on her schedule. And that, more than anything else, led me to the view that if we left it to the control of the universities and the students, they would use the communities to their service, to their own benefit. Sure enough, when the semester ended, this young lady and all the others exited the community and left those people disappointed.

So, first of all, my model involved working with community agencies that were not funded with public funds. Second, the students had to work full time under the control of the agency and provide service in the agency. Students couldn't go out and start their own projects. They had to be under the supervision and control of a community-based organization without public funds. That's how we provided the service.

Third, the learning came from the students' living in the homes of community people. They stayed in that community the whole term, living with a family and working with an agency. They would leave at the beginning of the term, go into the community, and live there for ten weeks. They would get full academic credit. They were under the supervision of those communities. That was the model. The learning came from the living experience. No more than two students could live with any one family. The university paid the student's room and board to the agency. The agency dealt with the family. We never did any direct dealing with the families. The agency found the families, and the agency supervised the students. Then they began to see the family's lives at the informal times— the times when they were not guarded. They learned the cuisine, the cooking. They became involved in social events.

We sent a young lady to Ridgeland, South Carolina. She lived in the home of a family that had no running water, and this was a young lady who was used to washing her hair every day. In order to shampoo her hair, she had to go out and pump the water and then heat it and all that business. Well, that experience began to raise questions for her as to how valuable and how important that daily shampoo practice was. It was this process of living in the homes of people who were very much unlike these students. Participating in their lives would be a learning process that would not only challenge the students' values but would offer them other perspectives.

The families got a great deal out of it too. First of all, they had the involvement of this individual who often became like another child. I remember going into this house, and here was a student in bed with five or six kids reading *Charlotte's Web*. For these kids in that community to have a pig that talked—I mean they didn't have TV and all that sort of thing. They were thoroughly fascinated.

One of the things that was very important was that no matter where we sent students, whether it was around the corner, to Alameda County, to South Carolina, or to Tierra Amarillo, New Mexico, the students always went by Greyhound bus. We found that college students were so used to traveling to other places and never leaving where they left that if you put them on a plane in the morning and they got off in the afternoon completely across the country, it took longer for them to make the transition into that community than if they went by bus. Let's say a student was leaving California and going to Beaufort, South Carolina. By the time he or she got to Bakersfield, just a few hours away, the student would meet a family getting on the bus going to Beaufort County. Now these people were doing it because they had to. So by the time the student got to Beaufort County, he or she had another set of friends.

The other side of the coin is that we made a commitment to the community for a minimum of five years. No project would be undertaken that we did not feel confident that we could keep supplying students for five years. As a result, we became so engaged with community people that as their kids grew up and they began to get a sense of what they would like to do in terms of higher education, many of them wanted to come to the university. Over the years 1968 to 1984, at least fourteen people from various communities completed college degrees who would not have done so had it not been for our students continually going out there.

In addition, our students could see the long-range consequences of their work. If they went out and spent ten weeks in a community, sometimes they couldn't see any impact. But if they could go back two years later and see that the kids they worked with were excelling or doing a lot better, then they could see the consequences.

Although obviously pleased with his model of community controlled service-learning, in reflecting back Blake identified some shortcomings:

> If I were to do it again, I would definitely arrange for more local situations, because there were students who could not get involved in full-time service—not because they were not committed, but because they were faced with other challenges. I think we did them a disservice.
>
> The other place I would put much more emphasis is on the learning side, the reflective side. There was no question that these students learned a lot when they were in the community. What we found was that usually about halfway through the term, the students would have to be visited. They would go through a tremendous depression, because they were out there with all of their enthusiasm and all of their idealism, and about halfway through they would suddenly realize that there wasn't going to be any dramatic change as a result of their presence. That led to questioning: Why am I here? Am I failing? We'd have to go out and help them work that through. We had three cases where students stayed two terms. In one case, the students stayed an entire academic year. It didn't matter what the length was; halfway through we'd have to do this. I made regular visits to all of these communities.
>
> I also had students who would go into these communities and find themselves so challenged by the realities that they became very racist. They could not accept the fact that people wouldn't do things the way they would want to do them. They would come back and say things like, "These people want to be poor." They would come back acting as if their values were unchanged.
>
> Indeed, it was ugly to the extent that change went in a different direction. I think this was due to what the students brought with them. We carefully screened and put the students through a preparatory program. What we learned with that helped us to

identify students who were clearly unsuited. But it never permitted us to predict what a student would do when faced with this reality. It's one thing to sit in California and hypothesize. It's another thing to be in Beaufort County, South Carolina, in that heat and humidity, living in a house where none of the amenities that you've come to appreciate are there. You've got to make that adjustment.

With one final anecdote Blake returns to the importance of his first principle of service-learning—community control:

> When I took a colleague, a social scientist, into South Carolina, that colleague could not make the adjustment. He was so used to controlling things. I'll never forget, because we visited a comprehensive health center where a student was working in the lab doing venal puncture. They welcomed Dr. Blake and his colleague. And this particular individual, in front of all these community people, walked up to the student and said, "We're really interested in what you're doing here, and we'd like for you to tell us more about what this community needs." It was as if the community people didn't know anything. You ask the outsider.
>
> Now these students had been well prepared. They understood that you never speak for the community, because they knew, and we knew, and we helped them understand it, that when the press or other people wanted some insights into the community, they weren't going to talk to community residents if they saw a white student in a black community. They'd try to get the white person to talk. These students were prepared to say, "You talk to so and so. I'm here in service." That's why the students had to be under the control of community people.

## Community Development and Institutional Change

> "We were about the business of institutional change, because our university was part of society. So while we were working at the community level, we also needed to work at the university level."

Like Blake, Dick Couto placed the primary focus of his work at Vanderbilt University's Center for Health Services on community development—in this case, in poor communities of Appalachia. But he was also concerned with how his students should be involved in these activities and what they could gain from the experience. Nevertheless, rather than develop and facilitate students' reflection on these experiences through a structured curriculum, such as was developed at Cornell, Couto focused his student development agenda on placing students in the "right" places with the "right" people:

> My focus has been to develop a high-quality program that could become a model and be disseminated. Doing it right means finding meaningful tasks that students can bring to some kind of closure and make a real contribution to community leaders and community organizations. These kinds of tasks lead to the greatest learning. Get something where there are real stakes involved, where the students are involved in something important to an organization and where the organization's leaders are effective and willing to give the kids time. When you bring all these things together, you can have incredible learning outcomes and make real contributions to a community organization as well. There's a synergism when you bring the best of both together.

Perhaps in Couto's case this emphasis on "right" placement and reliance on the power of experiential learning was a result of how he viewed his role at the university. Rather than seeing himself as a teacher, as the Cornell pioneers tended to view themselves, Couto often thought of his role as an organizer, "handing out the university's resources through an open window," with students being one major resource. Assuming that his students would learn important lessons from their service to grassroots community leaders, he could focus on organizing and supporting these leaders in their work.

> I tried to remain as sensitive as I could to what was happening within the community. We went beyond primary health care centers and found that many of the communities were concerned with environmental threats, and these sprang up in many different places. So we sat down and tried to figure out how we adapt this model of students working with community leaders and provide some kind of tangible service as a catalyst for further development of local leadership. How do we apply that to the environmental issue?
>
> We came up with the Student Environmental Health Project, where students, not in large medical teams of fifteen to eighteen, but in small groups of two or three, took samples and set up a laboratory at the university, so we could give people preliminary results. We sent students into local communities as interns with resources to do research and sampling.

Then in many instances, the next step was dictated by the experience. In one case, the legislature was about to pass a law that said nurse practitioners could not fill prescriptions, which meant they were going to be less effective. These nurses were in many cases the only practitioners in a rural clinic. All of a sudden, their patients couldn't get medicine. Something had to be done about that. So we brought people together to work on that issue. Out of that came the Tennessee Association for Primary Health Care Centers. There was a need to protect what we had established by paying attention to the policies that were affecting it.

When you organize something, after a while it has to make certain accommodations to existing factors. There's a change that occurs over time that changes some of the functions. We found that with enough time, we had to begin leaving a field, because it was no longer community based and no longer contributing to community leadership, or we had to begin organizing around it. One of the lessons with the primary health care center was that power gravitated to the physicians and to the administrator, and away from the community boards. I wanted to do another set of services where that would not be the case.

We put together what we eventually called the Maternal and Infant Health Outreach Worker program. The idea was to train local women in prenatal care and early childhood development, and prepare them to serve as go-betweens and advocates for women who were at high risk for problem pregnancies. We needed the professionals to come in and do the training, but these women could do a lot of the work with backup. We were very happy with that program. We started it in about 1982, and now some of them have staffs of twelve and fifteen women running Head Start programs in the county. They've become resource centers for educational reform. We not only found people who could do those services, but they were also entrepreneurs. They had the skills to gather other resources, and we supported them in that.

## Empowerment Teaching

"It started with my having the students analyze their own experiences and their own history."

As we learned earlier, Helen Lewis's single-minded focus on community development caused her to lose her job at two colleges. However, in spite of her strong community commitment, she was no less committed to students and their development or empowerment needs than other pioneers. Since her students were from the community Lewis sought to serve, it was simple: students' empowerment was community empowerment.

Lewis describes two ways she used a participatory action research approach to service-learning to empower her students, and therefore their community. First, we learn about her direct work with these students as a college instructor and later as an organizer for the Highlander Education and Research Center.

For my students, this was their home. It was their community. They brought the problems to the college, and I joined the students back with the community, with the problems that existed there. I took the side of the poor and of the coal miners, and not the coal companies. Other people on the faculty took the side of the coal companies. They played golf, and they went to the country club. The class thing more than anything else influenced where you put loyalty and what you called community.

When I first went there, there was this whole restructuring of the coal industry going on. They mechanized the mines. People were saying that the coal industry was dead. I would say, "Okay, let's look at it. There is still the same amount of coal going out." I had them add it up. Who's paying taxes? How much tax do they pay?

We started a movement for a sales tax on coal. It took quite a while for it to happen, but it finally did. Now there's a 7 percent tax on coal. It made a big difference. Now there's money for the school system. But it started with my having the students analyze their own experiences and their own history.

These were people who felt guilty because they'd lost their jobs. They figured that they'd done something wrong. This pedagogical process became the basis for my Highlander work in communities. You do economic discussions and start off with people telling their own work histories. You ask them what kind of development went on before, and what kind of development they want to see happen in the future. What kind of development did this company do when they were here? What was it like working there? Is that the kind of job you want now? You just put jobs on your list of what you wanted to see happen. What kinds of jobs? It's probing and pushing, questioning and making people answer. They know the answer, but they've denied it. They have followed the line using other people's explanations instead of using their own, which they already know in many ways. That's what it's all about. I was doing participatory research before it had a name of service-learning.

One of the major projects I did at Highlander was to develop a series of curriculum materials. I was working with community colleges to help develop outreach programs. I found that people in these communities, including highly educated people, felt that they couldn't understand the economy. It was something for some experts way off somewhere. I developed a curriculum for doing economic analysis of community needs and resources to help people develop an understanding of their economy from the bottom up, starting with their own work history.

If you start with people telling their own stories, then they soon realize they are part of that economy. Maybe they don't understand it in technical terms, but they understand and have repeated in their own lives a lot of economic history of the region within their lifetime.

Here Lewis describes how her clear mission of community empowerment influenced her work with field study students from outside Appalachia, who came to learn about her local students and their communities:

When I left teaching, I was still living on this farm with a group of people, some of them former Catholic sisters. We developed a field study center there, as well as a University Without Walls program. That was something that provided an education for a lot of older women in particular, who were very active in community action programs and grassroots groups, who were able to get credit, for their own experience and because they were the people to whom the field study students from outside Appalachia would come to learn from.

When the field study people came in from outside the community, they saw a completely different lifestyle. But I hated for them just to come in and be voyeurs. I would insist that my students be the hosts. They would take them home with them. They would be the bus tour guides. They would decide what they would show them.

I remember a photographer who came once and wanted to take pictures of poor people. I said, "The only way I'm going to introduce you to these folks is if you provide them with a set of photographs they can take on this march in Washington. They will tell you what to shoot." Well, he offered to do that. They gave him the most incredible pictures because they wanted to show their community to him. It wasn't him coming and showing it to the world. They were showing it to the world.

We called it field study, experiential learning. What does Paulo Freire call it? Conscientiousization. The thesis was that all education needed to be based on that combination of learning from books, libraries, and archives, and learning from people with experiences. You had to reflect on those experiences, because you did not just learn from them. You only learn from the experiences you learn from. That's what Myles used to say.

## Empowerment Planning

"We're concerned with capacity building of community-based organizations."

After leaving Cornell, Ken Reardon moved to the University of Illinois as assistant professor in the School of Urban and Regional Planning. With this move, he was able to combine what he had learned as a student activist, as a community organizer in New Jersey, in his graduate training in planning, and through his immersion in field studies at Cornell to develop a service-learning practice, which he calls empowerment planning. At Illinois, Reardon developed and still coordinates a focused partnership between community leaders in East St. Louis and the University in Champaign-Urbana, through which numerous faculty and hundreds of students assist East St. Louis leaders with their community development agenda.

As Reardon describes it, this long-term partnership ensures that the campus is directly involved in enabling these leaders to improve and strengthen their community, and on their own terms. Like Blake, he believes strongly and has structured his program in such a way that the community's agenda continually drives what the students and faculty both do and learn through the partnership.

> There are individuals within planning faculties who have always bridged the town-gown thing, viewing what they do fundamentally as supporting community efforts to change. Through ninety years of existence as a profession in the United States, there's been this countermovement within planning that focused on empowering communities through technical support and training.
>
> In graduate school I became aware of this history—the work of people at Cornell, like Bill Whyte [1955, 1991], people studying action research from a variety of disciplines. Then in the Cornell

Human Ecology Field Study Program, I found a very highly developed model that drew on a range of theoretical work in human development theory—Bronfenbrenner's [1979] and Kolb's [1984] models for example, the writing that Tim, Dwight, and Michele were doing about this thing called service-learning.

I applied for a job at Illinois in what was a fairly traditional graduate program in urban planning as an assistant professor to teach the community development classes. They had been asked by the university to help manage a troubled community assistance project in East St. Louis. Part of the attraction of going to Illinois— and I'm an East Coast boy, a New Yorker—was the opportunity to get involved in this very poor city, which had a tremendous tradition of resistance and mobilization but had really hit on hard times.

Empowerment planning comprises three dimensions, one of which is service-learning at its core. Through participatory action research, people define what it is they want to look at and how they're going to do it. They're involved in every step of the process. We're committed to capacity building through cooperative problem solving.

The second element is that it doesn't make any difference if you have good ideas of how to reform a situation or problem if you don't have the power to effect the change. So the second piece of it is an Alinsky-oriented [1971] commitment to community organization, using the process of intervention in communities to build the membership, leadership base, and political skills of community-based institutions.[4]

The third is a Freirian approach to education, being self-conscious about how it is that you go about your work, how the issues that you deal with are framed by larger societal forces. We try to do that with our students in the experiential education and service-learning aspects part of what we do.

So first, the problems are named by local residents. No project occurs that doesn't involve the local residents intimately and in every step of the activity. We're concerned with not only their power to decide what their focus is going to be, but also with capacity building of community-based organizations so they can maintain and extend these activities when the university's focus changes.

We have a community retreat every year where the community-based organizations, which are partners and collaborators, evaluate not only their own organizational development, but also the university as a technical assistance provider. Then they identify the projects to be done during the next year.

When we moved into East St. Louis, residents, who lead one of the most advanced community organizations, said to us, "We don't want you to come if (a) we don't set the issues, (b) we're not involved in all steps of the research and planning process, (c) there is no commitment to bring in new people to our organization, (d) you won't be there when implementation needs to take place, and (e) you won't help us establish primary relationships with area and regional funders that are not mediated or brokered by the university."

So, yes, we have a particular point of view, which is fundamentally looking at redistribution of resources and power within our society, bringing educational programs forward that help support the efforts of local communities to have the chance to participate in decisions and in the economy. It is political.

Like his pioneer colleagues, Reardon is not just an organizer and sustainer of this community-campus partnership. Although the community's action goals are primary, he never loses sight of the need to facilitate the learning and development that students can gain from assisting communities in this way.

We're also concerned with students' development, and how and when to bring them in. For example, a student who grew up in a very sheltered community may not be ready to go down and spend even a weekend in East St. Louis. But he or she might feel comfortable with enough support to go for a day. That might be a real stretch. We emphasize peer education; students who've been through more experiences help other students prepare for their fieldwork and think about it. And structured reflection is a component. We do annual "advances"[5] for students involved in the project, so they can reflect on how we're doing in terms of supporting their educational journeys. Whenever possible, we place strong emphasis on the reciprocal nature of the learning among community leaders, residents, and students. It is embedded in each of the activities, even if we go down for just a day.

The problems that we face are complex. I don't think anyone has the monopoly on answers. We also want to create critical thinkers who are committed to change that promotes social equality. How you do that, today or tomorrow, in this context or that, requires real thoughtfulness. I think in many ways these young students are a lot more aware of some of the false starts you can make and the unintended consequences of trying to do good than maybe we were. I think I was much more ideological. For them, because there's a range of controversy about what should get done, they have to think harder about what they think and why they feel that way, about where they think things should go. The students we're working with need to be very thoughtful as well as deeply committed.

## Must Service and Learning Goals Compete?

In this chapter we have heard from a group of pioneers who tended to emphasize first the empowerment of communities. They held a clear, primary focus on providing communities with needed university resources, especially students. These pioneers' approaches also exemplify concern with the nature of relationships between campus and community in service-learning, and a conviction that control of the service and the learning of involved students should be given to the communities in which they serve. As articulated by Blake, Lewis, and Reardon, this ceding of control from campus to community not only ensures "right" learning by students, but is also a prime strategy toward community empowerment. Thus, in this group we find strong confidence in the power of well-placed experiential learning. These pioneers share an assumption that students will learn the "right" things through their association with community leaders and organizations.

With these assumptions, with fierce commitment to communities, and with community bases or outreach-focused campus roles, these community development–minded pioneers focused more on the pedagogy of service than on the pedagogy of learning, the focus of their more student development–minded colleagues. As we shall see in Chapters Eight and Nine, these divergent emphases animated, and often complicated, the pioneers' approaches to sustaining and institutionalizing their work.

Whether they emphasized student or community development, or even institutional change, all of the pioneers held in common the belief that these two sets of goals were interdependent. The power of this approach to service and learning came from integrating the two. Bob Sigmon, who was, with Bill Ramsay, the first pioneer to articulate the term *service-learning* in describing his work, perhaps best describes this mutuality and suggests that rather than a competition of emphases between campus and community, the practice of service-learning is in fact the mutually interdependent integration of learning and empowerment needs of each partner in the relationship.

In their effort to establish service-learning within the Manpower Development Program at the Southern Regional Education Board (SREB), Ramsay and Sigmon were exploring what they called a "reflective internship model." As a community-based program primarily concerned with community development, they were less concerned with how to align their program with academic institutional needs. They wanted to ensure that their student interns delivered desired and useful products for the agencies they served. But they were also concerned that the students have opportunity for deep reflection on the meaning of these experiences for their lives as persons as well as students. Sigmon identifies his impulse to develop such an approach as coming from his experiences as both a student and a young missionary seeking to understand the concept and dynamics of the service act itself:

> There were two things I was interested in. One, the world is full of destitution, despair, and injustice, and something has to be done about that. The other is the "banking" theory of education: the telling, the lecturing, and the abstraction. We were searching for an alternative. Experiential education was our venue. We were linking our experiential education alternative with how you deal with destitution and despair.
>
> I got my first experience of this in the second grade, when I was asked to help another student, and in the way I had to work through high school. I had some theory stuff on service from my time in Pakistan and Bangalore, India, when I started doing a little homework with that. But my own experience was the key teacher at this point. Reflecting on Pakistan and this service thing, it was clear to me that something powerful happens when we learn in settings where we are asked to do something with people who define what it is they want. Something powerful goes on all the way around that mix.
>
> Then at Union Theological Seminary in New York, I did a lot of homework. I was thinking, "There's something missing in education. Every young person should have the chance to do what I had

experienced." I wanted to inflict what I had learned on as many young people as I could. I wanted to create conditions so young people could learn about themselves and others in a way that they're not hurting other people, that they are helping in some way.

At SREB we moved all over the South, bribing professors to get students out and to go out themselves and work on projects that community folks had designed. I don't take credit for that. I created the condition, set the model, and got other people involved.

The model was that communities define what they need. Then we went to the university and said, "Would you be interested, Mr. Political Science Professor, or Mr. Sociology or Mr. Law Professor, in getting a student or two to go out and talk to them? Can you reach an agreement in working on what they want? Can you provide some resources? On their terms? And, Mr. Professor, if you will work a learning agenda with these students and give them credit, we'll give you three hundred dollars for the summer to work with these kids. We'll pay the kids a hundred dollars a week. But the community owns the product of what they do. What you do on the reflection and learning side is your business."

There were two notes. One, we were trying to tweak higher education toward using the experience of service. Learn how to learn through your own experience and be honored by your own learning. I didn't know how to stress that very well, but I was aware of it. The other was that if you got involved in something interesting, you were going to do something productive, and that was going to make you feel good. You were going to be contributing. You could see it. You could document it. You could watch the young folks deal with it. You could watch older folks take pride in helping the young figure that out. You could see success start to come alive.

The best part of SREB was that we got kids from all over the South—black and white—for a two-day seminar. We'd bring twenty-two or twenty-four of them together at a time in New Orleans, Miami, Washington, D.C., Memphis, or Atlanta. We'd meet at Pascal's in Atlanta. That was a good trip right there. Pascal's was black owned, black operated, and this was 1967–1968.

We'd ask two questions in this seminar. One was, "What's the most important developmental issue that's facing you and the people you're working with?" For some, they were working in education, so they said, "The kids have got to learn to be well educated, or else they are not going to be healthy or have a job." Students working in health would say, "The kids have got to be healthy, or else they can't learn." Students working in job development would say, "The kids have got to have a job before they know that they've got to learn to be healthy." The students would fuss and fight for hours about which of these issues is most important. They would fight like cats and dogs out of their own experience and not come to any conclusions.

Finally, the question got turned around to, "How is your education helping you deal with these issues that we've been talking about?" And they would bitch and moan some more about how unhelpful their education had been. Then we talked about what they could learn from this experience about what they could do about what's happening in the world, and how they could create their own learning design. We'd put those two things together. It was an incredibly simple design that stimulated so many of these students to think at a level they never thought at before. We watched kids grow and learn and teach one another.

There was something that needed to be done out here in these communities, which we were labeling service. But I was clear that there was an extraordinary learning that was going on too. So we came up with the term *service-based learning*. What's distinctive about learning when you are in that kind of service relationship? That's what we thought about, but we didn't have a set design.

## Notes

1. Campus Outreach Opportunity League (COOL) was founded in 1984 to galvanize college students into public and community service in their communities. Staffed by students and recent graduates, COOL's philosophy is to work with community leaders to identify issues, train student volunteers to accomplish meaningful activities, and reflect on and evaluate the effect of their actions.

2. Through Alternative Spring Breaks, students spend their spring vacations on intensive projects focused on topical issues or policy areas (for example, homelessness, hunger, or literacy), providing direct service and meeting with policymakers and activists. Projects take place both far from and adjacent to campuses.

3. In 1956 at the age of fifty-eight, Septima Clark was fired from her teaching job in Charleston, South Carolina, for refusing to renounce her membership in the National Association for the Advancement of Colored People. She went on to work with Myles Horton as director of education for the Highlander Folk School and in the 1960s worked for the Southern Christian Leadership Conference, where she was a close colleague of Dr. Martin Luther King, Jr.

4. Saul Alinsky founded what is known today as the Alinsky school of community organizing. Through the Industrial Areas Foundation, which he began in 1940, Alinsky and his staff helped to organize communities throughout the country and train a next generation of organizers.

5. "Advances" refers to annual reflection and planning meetings between project faculty, students, and local activists.

# Chapter Eight

# Mainstream or Margins?

## The Dilemma of Institutionalization

With deeply rooted values, commitment, skills, courage, and some-times plain good luck, the service-learning pioneers designed and established diverse approaches to combining service with academic study in postsecondary education. This work was difficult, with no road maps to follow and no models to replicate; it was often lonely as well, because the pioneers were usually the only ones, or part of a very small group, in their institutions or locales seeking to inte-grate social change–oriented action with critical learning, activi-ties that traditionally had been thought of as discrete, if not at odds with each other.

The work of these individuals was also dangerous. Running against the grain of institutional practice cost some their jobs. Oth-ers experienced occupational and personal strain while trying to establish toeholds in the academy. And others opted out of post-secondary education altogether, viewing the academy as imper-meable to change, or at least not relevant to their community development objectives.

Almost by definition, a pioneer's life is not easy. Not only must new trails be blazed through uncharted territory. Once the new land is "mapped," it must be "settled." Communication must be established between the new and old worlds. In this chapter, the pioneers describe their entrepreneurial efforts to "settle" their new lands and establish relationships with their institutions, the "old worlds." Some of these efforts to connect these new margins to the old mainstreams of postsecondary education were more successful than others. Some pioneers focused on building a safe, permanent base for service-learning within specific institutions. Some focused on building a national movement to support local efforts. Some saw their local work as strengthening the larger movement.

A few pioneers held contrary views on institutionalization. They viewed efforts to move service-learning from new margins to old mainstreams as too difficult and too distracting from their community focus. They worried that institutionalizing relationships with the "old world" would corrupt the "new," robbing service-learning of its power to develop students and communities. Some did not view postsecondary education as an adequate base from which to pursue their social change agendas.

## Settling New Territories: Institutionalizing from Within

> "So you headed up the wagons and went out over the mountains in the hope that ultimately they would follow."

This statement from Michael Goldstein describes many of the pioneers' approaches to establishing their programs and practice. Working in institutions where nobody else may even have been listening, they set out on their own, hoping others would follow, or at least hoping that no one would get in their way. Gib Robinson was one of these individuals:

> When I got to the English department at San Francisco State, what I found was that most of my faculty colleagues didn't see the problems I was trying to address, so we couldn't even have a discussion. What that meant was, after a while, I stopped trying to talk. Then I thought, "Well, at least I could go out and do it, and then I could point to it and say, 'See, that's what I was trying to talk about.'"

### Collaborative Entrepreneurship

> "It's like crashing a fraternity and making the fraternity change its way of thinking, recruiting, and sustaining its membership."

Jane Permaul established the Field Studies Development Program at the University of California at Los Angeles (UCLA) in 1980. She used this base to pioneer with UCLA faculty a field studies approach to service-learning, fusing community-based experiential learning with subject matter across UCLA's curriculum. From the start, Permaul targeted faculty as her means both to establish and institutionalize service-learning pedagogy. To get their attention and participation, she funded and trained graduate teaching assistants (TAs), and "gave" them to faculty willing to insert service-learning in their instruction. The TAs placed students and monitored their service in the community. They led reflection sections that students attended in addition to regular classroom lectures, which were designed to help students think critically about their service experience in the context of course subject matter.

This approach to service-learning development proved to be highly successful at this research university. Faculty did not have to revolutionize their approach to instruction. They could rely on Permaul's trained, "free" TAs. As a result, they participated in large numbers, and numerous innovative course designs emerged over the years. However, the success of Permaul's strategy was due to more than the fact that it fit well with its institutional context. Another critical success factor was the entrepreneurial spirit and style that Permaul brought to her work:

> Despite the fact that higher education is supposed to be at the leading edge of everything, it has some very entrenched traditions. A good example is the tradition that faculty are the sources and deliverers of knowledge. Administrators and staff are supposed to make sure that faculty do that. Students are just a transient sponge that absorbs the knowledge, then leaves, and that's the way it is.
>
> To suggest that perhaps students and, in some cases, staff have something to say about the curriculum directly confronts that tradition. Then, of course, when you look at service-learning, after you begin to organize it better and institutionalize it to a certain extent, the community partners want to have a voice about things—and rightfully so. So you add another player into what used to be an exclusive terrain of the faculty. That's difficult. There are different criteria and requirements for these new players who now want to have a say. It's like crashing a fraternity and making the fraternity change its way of thinking, recruiting, and sustaining its membership.
>
> One thing I learned along the way is to read the organizational environment, knowing where the influence and change agents are,

rather than looking at it as a formal structure—to look at UCLA as an organism, a dynamic community where there are change agents. I'm not bothered so much if a chairman is here or there. I don't ignore them, because there is the formal structure. But there's also the real structure. I work through that real structure, and my approach is not confrontational. It's not cause and effect. Rather than seeing things as having tension, I look for common ground. That's how I got my reputation here. It's how I earned respect.

There are other things I've learned. One of my graduate program practicum supervisors said to me, "Jane, remember, you are hired to make decisions and to do what you think is best, because you're trained to do that. That's why you're in the position you have. Don't ask; just do it. Continue to do what you think is best until somebody tells you can't."

That's a very important piece. Another has been brought out in Helen Astin and Carol Leland's book, *Women of Influence* [1991]. They studied a variety of women, mostly in education, who had risen to high levels of leadership and tried to find out what their qualities were. One of these was not having to feel that you always have to have recognition. Collaboration is important too. But whether you collaborate or whether you do it all, you should try to get somebody to feel good about it. That's the important part. We've been socialized to put people on a pedestal: up there, they're all good. But competing for that pedestal creates a major barrier to getting there. I've learned not to think I have to get all the credit. Teamwork, collaboration: it's critical.

## Organizing and Supporting the Faculty

"I find informal opportunities to get faculty together to talk about these things so they aren't isolated."

Sharon Rubin played a similar role to that of Permaul as an academic administrator in three institutions: the University of Maryland, Salisbury State College, and Ramapo College of New Jersey. As an assistant dean, a dean, and now as vice president for academic affairs at Ramapo, she used her resources to interest, organize, support, and gain legitimacy for faculty who use service-learning pedagogy in their instruction.

There are several things I do with both my faculty and other faculty. One, I start them when they're young; that is, if you have first- or second-year faculty and you do faculty development activities on teaching and learning, include service-learning. First of all, they're very grateful, because it's a big challenge to figure out how to be a teacher. Their minds are more open to some of these ideas than might otherwise be the case. Start with the new ones.

Second, I find informal opportunities to get faculty together to talk about these things so they aren't isolated. Every semester we have an opportunity for people to learn from each other and share materials.

Third, I have a faculty member who owes me a credit's worth of work. He's really interested in service-learning, so I suggested that he develop a set of resources. There are books on the shelves, but what would a faculty member really want to know? What are six or seven really wonderful sources? He's pulling that together.

Then I talk to other administrators and to promotion and tenure committees about experiential learning, so they know it's okay to accept it as part of a person's packet.

While developing, managing, and teaching in Westmont College's San Francisco field study program, Jim Keith played a faculty organizer role as well. His organizing was necessary to gain both personal support for his students when they returned to Westmont's Santa Barbara campus and political support to ensure that the college continued his program:

I invited faculty who were doubters to come visit our program. My aim was to have them get to know the students there, because we discovered that when students returned to Santa Barbara, they needed to feel there was somebody on campus who understood what had happened to them while they were in San Francisco. I also discovered that those faculty were able to pinpoint these students in classes. They discovered that they were the students they most liked to teach, so they became very supportive.

Academic communities so easily become ingrown. Faculty can get totally engaged in fighting the administration, nitpicking about the admissions office's admitting ill-prepared students—issues that are real but get blown out of proportion to what the education process could really be. Having a strong community base corrects some of that ingrownness. In North Carolina, my wife and I would invite somebody from the community and six or eight faculty to sit around and talk. This doesn't happen so often on campus. I think of these conversations as faculty development.

## Fundraising as Validation

"I've been able to institutionalize the program through outside funding."

Garry Hesser's entrepreneurial work focused on fundraising:

At Augsburg there was generalized support for experiential education, for urban semesters, for internships, for community service. But the program was floundering for lack of resources. What I brought was not only a commitment to experiential learning, but an entrepreneurial spirit. I've been able to institutionalize the program through outside funding.

I helped find a co-op grant, so we were able to staff the internship program with two full-time people. Once I got the staff paid for, we started leveraging Work-Study money. I had arrived in a city that already had an Urban Corps. We channeled people into that.

I helped Campus Compact host the first faculty service-learning conference in the state at Augsburg. We got a modest grant that enabled us to hire a person to give full attention to the community service piece. We used Work-Study money as a matching grant with state money, got a Fund for the Improvement of Postsecondary Education [FIPSE] grant, got a Literacy Corps grant. We went through several iterations of funding at a time when the college was in pretty dire economic straits.

What the external funding did is validate our work. Over that period, we got to the point where the college was willing and able to see its value. Faculty became advocates for fully budgeting it. I feel that if I walked away from this tomorrow, there are four staff people who have become highly recognized by my faculty colleagues. This would continue. That's the impact I feel best about. We have in place something that's validated.

## Continuity and Community

"It's hard to build community when you are a professional gypsy."

Continuity was Dick Cone's strategy for sustaining and institutionalizing service-learning through the University of Southern California's Joint Education Project (JEP). Sticking it out was at first a personal challenge, but over time Dick came to see his long-term approach as his greatest asset:

I taught for ten years, straight out of college and the Peace Corps. I did three two-year stints and two one-year stints. I was a gypsy. What I liked was to go into a school that was a mess, make my contribution, and have everybody say, "Wow, this is great." Then I would leave before anything could fall apart. So after my first few months at JEP, I decided I should stay a while. My goal was to see if I could stay for more than two years and get beyond that whiz-kid syndrome—the quick-fix guy who moves on—to see if I could work with something without ending up with mud all over my face. I've been able to do that, and I've come to believe that continuity is something we need in this field. It's hard to build community when you are a professional gypsy.

Higher education institutions are incredibly complex. What I do in the institution today could not be done by somebody new who came in with the most brilliant ideas. I can do it because I'm part of the community. I know where to go. I know who to talk to—and who not to talk to. I know whether to put something in writing or use e-mail—all these little but complex things you do to get things through an institution. It's the same working in the community.

I've been here long enough to see that we change our focus periodically. This can be the most important agenda right now, so we will focus on it for a year, two years, three years. Then some other agenda will come along. But we don't lose ground. We circle back and work on it again. And not only me. The rest of the JEP staff has that kind of longevity.

I have much more appreciation of the complexity of our work, much more of a sense that this is beyond a quick fix. I have trouble with that notion that we just lay out objectives and move on and do it. This is a human enterprise. I think institutions are the way they are because they involve humans. They tell us something about human nature.

What are faculty like, and what are they searching for? Why are they so comfortable being isolated? Why are they so intimidated by the notion of community or working with the community? These are issues we have to address. We can do that only by being a part of a community. You can't come in with a model. I don't think models have much service other than provoking our thoughts, getting us to look at other ways, to see the world through different perspectives.

## The Hazards of "Open Field Running"

"There was noise in the system, and I was the cause of it."

Dick Couto is one of the service-learning pioneers most fiercely committed to the community development outcomes of his work. He viewed Vanderbilt University's Center for Health Services, which he directed for thirteen years, as a base from which to support, organize, and advocate for poor Appalachian communities. With his focus outside the academy, organizing on the inside was often secondary to Couto, and it was something that ultimately affected his ability to remain at the center.

It's a little bit like open field running in football. You don't have a whole lot of blockers, but if you keep moving, that was just a thrill. Some people at the university actually envied me, and I said, "You can have it the same way any time you want. Just forgo your salary and all your institutional support. That's when they allow you your freedom."

But I also wanted to get more into teaching, to bring some of the lessons of community change into the classroom, because that was completely missing in our program. None of this service-learning was for credit. It was all in the summer months. Service-learning was a profound pedagogy, but I wanted to tie it into the classroom, so I started teaching at Peabody College in the human development major. But here I ran into the university again. They asked me to teach a course on community assessment. To make a long story short, the class took as its project a study of diversity at Vanderbilt. The university was the community that we were going to assess. Well, the chancellor heard about the study and called the vice chancellor, my boss, and inquired about it. That was all my vice chancellor needed to hear. There was noise in the system, and I was the cause of it. He called me in basically to tell me to stop the study, which I didn't, and couldn't, do. At that point the Center for Health Services received money from the university, and he talked about taking it back. So I said, "I won't stand in your way. I'll just step aside and resign." I did that and went completely over to teaching.

Couto's experience suggests that the more deeply committed a pioneer was to the community development goals of service-learning, the more likely it was that he or she would focus on community impact, at the expense of establishing and sustaining support for service-learning inside the academy. Couto's experience further suggests that his strong focus on the community side of service-learning may ultimately have caused the university to reduce its support. Indeed, after leaving Vanderbilt, Couto moved to the University of Richmond to a faculty role, where he focused on service-learning curriculum development on his own and with other faculty. Although this was a conscious choice, Couto acknowledges that it required him to attend less intensely to what was happening in the community.

> This job at the University of Richmond meant an opportunity to develop a brand-new curriculum and train people for service to society through leadership. We've instituted a six-unit service-learning internship that students do in nonprofit organizations. We've done action research and other programs that incorporate community issues and community needs into our instruction. The university has been pretty supportive; for the first time in my experience, a president came to me with funding. We can now lend technical assistance to other faculty to integrate community service into their course work.
>
> My focus has changed. It's more on the educational institution, bringing about changes on campus. Previously I gave my strongest attention to the community organization, putting something in place that would be sustained. Now I put that attention to the university.

## Strategically Enabling Others

> "If we truly want to change higher education on behalf of service-learning, then we have to let go of the doing of it and encourage, bribe, and support the faculty to take up the work."

Tim Stanton reflects on the change in his role when he went to Stanford in 1985 to help establish what became the Haas Center for Public Service. He describes how lessons learned in a contentious struggle to sustain the Human Ecology Field Study Program at Cornell enabled him to develop a careful but ambitious organizing strategy designed to integrate the values and practice of service-learning across the curriculum at Stanford:

In 1983 Stanford's president, Don Kennedy, wrote a manifesto on public service in the Stanford alumni magazine in which he talked about the social obligations of students who attended places like Stanford and the obligations of such institutions to help students develop the commitment and capacity to serve. I was struck by this article, and decided to write him back. The gist of my letter was that Kennedy's initiative was the first thing Stanford had done since my graduation that made me truly proud to be an alum. But, I said, "If you're serious about this, there are issues that need to be addressed, with the primary one being the need to connect the public service initiative directly to Stanford's academic mission, and to involve faculty."

Kennedy responded, although I think Catherine Milton, his special assistant, actually wrote the letter, and said, "Thanks for your thoughts. If you're ever in the area, come talk." I pursued the invitation and ended up going to Stanford, meeting with Catherine and others. They were in the process of thinking through the public service center, and I joined in. The main issue I pushed was, "If you're serious about making service a critical part of the Stanford fabric, you've got to deal with the curriculum. You've got to deal with faculty."

Fortunately, Kennedy and Milton recognized this as an issue worth considering. They needed somebody who could work with faculty, and that's what I brought from my Cornell experience. I had learned so much about academic political fighting during my time there.

I thought long and hard about going to Stanford. I had become very upset with higher education at Cornell, quite discouraged. I had an offer to do something else. But I remember thinking it through and deciding Stanford was worth a try. I had a feeling that service-learning, or whatever we called it, could grow at Stanford. There was a brand-new program. There was presidential support. I also thought that if I could make service-learning work at Stanford, that would make it safer for others to do this work elsewhere.

I discovered the term *service-learning* in the 1970s through the National Student Volunteer Program and the Society for Field Experience Education (SFEE). This was four or five years after I started working with youth volunteers and experiential learning. I accepted the term as an explanation of the work. But at Stanford we shied away from terms. For instance, we didn't use the words *service-learning* or *experiential learning* for several years, consciously, because at Stanford, words count. They can get you in trouble. We did not want our efforts to connect students' service with academics to appear to faculty as some sort of "touchy-feely" exercise, which is what those words would connote in their minds.

At Cornell we had free rein to develop a wonderful program, and we did. But because we did it so well, we caught a lot of flack. At Stanford, the strategy was different. We had this attitude that we were going to change the university, but we were going to do it through others, the faculty. We had to find allies, build alliances, have a real organizing strategy.

Sometimes I feel that working in this way is really hard work. I get tired. I sit down and think, Gosh, I could do better teaching a service-learning course myself, so why am I trying to help this faculty member when he doesn't even understand it? Sometimes I think of those Cornell days as a most creative luxury, because we could just do it ourselves. But what I learned at Cornell is that if we truly want to change higher education on behalf of service-learning, then we have to let go of the doing of it and encourage, bribe, and support the faculty to take up the work. I find this strategy harder to carry out than simply doing it myself, but I hope it will have a larger impact.

## Settling New Territories: Developing a National Movement

While some pioneers focused their attention on maintaining and sustaining service-learning within their institutions and on behalf of selected communities, others recognized the need for interinstitutional networks through which practitioners could share information, give and get collegial support, and develop a movement that perhaps could influence postsecondary education nationally.

### Building a National Network

"To get started, we just issued an invitation."

In the early 1970s Jim Feeney was working to identify experiential learning programs outside Florida for New College students. He traveled around the United States to examine programs such as the Great Lakes Colleges Association (GLCA) Philadelphia Urban

Semester to make arrangements for his students to participate.[1] Through these travels, he noticed that people running these programs, such as Steve Brooks at GLCA and John Duley at Michigan State, were dealing with many of the same issues, but in isolation. Perhaps, Feeney thought, they should be brought together. He took on the organizer role and called them together. Those who attended formed the Society for Field Experience Education (SFEE), an organization that evolved to play a critical role in the development of service-learning, both in its practice and as a professional field.

> I got the idea that we should build a network so people could start exchanging ideas about what makes a strong experience for students. There were all these people trying to get field-based learning started, recruit students, defend their work, but most of them were working on their own.
>
> Ken Lingle, a member of the New College board of trustees, gave us money to support it. He was a network builder. His philosophy of problem solving was to build networks of people who were engaged in a problem and let them solve it.
>
> To get started, we just issued an invitation. There wasn't anything very complicated about it. We had money, so the message was, "Come down to Sarasota and talk." There must have been an agenda, but I don't have clear recollection of one.
>
> We didn't want to follow the conventional path toward a professional association where people put out great energy competing for prestige within the organization, or have it become primarily a job market thing. We wanted a place for dialogue, where each person can be strengthened on his or her own ground through talk with other people, networking, a phone call, and that sort of thing. We wanted to be countercultural in terms of the professional world.
>
> Bob Sigmon was the lead advocate for this kind of an organization. There may have been disagreement on how you accomplish this, how you create whatever this other culture is, but I think it did ultimately happen. To this day, feedback on National Society for Experiential Education (NSEE) conferences supports the notion that they are different. People get to talk to more people. There is more sharing, less competition. NSEE people still worry about how to preserve that.

## Competing Networks, Limiting Language

> "What particularly concerned me was that we were getting fixated on terminology."

Simultaneously, but separately from the birthing of SFEE, practitioners of internship programs that focused on government organized the National Center for Public Service Internships (NCPSI). While SFEE people represented more of the field study, cross-cultural learning, and service-learning strands of the work that was developing, NCPSI represented individuals working in programs such as Urban Corps and statewide government internship programs. Some practitioners, and some of our pioneers, became members of both organizations. Michael Goldstein describes the different philosophies and roles taken by the two organizations, and how he and others came to feel that the field would be better served by bringing them together:

> There was an interesting dichotomy that developed between SFEE and NCPSI. For many years, each organization felt that it had the holy grail, and that the other organization was somehow running astray.
>
> What particularly concerned me was that we were getting fixated on terminology. What you called your program defined it, rather than what your program was. The internship people wouldn't talk to the field experience people, and so on.
>
> It seemed to me that except for this kind of rhetorical distinction, there really wasn't any distinction. The programs conceptually overlapped, if not 100 percent at least 80 percent. So folks like John Duley, Bob Sigmon, and others and I started talking about whether these two organizations could get together. The distinction was that SFEE ran the grand national conference and brought together lots of people. NCPSI had a staff, had some resources, and provided a rather high level of service to experiential education programs. We made several abortive attempts to get the two organizations together, but there was always this semantic notion on both sides: "Sure we'll merge, but you have to give up your heretical notion and adopt the true faith."
>
> Ultimately people began to agree that they would be better served by getting together than by staying apart. I remember the meeting in 1980 at which we decided on the most critical issue,

which, of course, was the name of the merged organization. I remember writing the words that were in the names of each—National Center for Public Service Internships and the Society Field Experience Education—on pieces of cardboard and then putting them up on a long bulletin board. Then we all got up and played with mixing and matching the words. We came up with a name—National Society for Internships and Experiential Education—that everybody felt embodied enough of each organization. Interestingly, from that point forward, there was substantial convergence among the programs and a willingness of people to say, "You can call it whatever you want as long as when we look at it, we can recognize it."

With the merger settled, the new national organization began to focus on how best to support its members in their struggles to sustain experiential learning in the academy. Jane Permaul, who served on the board and as president following the merger, recalls discussions at the time:

When I got involved in SFEE, we all were very much front-mind pranksters, very intense in terms of what we were about in a particular program or set of programs. While I admired that intensity and dedication, I felt that for the field to flourish and have larger impact, we had to broaden our perspective. We had to see each piece as part of a larger puzzle. So the agenda I had, both when I got on the board and then become president, was to start talking about education in general rather than just the experiential piece. We had to view service in the broader context of education.

Another piece was to have a large umbrella. You remember the history—the merging of the society with the national center. We wanted to merge because there were a lot of common threads. But still, in the earlier days we had the international, intercultural education people; we had the co-op people, experiential education, service-learning, and so on. My sense was that rather than separate them all, we needed to integrate. But we also had to keep learning from our diversity while we brought in a unifying sense of what we were all about.

Then the third thing was the research piece. What are we all about? Can we generalize? What is it that we have collectively learned? Can we put it in some organized fashion, so we can see where to go next? So we formed the first special interest group on research.

## Building a Broad Community of Support

"I was creating a place for storytelling."

Jane Kendall became the first full-time executive director of the merged organization:

> I was directing a liberal arts internship program at the University of North Carolina, working with faculty in specific fields and was a member of both the society and the national center. At that time, in 1976, there were various economic development internship programs in Virginia, Alabama, Kentucky, North Carolina, and Georgia leavening from that Manpower Development Internship project. Then the EDA [Economic Development Administration], which had been funding in other parts of the country, approached NCPSI about funding internship programs in the South. I was hired to come to Washington and work with NCPSI to get that going.
>
> When we had to close that office and move everything back to Raleigh in 1983, I became director of what had become NSEE. The organization was on a roller coaster financially. At one time, we had only six months of funding; we went from nine staff to two. I stayed as director for twelve years.
>
> Some of these years were hard ones for service-learning. Careerism became very strong. One role I saw myself playing was to keep the story alive. There were a lot of people moving in and out of the field, and there was an oral history developing. A lot of what I did was listen to people's stories and connect them to other stories. In some ways that's what NSEE was—a storytelling community—telling the stories that kept it alive during some of the leaner times.
>
> I encouraged people to tell their stories because often they felt alone on their campuses. The fact that there was a community of support was wonderful. I know that when I first found that community, I was like a kid in a candy store. So I was creating a place for storytelling.

We shall learn in the next chapter how important this storytelling community was to sustaining the work of the service-learning pioneers.

This nascent field now contained a variety of approaches to practice in a variety of institutional and community settings. A fledgling national network was committed to the support and development of practitioners, and to enhancing their ability to institutionalize experiential teaching and learning within post-secondary education.

On some campuses and within the network, people were realizing that developing programs and supporting those that develop them would not be enough to sustain innovations that raised fundamental questions about the quality and effectiveness of traditional forms of instruction and the role of the academy in society. The forces of reaction and institutional inertia could be strong, especially in tight budget times. If innovations represented by the service-learning pioneers and pioneers of other forms of experiential education were to take hold and become institutionalized, the field needed substantive advocacy. And that advocacy needed to be theory based—even, as Permaul had recognized, research based. Practitioners needed a clear concept of how and why experienced-based pedagogies worked and could contribute effectively to the academic missions of their institutions.

## Building a Theory Base

"We had to develop the kind of assessment procedures and theories that would stand up to criticism by people who hadn't even thought about this."

John Duley recognized the critical importance of this need, for his own work at Michigan State University and for the wider field, and decided to take it on:

In the late 1960s, there just weren't any other people I knew who were involved in trying to provide service-learning opportunities for undergraduates. They just weren't there. If they were there, they were hidden in the woodwork someplace, not available to use as models or reference points. Nobody was writing anything about assessment or the competencies that people ought to acquire from service-learning, or the skills that people could acquire that were important to successful performance in the world of work, as well as academically.

Because there wasn't anything out there, my dean encouraged me to pull together a case for granting college credit for the learning that was acquired in off-campus experiences. That was the challenge that confronted us in our particular situation, because we had this course for which a full semester's credit was given to students spending eleven weeks off campus in another cultural environment, trying to learn as much about that environment as possible. We had to justify to the powers that be in the university that this was worth a full semester of credit.

The greatest help I had was from a man named Paul Dressel, a key figure in evaluation of academic performance. After World War II, he had developed a methodology for granting advanced standing to returning veterans on the basis of math, science, and other skills they had acquired in the military. I went to him and said, "Paul, how can we provide for assessment of learning that's acquired in field programs?"

He said, "There are two things. One, look at the work John Flanagan did in the Aviation Evaluation Program for the air force in determining the capability of people to become pilots. There is a critical incident technique [Flanagan, 1954] that he developed to document learning acquired through experience.[2] Look at the Peace Corps, and what was happening with the people who returned from service overseas. What kind of cross-cultural learning skills had they needed and acquired?"

That challenge, plus the opportunities that were available, led me to be a part of a national effort to develop assessment techniques and identify skills and competencies—like the higher ranges of knowledge acquisition, synthesis, and practical application—the things at the highest level of Bloom's [1956] domains of learning. What could students learn in the field that they couldn't get in the classroom? How could students demonstrate that they had, in fact, acquired these skills when they were involved in off-campus learning?

I started working on this in 1968. SFEE began in 1971. It was my privilege to host the 1973 SFEE national conference at Michigan State. I got Jossey-Bass to publish the papers from the conference [Duley, 1974]. That was the first step to building a literature on assessment of experiential learning. Then I got involved with the Council for Adult and Experiential Learning[3] [CAEL] in 1975 and wrote with Sheila Gordon of LaGuardia Community College a CAEL handbook, *College Sponsored Experiential Learning* [Duley and Gordon, 1977]. These opportunities made it possible for me to make a contribution to justifying this kind of learning as college creditable and determining how much credit it was worth.

I'd heard about David Kolb and invited him to come to the SFEE Conference in 1977. Kolb came into a vacuum in which we had no theoretical framework in which to try to understand how students learned from experience. He provided a conceptual framework [Kolb, 1984] with which we could visualize what was happening in terms of students' observation and reflection on experience, how they could interpret it, which would lead to further observation and analysis. This began to make clear that skills in observation were very important. Skills in recording were very important. So one of the skills that you needed to teach students in order to help them learn from experience was the ability to observe and to know the difference between observing and making snap judgments about what they saw.

Kolb's theory sharpened for us the kind of skills that were absolutely necessary if people were going to be able to be experiential learners on their own and take charge of their own learning. That was important, because we were saying to universities that commencement ought to be a time not of ending education, but of beginning a life-long process of learning. If you're going to do that, then you have to teach people to learn on their own. Field experience education was one way to do that, because it requires students to observe accurately, record only observations first, and then make reflective judgments and see alternative meanings for what they've seen and recorded before they interpret that and go on to apply and experiment again.

Although I came to feel Kolb's cycle of continuous learning was overly simplified, it helped us make sense of what was happening with our students and interpret that to faculty colleagues in ways they had never thought about before. It was a very useful tool.

We began to look at other skills too, which we picked up from Peace Corps. There's an article written by Harrison and Hopkins [1967] in which they did a comparison between traditional higher education and cross-cultural learning. They pointed out that the kind of skills necessary for successful cross-cultural learning had to do not with getting the right answers but with being open to accepting information from the environment and not making snap judgments about it. The goal in cross-cultural learning is not having the right answer, but having the appropriate answer for that moment. To do this, you need different skills from the ones needed to succeed well in higher education. In the classroom, it is the right answer, and there's only one. But this isn't true in the

field. There are appropriate answers, approximate answers.
You must use your intuition and not depend only on objective
knowledge.

Then George Klemp came along with his analysis [1977] of
the skills necessary for superior performance in the world of work.
These skills were in stark opposition to those you gain in the classroom, but they were at the heart of what students gained through
service-learning and field experience education.

We began to see things you could put together to make a
strong case for the value and need for this kind of education, to
supplement in a creative way what was done in the classroom. Not
that there was anything wrong with what was happening in the
classroom. It was just incomplete.

Mary Edens, who was pioneering service-learning at Michigan
State University (MSU) at the same time, comments on the important role Duley's work played for her and her colleagues:

What John did was bring faculty together to talk about experiential
learning. That helped integrate volunteer programs more with
experiential learning. It also helped to educate us. I don't know if
I would have connected the similarities between the counseling
model and experiential learning if John hadn't been there to pull
that together.

The other thing that John and I think the experiential model
did was help faculty create a structure that wasn't there. Up until
then, students could get credit for the experience alone, without
really analyzing their performance. I felt that students were volunteering without knowing what it was they could contribute. They
didn't know what they could learn from the experience. We had
to figure out ways we could build in thinking about learning
objectives prior to students' going into a placement.

John helped create those materials for faculty. He worked
with them to integrate experiential learning in the classroom.
Through that work, he opened up a means for redefining volunteer programs as experiential learning and then helped legitimize
experiential learning.

John opened those doors for me in ways that I probably didn't
even recognize at the time. It was an "Aha!" experience. We could
have boxed ourselves into career services or volunteer services.
But John helped people get out of those boxes; the boxes kind
of peeled away. Experiential learning, service-learning: these are

variations on a theme of learning in a nonformal setting with formalized opportunities to establish, monitor, and assess progress toward a set of learning objectives, with or without faculty. I give John a lot of credit for helping us see that.

## Technical Assistance

"Helping people figure out how it works and how to make things happen in their institution was what was important."

With theoretical frameworks developing along with ever more varied approaches to practice, those working at the national level began to consider ways to think conceptually about how to institutionalize these innovations. How could practitioners get assistance in working at this on individual campuses? Sharon Rubin describes NSEE's response:

Jane Kendall wrote a grant to FIPSE for NSEE to have a small group of us work intensively with about eight colleges over the course of two years to get them to make experiential education more central to their campuses. Through our work over two years, we learned a tremendous amount and wrote a handbook, *Strengthening Experiential Education* [Kendall and others, 1986], based on what we had learned.

The book turned out to be longer, more complex, and more interesting than we thought. It became a basic set of informative chapters for anybody who was running a program or any faculty member who wanted to know how he or she fit, or for students who wanted to know how to make use of it. I don't think we used the term *service-learning* more than once or twice in the whole book. But a lot of the principles were very solid and have influenced the way service-learning programs have been designed and developed.

That program was so successful that we got another three-year grant from FIPSE to work with many other schools using another set of models, because not everybody could afford or was ready for a very intensive on-campus consultation of the kind we did in the first proposal. This one was conference presentations, workshops for consortia, faculty involvement workshops. We tried all different kinds of things—and, indeed, found out that they all work, for different purposes and different ways.

This project helped us become clearer about NSEE's mission, which was to provide a very high level of technical assistance to the field. Until then, there was always discussion about what we should do for students and various other constituencies. Instead, we said, this will be mainly, if not exclusively, a professional development organization for people who are running programs. Whether they're faculty or administrators, we need to give them very high levels of technical support so they can do what they're doing very well. Every college is different. Helping people figure out how it works and how to make things happen in their institution was what was important.

## Principles of Practice

"It was like making the field reflect on itself in the same way that we try to get students to reflect on their experience."

Through the FIPSE project, NSEE and its involved practitioners began to learn and disseminate both approaches to effective practice and strategies for successful institutionalization. This developing field needed to discuss and develop principles of good practice. It needed to collect and disseminate its developing literature. Given the diversity of those involved in terms of goals, approaches, and populations served, the process of developing these principles and collecting and selecting the literature needed to be both broadly representative and collaborative. Jane Kendall picks up the story by describing her next moves:

> There was a lot of stock to put into service-learning in the 1960s and early 1970s, but there was always this feeling that do-good service came first, and then the learning part was a next step. In the mid-1980s, when the student service movement took off, I felt it was sort of kamikaze service. Something about it deeply offended me, because it seemed like an unintentional manipulation or presumption that we, the volunteers, were needed and can help, whether you want it or not.
>
> I started to feel real old. But also I started feeling that we didn't always have to start all over. I'd been to some extent one of the keepers of the literature, because of the NSEE resource center. We tried to collect and encourage writing for papers and the newsletter. I knew a lot of that could be useful.
>
> I thought we needed a resource book with two parts. One was principles, and the other was a body of thought. I wanted to

capture those at a point in time, with the idea that each generation would not have to recreate them for themselves. English literature doesn't have to start all over every time there's a new Ph.D. I started to feel I should play that role.

I enjoyed trying to draw participation in this process from different parts of education, from different community-based groups. Some of them didn't know what they had in common, but through the process they could say they were involved in reviewing or commenting, or getting very angry at something another group said. The process reminded me of how many strains there were in the field and how we had language problems. Until you can find ways to talk about it, it's very hard. I don't know if the principles [Honnet and Poulsen, 1989] that we came out with were the principles, but they represent a very broad grassroots process of teasing them out from the very different strains. That felt good to me to see people being reflective like that. It was like making the field reflect on itself in the same way that we try to get students to reflect on their experience.

Sharon Rubin comments on Kendall's collaborative approach to developing the field, in this case her compilation and publication of *Combining Service and Learning: A Resource Book for Community and Public Service* (Kendall, 1990).

The inspiration was Jane Kendall. She had a strategic mind about what the field needed. She was always way ahead of where the rest of us were, and we scrambled to catch up. For example, she said the resource book is what the field needed. She didn't think it was going to be three volumes, and none of us thought it was going to be three volumes. We thought it would be a hundred pages. But in her thorough way, Jane called on many, many different organizations and individuals and said, "Send the best stuff. Send what you think is going to last." At one point, all around her dining room walls there were piles about four feet high because there was a tremendous amount of material.

Jane did most of the editing herself and made choices that were very wise. The books have been an incredible help to people who wanted a library in one place, a place to start. Even I, as familiar as I am with this field, often take down a volume and look through it to find a quote, the inspiration, a new way of thinking about things that I am not sure about. I still use it.

## Building a Research Base

> "If there was going to be research, there ought to be a plan,
> an agenda."

As Permaul recognized in 1980, an emerging field needed more
than a vibrant professional association and agreed-on principles of
practice. Research was needed to describe the outcomes of service-
learning and confirm the theoretical assertions developed by Duley
and others, which were being used to promote it. Dwight Giles
played a critical role in organizing and catalyzing this research:

> In 1988 I was asked by the president of NSEE if I would chair the
> research committee. I had once before been asked to chair the
> research committee of a practitioner organization. Essentially
> what happened is that two people gathered every year to have a
> research committee meeting, lamented the lack of research in
> the field, and vowed to do something about it. We came back next
> year and repeated the process.
>
> Jenny Anderson and Jane Permaul had put together a research
> bibliography [1984] for NSEE on experiential learning. Janet
> Luce at Stanford produced a bibliography of service-learning
> [1988], which had a lot of research in it. The question was, Do
> we need an experiential learning bibliography more focused on
> research, now that service-learning was emerging, now that it had
> became a more dominant part of NSEE? It was hard to go to
> NSEE anymore without seeing that two-thirds of the sessions were
> service-learning.
>
> My main accomplishment was working with Ellen Porter
> Honnet at The Johnson Foundation and Sally Migliore of NSEE
> to organize a Wingspread conference in March 1991 to develop
> a research agenda for service-learning. If there was going to be
> research, there ought to be a plan, an agenda, and this conference
> could bring attention to this need.

## Defending the Turf

> "A lot of us were happy to see college presidents organizing
> to advocate for public service, but we were mad at the concept
> of service they were putting out."

After settling new lands, pioneers often find themselves having to
defend the new territory from the encroachment of others. The

service-learning pioneers found themselves in such a situation in the mid-1980s with the establishment of Campus Compact: The Presidents' Initiative for Public and Community Service.

Campus Compact was established by Presidents Timothy Healy (Georgetown), Donald Kennedy (Stanford), and Howard Swearer (Brown) in response to a sense of disengagement by students from public and community service in the early 1980s. They were concerned with indicators of student apathy, which they felt would be deeply problematic not only for colleges and universities but also for society at large. They established the Compact to organize their colleagues to draw national attention to this problem and to develop and support measures on campuses to encourage and support student volunteerism. Postsecondary education institutions, in their view, needed to be reconnected to their original mission of preparation of citizens to participate actively and effectively in a democratic society.

This initiative for public and community service was welcomed by the service-learning pioneers. Finally there would be institutional leadership on behalf of at least the service side of service-learning and, they hoped, increased institutional support. But these "new kids on the block" worried the pioneers as well, because the concept of service they articulated was one of pure voluntary action. There was no mention of the learning students might gain, much less need, in order to serve effectively. There was no mention of the need to connect such learning with that sponsored by the academy, and no sense that perhaps the academy, with its deep divide between doing and learning, was part of the problem itself. The pioneers worried that this high-profile support for a narrow concept of voluntary service could undermine many years' effort to advance the concept of service-learning.

Tim Stanton recalls how he and other pioneers plotted to defend this newly settled turf:

> Dick Couto, Michele Whitham, and I were at the Pittsburgh NSEE meeting in 1985. Campus Compact was just starting up. A lot of us were happy to see college presidents organizing to advocate for public service, but we were mad at the concept of service they were putting out—one that appeared to be pure volunteerism separated from the curriculum, separated from the academic purposes of institutions. We feared that if that concept prevailed, it would

undermine the work that NSEE had been doing for many years to build experiential service-learning into the curriculum. If institutions could get away with pushing service as co-curricular noblesse oblige, the service students would undertake would be ineffective and the learning students would derive from it would be incomplete.

Dick, Michele, some others, and I sat around a table one night in Pittsburgh and strategized how we could influence Campus Compact's thinking so that it would embrace and support service-learning as well as voluntary service. Dick and I went after Susan Stroud, director of the Compact. Susan invited us to Washington for a two-day meeting. Michele and I, and, I think, Dick were there. A small group of us sat around the table with Susan for two days talking about service-learning. She asked questions and seemed sincerely interested.

I decided, for both my own needs at Stanford and to continue that strategy, to capture Don Kennedy's attention as well. Catherine Milton was helpful and got me in to talk with Don about it. We got him interested in taking up the flag for connecting service with academic study for the Compact. Susan hooked him up with David Warren, president of Ohio Wesleyan University. They started a Compact task force on combining service with academic study, which I staffed. We did a national survey on these issues with all the Compact institutions and issued a report [Stanton, 1990a] calling on the Compact and its membership to make the establishment of study-service connections through service-learning a high priority.

## Defending the Students

"I found myself in the role of protecting students."

While many pioneers took on the task of staking out and defending their new land, others remained focused on the goals of their work—developing students and communities—on whose behalf the struggle was supposed to be about. As we shall see, many of these pioneers were those most committed to communities and their development. Greg Ricks, however, remained steadfastly committed to the young people involved in service-learning, especially those who took national leadership roles through such organizations as COOL (Campus Outreach Opportunity League) and SCALE (Student Coalition for Literacy Education).

I felt adults were somewhat "adultist" with regard to young people's capability to deliver on issues, on their ideas. The kids had great vision and ideas, but older people thought it was their job to interpret the young and get money for them. For example, I used to argue with Roger Landrum at Youth Service America (YSA) saying, "You're doing a really good job, but you should never compete for a grant against COOL or SCALE, or any young people's group. Your job is to lobby Capitol Hill; do those kinds of things, and let young people interpret for themselves."

I found myself in the role of protecting students. Basically I was running around the country, kind of committing political suicide with my career, because I was bashing colleagues my age for blocking student leadership in this movement.

I remember being on a panel one time. I had heard just the day before that COOL was in for a $500,000 grant and YSA was in for one too. When the grants were given, YSA got $850,000 and COOL got $65,000. So I called the funder out in front of four hundred people and said, "Why would you give one group of older people, in this case older white men, $850,000 to interpret these young people and only $65,000 to the young people themselves? What signal is that sending? This is not a platform for young people to lead at all. What's going on?" I spent a lot of time fighting that.

Still, the vision young people had needed to be more visionary: to go beyond students to institutions. That institutional vision was left to groups like Campus Compact, and that was a mistake. That's why a lot of students became frustrated. They learned how to set up the office, get the file system going, get on-line, have a community service fair and do projects. But—and here's where COOL failed— they didn't offer a collective vision beyond what students could do. I think a reason for that was there was no funding. Kellogg, for example, gave the first serious grant to COOL for a million dollars for Into the Streets,[4] because our generation was willing to acknowledge that young people can get other young people mobilized. But we were not willing to help them learn how to run a program and design a curriculum that would educate them. No sizable grants came from anywhere else other than a few literacy grants, and again, they were all focused on direct service by young people.

There wasn't any kind of push to get students thinking about the larger issues.

## Margins: The True Frontier

"I liked it better when it was more marginal, when there were fewer rewards, when students came to it with a more fiery desire for change in the institution and the world."

Although most pioneers worked to mainstream service-learning within their institutions and to develop the field nationally, others preferred to remain at the margins or outside the academy altogether. Whether by choice or as a consequence of where and how they did their work, institutionalization of service-learning and settling the field were not goals for these pioneers. To them, efforts to move service-learning into the mainstream of postsecondary education were at best irrelevant to what they wished to pursue and at worst corrupting of it.

For these pioneers, the margins were where the action was. They held no hope that mainstream postsecondary education could be an engine of social change for students or communities. To institutionalize service-learning would ultimately rob it of its power to radicalize students and bring justice to society.

Jack Hasegawa's reflections on his experience at Dwight Hall at Yale University exhibit these concerns:

I came to Dwight Hall in 1980 from Friends World College, which was a 100 percent experiential, no-classroom place, so it was easy for me to operate Dwight Hall as if it were a separate entity, which it legally was, removed from Yale's academic life. I resisted credit for Yale students' service, and in a pretty direct way I dropped out of national associations like CAEL and NSEE. To a real degree they didn't have much relevance for us.

I came to Yale at a time where students who were active were looking for an alternate model. My civil rights work had real resonance with that. The men who were in Dwight Hall still had long ponytails. It was the last gasp of guitar playing, sitting around, singing freedom songs. By the time I left, Dwight Hall had become such a central activity at Yale that the student cabinet contained people who were also, for their other extracurricular activities, captain of the debate team, head cheerleader, students who were in the secret societies. It had gone full circle back to what Dwight Hall had been in the 1940s and 1950s when it was one of Yale's premier social institutions.

I was uncomfortable with that shift. I liked it better when it was more marginal, when there were fewer rewards, when students came to it with what seemed to me to be a more fiery desire for change in the institution and the world. I was not seeing this by the time I left. Students were much more reactive, protective, and self-protective, wanting to know, sometimes in great detail, what the benefits of service would be for their careers.

There was a lot of pressure to make the delivery of service more convenient. We started spending money on cars, because, as students perceived Yale as becoming more dangerous, they refused to walk from the campus. We had a long tradition of having only service projects that were within walking distance, trying to create a sense of local community for Yalies' work with their neighbors. But we found ourselves looking at projects that were more interesting, and they were farther away. That replicated a pattern that was going on in the late 1950s and early 1960s, when a lot of Yale volunteer work was driving to Middletown, forty miles away, to the state mental hospital to deliver cigarettes to mental patients, or to the veterans' home, which is forty-five minutes away. Or what we used to call the Bethany movement, where Yale students would teach Sunday school in surrounding small towns.

## Inside Critic

"Service-learning is a continual process. To the extent it becomes institutionalized and you begin to evaluate it and encapsulate it in any formal structure, you begin to limit its capacity."

Herman Blake had deep worries about efforts to institutionalize service-learning as well. Concerned that mainstreaming this pedagogy would remove the possibility that communities could exert control over students' service and learning, he took on the role of inside critic:

To the extent that service-learning is more talked about in higher education, I would rather be engaged in criticizing it, trying to improve it than stand by and let it inflict itself on communities. I have a lot of problems with service-learning and have always been opposed to its assumptions and many of its practices. In that sense, I don't have hope that higher education is any place for it.

My strongest criticism is that practitioners do not look at the community as a place of integrity, with strengths, and a consistency and continuity that have to be respected. So often service-learning talks about students, institutions, and faculty, and the community is almost an afterthought.

I was involved in a Campus Compact project trying to get faculty committed to and involved with service-learning. I think that was a noble effort in many, many respects. But it seems to me that what we needed to do was to get faculty out into communities where they would have insights and understandings of communities.

Let me give you an example of what I mean. One of the pioneers in this field, who did a wonderful job at UCSC, was Nick Royal. He developed a field studies program at Merrill College. Now, Nick and I had differences of opinion, and I would not have done things his way, and he didn't do things my way. But Nick had one thing that was precious. When Merrill College was founded, they would not accept any person on the initial cadre of faculty who had not spent at least two years living and working outside the country. That meant that faculty had an understanding of the powerful consequences of this multicultural experience. You didn't have to persuade them. Something happened, and they knew it.

When we were trying to engage faculty, I was continually trying to put the community perspective into their perspective. For example, I remember that summer at the Campus Compact Service-Learning Institute at Stanford, when we brought in some community people to talk with faculty and one of my former students made a presentation. One woman was the community person supervising our students in Stanslaus County, California. As a thirty-eight-year-old grandmother, she came to the university and got her bachelor's degree and went on to get a master's degree in counseling. She's now a counselor at a state college. She came and talked to the faculty from the community perspective, and faculty asked her a lot of questions. She kept saying, "The thumb of the rule is this, the thumb of the rule is that, and the thumb of the rule is the other." When she left, people said to me, "She just didn't understand. She just kept talking about the thumb of the rule. It's the rule of the thumb." And I said, "No, *you* don't understand. It's the thumb of the rule. If you're going to make an adjustment to that community, *you* adjust to *them*. You don't expect them to become a part of who you are." You can't look at the community in terms of its deficits rather than in terms of what sustains it.

I sent one of my students out to Daufuskie Island [South Carolina] years ago. Because they had no telephone, the family the student was supposed to stay with had left the island the morning of the day he arrived. Now he arrives on the ferry that runs twice a week, Monday afternoon, and the family he was supposed to stay with is gone—gone to the mainland for three weeks. He has an assignment and people to supervise him but no place to stay. Well, this woman looked at him and said, "Come on, stay at my house." She didn't charge him a dime. She took him there and kept him for three weeks.

I went to see her one day and said, "Why did you take that stranger into your home?" She looked at me, puzzled by my question. I came back at it several times: "Why did you take that stranger?" I was trying to take her activity, her action, into my frame of reference, and I don't claim to be any better at this than any of my colleagues. She looked at me and said, "I looked at that boy, and I said to myself, 'That's a mother's son. Boy, come home with me.'" To me the student was a stranger to this woman. But to this woman, the boy was a mother's son.

There are values and perspectives on social behavior that come out of that experience that we just don't hear in the academy. It doesn't mean there aren't problems, because the woman who did this was the local alcoholic. She was known for some rather strange behavior. But what she came through with was extraordinary. What I'm saying is that so many of our assumptions start out with a deficit approach.

Service-learning is a continual process. To the extent it becomes institutionalized and you begin to evaluate it and encapsulate it in any formal structure, you begin to limit its capacity. There's something about what goes on between students, universities, and communities that must be constantly dynamic. We have to learn continuously from new issues.

## Institutional Emigration

"It's why there are so many of us who put on our résumés, 'educator in private practice.'"

While Blake remained in postsecondary education as an inside critic, Judy Sorum Brown and Michele Whitham "emigrated" from institutional life. With concerns that were more epistemological than political, Brown did not see the academic mainstream as a place to work for educational change. She decided to become an "educator in private practice":

> I have a traditional doctorate. I always assumed that I would take an administrative post, partially out of this misguided view that if I was going to be part of one of these institutions, I might as well run it, which is a terrible attitude. When I think about it, I think, "Holy cow, Judith Ann!" But there was a sense that what I really wanted to do was be in a leadership role. I taught a leadership course at Michigan State, and I always taught an English course. When I came to Maryland, I did the same thing: always a course in English, usually Women in Drama or Shakespeare, and always a course in leadership in the education school. The path I ended up following at Maryland was probably instructive of what was happening with the movement. I went from being director of community service programs to being the founder and head of the Center of Experiential Learning, which developed and accredited arrangements for learning of various kinds.
>
> After that, I became a dean for students who designed their own majors, which were contract baccalaureates. Now if you think about it, that's a movement from focus on service to a focus on student-led learning, self-directed learning of various kinds, with high faculty involvement, which was a way of backing into faculty transformation and faculty development. I did that for awhile, and then I was nominated for a White House fellowship and got it. That was 1978.
>
> I've learned never to say *never*, but I would be wildly surprised if I ever go back into an institution. My work is about education for connection. It's about relationships across difference and across sameness. We need to understand that real energy is in the space between things, to understand the space between the two words of *service* and *leadership*. We need to attend to the space between things outside us and also among us as human beings. We need a much more respectful, emergent view of learning that's not so focused on objectives.
>
> My worry is that our traditional views of service and our top-down, teacher-oriented view of education confound our understanding of the relationship between teacher and learner or servant and those that receive service. We need to get those mental models out of the way; we need to get away from what is probabilistically

likely when we bring people together around honest and interesting questions. The difficulty is that learning institutions, and all other institutions to some degree, are at odds with that. That's a real challenge. It's why there are so many of us who put on our résumés, "educator in private practice."

Michele Whitham left the academy, both because she found herself wanting to take the activist role in which she had formerly been placing her students and because she increasingly came to view education as too far removed from the problems plaguing society:

> I was at Cornell from 1976 to 1988. I was helping my students, and the community groups they worked with, to accomplish all these wonderful things. But my activist soul wanted to be *doing* the work. I didn't want to be helping people reflect on it and develop their consciousness about it. I wanted to do it. I had become less convinced, less interested, in helping people to change their minds and more interested in changing their behavior.
>
> Like a lot of other people who grew up during the civil rights movement, I had strong feelings about the power of law. I grew up in the Warren Court era, and I believed in what the legal process could accomplish. In the back of my mind, I always thought that maybe someday I'd go to law school. That day just came. I went thinking law would be a tool I could use to work on the other side of the action-reflection practice that was so much a part of our service-learning work.
>
> I wouldn't go back to higher education. I've had opportunities to go back and I value that work. I value what I did. I value what other people are doing. But I have very profound questions about whether those institutions are close enough to the core issues in this society to make a difference. The problems of racism ultimately are due to the inefficiencies and inadequacies of our economic system. I don't think they're being affected by academic institutions. I don't have time to waste. I'm not getting any younger. If I'm going to have an effect on any of that stuff, I can't afford to go back into those institutions, which are two layers removed. It's like working through cotton candy.
>
> That was the impulse—that desire to go into tough situations where the stakes are high and say, "This is how it's going to be, people." That galvanized me to pursue the law. I like being able to use that tool in order to foster the behaviors that people ought to be manifesting. Then their hearts and minds will follow.

There are strongly held differences among the pioneers about how best to achieve their goals for students, communities, and ultimately the academy. From the stories told here, we learn that these differences animated the pioneers' efforts to settle the new territory between campus and community, which they had staked out, and to establish and institutionalize a new field. In a sense, as much as the pioneers held in common, their differences exhibited a kind of tug-of-war, with some seeking to pull an innovative, marginal practice into the mainstream and others pulling back, worried that the mainstream would inhibit, even co-opt, the power of the practice.

Although John Duley and other pioneers sought to discuss these differences through NSEE conference workshops and collegial discussions, they were not greatly debated. Rather, each pioneer seems to have made his or her choice of how and where to engage individually. As we shall learn in the next chapter, many pioneers regret this lack of debate. Perhaps open public debate on conflicting approaches to both practice and institutionalization is needed if the field is ultimately to achieve its educational, political, and strategic goals.

**Notes**

1. Founded in 1967, the Philadelphia Center (formerly called the Philadelphia Urban Semester) is a liberal arts–focused off-campus internship program, open to students from all majors and disciplines. Affiliated with the Great Lakes Colleges Association, the center is open to undergraduates and graduates from all colleges and universities. To date, more than five thousand students from fifty-five schools in the United States and abroad have attended.

2. The "critical incident" technique of journal writing is a structured approach to reflecting on and writing about experience. Rather than simply describing and interpreting an incident and the people involved, this reflection technique enables the writer to use the incident and its impact as a means for self-monitoring, personal exploration, and learning assessment.

3. Morris Keeton founded the Council for Adult and Experiential Learning in 1974. This organization, now specializing in adult education, provides training and education to individuals and organizations.

4. Into the Streets is a national service day program designed to introduce students to volunteering through hands-on experience in an area

of their choice. Operating under the motto, "Try it for a day, you may love it for a lifetime," Into the Streets combines service with education and reflection in order to encourage continued student involvement throughout the year.

# Chapter Nine

# Helps, Hindrances, and Accomplishments

## Reflections on the Pioneer Experience

The stories of the service-learning pioneers paint a picture of both accomplishment and sacrifice. New, uncharted worlds in education and community development were explored, settled, and established, but as with any other pioneering effort, the road to accomplishment was hazardous. Trailblazing could be lonely and painful. Sometimes the pioneers lost both their compasses and their paths. Some of the pioneers were driven off the trail, and others turned back to find different arenas in which to continue their explorations. In this chapter the pioneers reflect on these experiences, seeking to identify the forces and resources that helped them along their way and those that presented considerable barriers.

## Sustaining Resources

In Chapter Three the pioneers identified early experiences, motivations, and commitments that inspired them to seek change in students, communities, and postsecondary education institutions. Adult role models, youthful experiences of community and service, alienation from schooling, social concerns, religious faith and training, and the social and political movements of the time propelled these individuals into innovative work that brought them up against traditions and structures in both universities and communities. In looking back at their experience, many of the pioneers identified these same kinds of commitments and motivations, internalized over many years, as critical to keeping their "eyes on the prize," as they maneuvered around hazards and coped with stiff opposition.

## Personal Characteristics: Anger, Hope, and Faith

Nadinne Cruz has already described the inspiration she received from her youth from work with Philippine peasants. The other side of that inspiration was anger at the conditions of the poor, something she identifies as sustaining her commitment to service-learning over three decades.

> It started as rage and continues as fury in some form at all the unnecessary suffering in the world. I don't buy the notion that there are misfortunes much like a volcano eruption, an act of God, or a tragedy of nature. Poverty and suffering exist due to acts of human design. They can be undone by human design. To continue an order that seems unnecessary is an outrage.
>
> The Philippine peasants have been an infinite source of inspiration because, as formally unlettered as they were, they thought about the world in ways that could help them shape their destiny. I was inspired by their wanting to learn and their goodness of heart. They were not victims or recipients. They were acting on their lives just as the Greeks conceived of the civic arts. They were the epitome of what it means to be fully human.

Dwight Giles identifies "transcendent hope" against all odds as key to sustaining his commitment, a trait expressed by many other pioneers.

> I guess there's a difference between hope and optimism. Ann Colby talked about that in *Some Do Care* [Colby and Damon, 1994]. I was inspired by that book. One of the things that she and Bill Damon point out about the people they interviewed was how they think about life. They didn't have much optimism. They worked in a world that was going to hell in a handbasket. But somehow they sustained hope. Colby and Damon use these words, and I would use them, too—a "transcending hope," because the people they talked with felt things would go right in the long run.

Helen Lewis used her focus on the long-term nature of social change to sustain herself as well:

> I don't expect victories. My philosophy is like my grandmother's: that human beings are born to struggle. I enjoy the fight. I enjoy pushing the barriers. Myles Horton always said that you had to be in it for the long haul. You can't count on short-term victories. It's kind of self-righteous sounding, but you don't expect to win. Victories come, but they build on little things. You're just adding to it. Somebody else will push it further along. You do what you can under the circumstances where you are, and you don't give up.

Other pioneers attributed much of their ongoing commitment to a calling. One of them is Bill Ramsay:

> At a conference I went to, someone gave a speech on careers and made a distinction between vocation and job, which was more than different jobs in a career. The idea was that you have a vocation, a calling—something that you want to see done or something you want to relate to, that can take place in any number of expressions. It can be a job; it can be community service as a volunteer; it can be as a researcher or writer. There are any number of ways that find expression.
>
> As an administrator, as an educator, I've always been interested in empowering other people. My commitment is to help other people identify and realize their goals, to influence them in those areas where I feel I've learned something and have something to offer. I started out as an intern, and one of my first tasks when I went to Oak Ridge was to supervise the public administration interns. I've always tried with the staff I have the privilege to work with to empower them, and help them grow—to live a life responding to what you feel you're called to do.

John Duley identified deep, socially oriented faith as an important sustaining resource.

> One of things I've learned as I've reflected on my life journey is that my Christian faith has empowered me to say yes to life—to accept life as it comes and to affirm it, rather than to try to hold it off and protect myself from things that happen.
>
> But I can't do just that. I can't exist without a deep sense of social responsibility, trying to work for peace and justice. That's

what I mean by "socially responsible hedonism." It's got to be fun, but it also has got to be socially responsible. You've got to make a difference.

## Closed Doors: Calls to Action

This urge to make a difference arose repeatedly in the pioneers' reflections on their lives. Here Mike Goldstein and Garry Hesser discuss what it meant for them. First is Goldstein:

> I think part of it was not knowing enough to realize that what you were doing was impossible. I suspect many of us in our early years had a guiding theory: that the door that says "do not enter" was a challenge. We saw closed doors as waiting to be opened. The barriers and challenges were that it obviously couldn't be done. We just didn't know it at the time.
>
> We were setting up a large program in an immensely complex bureaucracy with a total absence of resource support. We had colleges not wanting to release Work-Study funds. The Office of Education said it wasn't a good idea. We didn't know enough at the time to realize that those were barriers. We viewed them as challenges.
>
> Our assumption was that of course we could do it. If someone got in our way, there were simply two alternatives: go around them, or go over them or through them, which was what we did. My name for an awfully long time was cursed in financial aid circles, because we essentially went over and through them. There were immense challenges and barriers, but one of the great virtues of doing that at that particular stage in our lives was that to us there were no barriers. There were just challenges.

Garry Hesser:

> I think arrogance would be another way to describe it, but that is a positive. I think pioneers have arrogance, want to change, make things better. We thought we could, which is almost by definition intellectual arrogance. That's a distinguishing characteristic of people who want to change the world, want to make things better, or have an impact. Call it arrogance; call it intestinal fortitude, stupidity, or simply lack of knowledge and therefore blindly going into the desert. Whatever it is, pioneers try to get through.

## Sponsors, Protectors, and Funders

Just as Lewis and Clark had the sponsorship and support of President Jefferson, several service-learning pioneers gained critical support from individuals, usually older, who were their bosses, mentors, or sponsors or who otherwise created an environment in which they could go about their work. From these people the pioneers received funding, protection, and good advice. Page Smith, provost of Cowell College at the University of Santa Cruz, played a critical support role for Herman Blake by providing academic sponsorship for his students' service-learning. According to Blake, "Page was the kind of person who never let bureaucratic procedure, academic policies, or rules stop or even delay him once he made up his mind. His philosophy was damn the rules—full speed ahead. Students received full academic credit, and Page registered them. When it came to getting faculty engagement, when it came to getting academic credit, Page handled it."

Jane Permaul cites the long-term leadership of Chancellor Charles Young at the University of California at Los Angeles as setting an environment in which she could organize faculty: "It's important to have sustaining leadership even though it may not agree with you on important priorities. Then you don't have to change the rules constantly in terms of how you play the game. Chuck Young provided an environment that allowed people, and certainly me, to explore, learn, and try new things."

Tim Stanton comments on the important role played by President Donald Kennedy at Stanford in setting a vision, encouraging faculty involvement, and funding.

> Organization behavior theories, which talk about the importance of the person at the top putting out the vision, are right on target as they apply to Stanford. Kennedy's leadership was critical to establishing what became the Haas Center for Public Service. But just as important, almost single-handedly he changed the culture of the institution to support service involvement, and that made our work so much easier. He was a very "out there" president in terms of style, and in those early years he was "out there" on behalf of public service with students, faculty, alumni, donors—you name it. He talked about it all the time, and pretty soon everyone else was talking about it too.

He helped us in another important way to get faculty engaged in service-learning. I remember he would invite what he called "opinion leaders" in the faculty into his office for Friday afternoon salons, or that's what they seemed like to me. He'd give them a glass of sherry, and then lead them through a most invigorating Socratic dialogue about how we could educate students through service. How could we help them learn from these experiences? How should that learning be connected to the curriculum? I think those sessions got people thinking. So when we had funds to give to faculty for service-learning course development, which Kennedy also provided, faculty were ready to take off. They knew they would have support.

There was no better person to work with on this than Don Kennedy. I remember when we were just getting started, I went to Washington for a meeting where Don presented what was basically my paper on the need for study-service connections to a group of Campus Compact presidents. Don sat up there with David Warren, and the session went well. There were lots of good questions. Toward the end, Don made me stand up and he said, "I'm really indebted to Tim Stanton." Well, that was great, but what was better was that he came up afterward and said, "Was it okay that I did that? I didn't want to embarrass you." And I said, "Oh, that was fine. I really appreciated it." Then he said, "Well, I just wanted to make sure they liked it before I told them that the work was yours." That was so gracious.

Funding was a critical resource or a critical challenge for all the pioneers. As described by Garry Hesser in Chapter Eight, it often became the route to legitimizing service-learning with faculty and administrators. For Gib Robinson, the funder was as important as the funds themselves:

In 1971 when I started, the most obvious barrier was that people had no idea that service-learning was something that we should be doing. They had no sense of its value. Certainly in my own department, there was precious little interest. The English department was not the logical place for that!

What overcame that were two things. First of all, money, and that came from outside resources. The university at that time, particularly the English department, did not solicit. There wasn't a whole lot of outside money. So when I got funded, the university said, "Well, we don't know what he's doing and we don't know why he's doing it, but he's got money, so we'll let him do it." That was crucial.

Just as important was Ruth Chance, director at Rosenberg Foundation, who was a crucial mentor to me. She asked hard questions and then empowered me to go do what I wanted. She basically gave me a check and said, "Go do it." That kind of trust was terribly important, because my faculty colleagues did not understand and could not even ask the questions that Ruth did.

## The Power of Success

Another critical force propelling the pioneers along was the impact of their work, which they perceived in the students and communities with whom they worked.

Mary Edens:

What sustains me are the students and their reports of outcomes. That sustains and drives all our staff. I sense that students are making a difference in the community, but we don't have them long enough to see a real difference there. I don't know if that would be a realistic expectation. But talking with students as they report their growth, their learning, their enthusiasm, their excitement, or even their discomfort and puzzlement with issues that they're exploring and wrestling with is still a driving force.

Rob Shumer:

Student outcomes, students' expressions of enjoyment of learning, of connecting kept me going. When I was running the alternative high school, I had a chance to meet with the parents of all of my students every ten weeks. I would go to their homes, and they would talk about the transformation of their kids and how much they liked learning. It was a whole different relationship. It showed me that school is an artificial place, and parents didn't like to come onto campus. But when you went to their house, it was different. You were extending yourself to their world.

Tim Stanton:

Students keep me going. The first year I was at Cornell, I taught the New York City program. I was commuting from Ithaca, running this fifteen-credit, full-time powerhouse course, trying to train students how to think critically about their experience, and use what they learned to be more effective. I got a letter from one of those students a couple of years after she graduated, in which she told me how she was trying to organize things where she worked and how she was taking the curriculum that we had taught them in New York and applying it, and how well it was helping her. Outcomes like that make me feel like it's all worth it.

## Greg Ricks:

Seeing young people go on to be incredible leaders. Goodwin Liu: what can I say?[1] Goodwin was a sophomore when I met him, and he was one of my kids. To see him today as one of the best minds in America thinking about this stuff for the last twenty years brings tears to my eyes. I feel incredibly proud and a piece of who he is. There are a number of students like him who I see now becoming major players. That sustains me.

Other pioneers gained sustenance from accomplishments they perceived in the community.

## Dick Couto:

I spent a whole lot of time raising money, dealing with problems, being very, very reactive. Sometimes I wondered if it was really worth it, especially on those days when you came in with the bookbag full of work, and somebody came in first thing and gave you a problem that you spent the whole day working on. And several other problems came across your desk, and you left late at night with the same work in the same bookbag without even having touched it. At times like that I asked, "Is it really worth it?"

I made a point of visiting all our projects at least once, if not twice, during the summer. I would come back after talking with community leaders and listening to the impression they had about the difference the students were making, after having talked to students and setting my eyes on the places that they were at. There was just no doubt about it: it was worth it. But very often I had to leave the university to convince myself of that and get immersed in both the resources and the problems that were going on at the local level.

## Ken Reardon:

One of the most important things is the relationship I have with residents or leaders in communities that have experienced wrenching social problems, who throughout those changes continue to provide highly constructive, even heroic at times, leadership around those issues. Take the chance to work with Celia Davis, who's been in the same neighborhood in East St. Louis since 1961 as a community organizer. She is a legend. She's our Mother Teresa, our Mahatma Gandhi. To have a chance to work with somebody who understands the nature of the problems and every day has been at it is an honor. It's spiritual; it's personal; there's a great sense of joy when we're able to do things together, to be engaged in that way in the world is gratifying work.

## Colleagues and Comrades: The Importance of Community

Repeatedly the service-learning pioneers pointed to other colleagues as perhaps the most important sustaining resource. For example, the four Cornell pioneers point to each other as their main supports.

Tim Stanton:

The great luxury and opportunity at Cornell was to be able to build a program with Michele, Mady Holzer, Dwight, and the others. It was this great collaborative. We were very simpatico. We energized each other. I've learned an immense amount from them. And because we were under attack all the time, we were very bonded as group. That's really important to me. I find I do my best work when I surround myself with really good people. I don't do as well when I'm totally on my own. It was important in my Marin work, it was important at Cornell, and it's important at Stanford.

Unlike these Cornell colleagues, however, most pioneers worked on their own. In the early years when service-learning projects were few and far between, they were the only ones on their campus concerned with service and academic learning. They had to reach out beyond their institutions to find collegial support. In the early 1970s, Hal Woods found such a network through the National Student Volunteer Program (NSVP):

There was a group of us who were volunteer consultants with NSVP, and we met in Boston. For the first time, I began to feel that there were other people involved in this and that there was something to learn. We had opportunities to write articles about our experience.

We had a chance to do training, which deepened our experience. We were developing a sense of colleagueship, sharing information, techniques, materials, and so on.

Jon Wagner describes a collegial network that he discovered through a friend, which played an important support role for him:

The New Faculty Program of the Church Society for College Work was started back in 1971 or 1970. It was an ecumenical church organization. They wanted to help new faculty members and graduate students carry forward a socially engaged agenda. It was based in the Northeast. There were annual conferences some place around Cape Cod or Boston for four or five years. I was involved through an undergraduate friend, who was at Brandeis. People from the Brandeis sociology department were involved—people from graduate theological seminaries.

The first meetings were extremely intensive. The women's movement was hitting a crest at that time, so there were tremendous arguments about gender. There was also a feel for development of engaged university people—graduate students, faculty members. How do we do this? How do you link community organizing and university work?

Later it became the Life Work Network for Social Change. Then somebody had a dog named Farfel, so it became Friends and Resources for Everyday Learning. There were several different incarnations. But as a sustaining thing, this was a place people kept coming back to every summer. We called it summer camp. It was a way some had vacations. The major institutions needed to be reformed, and we saw ourselves as a vanguard moving through higher education. We would do this work together at these conferences, and then we would go back. The notion was that this was our school, our place to heal and grow and learn as we worked together in the long march through our institutions.

The organization most often cited by the pioneers as a place to give and get support was what is now known as the National Society for Experiential Education (NSEE) and its antecedent organizations. In Chapter Eight we learned from Jim Feeney and Mike Goldstein about how the society was organized and the merger that brought together government internship people with those who identified with the terms *field study, experiential education,* and *service-learning.* Here the pioneers discuss how their association through the society supported and sustained their trailblazing work.

### John Duley:

One challenge we faced was isolation, loneliness, and a sense of being a pilgrim, and the main antidote was the Society for Field Experience Education [SFEE]. It became a network of mutual support for all of us. The field was so new and unexplored that we needed one another to keep our heads above water. There was no hesitancy among members to share resources or program ideas. The strong, collaborative leadership of Jane Kendall set the tone. The supportive fellowship the society provided was extremely important, and the publications and resources were a great boon to the movement.

We were all wrestling with the same questions. We fed one another, supported one another, criticized one another. It was the most free-flowing society of professionals that I had ever met. There wasn't any one-upsmanship. There was a desperate need we all had to learn from one another and gain as much knowledge and insight as we could by picking each other's brains and sharing with each other what we knew. So whatever learning took place about theory and practice, it was enhanced, strengthened, and criticized by the community that developed.

### Sharon Rubin:

The community of people in NSEE has sustained me enormously. No matter what was happening on my campus, I could call Jane Kendall or I could get a call from Dwight Giles, or somebody else, and get some perspective of what was going on, get encouragement, and get told I really did know something and I wasn't a total idiot. Just having that psychological and then intellectual support from very thoughtful, intelligent people, who want to think as deeply and as well as they can about these topics. I've never felt all by myself. I've always felt there was a whole community of people who were doing this wonderful work even if I'm not in contact with them all the time.

I wish more faculty had a group like this one—not necessarily NSEE, but a group of people who were sustaining them like this. Faculty go to disciplinary groups. They have friends from the department or across departments. They say, "I'm going to do something that's not ordinary. How am I going to be understood, and how am I going to be valued for it?" It's very hard. They are very isolated. So the thing that's sustaining is not only my friends, but getting people into a group, so they can talk about this stuff and not feel that in some way they're peculiar or that something terrible is going to happen to them for wanting to do teaching and learning very differently from the way other people do it.

## Jane Permaul:

I'm attracted to service-learning, because the essence of service-learning is team. It's collaborative as opposed to egocentric and individual. I don't know which came first: whether the philosophy attracted me to service-learning or service-learning influenced me. Maybe it's both ways. One reaffirmed the other.

NSEE had a great deal to do with it. Somehow this collection of people has those qualities. This group is very different from the American Sociological Association or the Historians' Association. Let me suggest a theory, because I don't know the real answer, but it's a way of asking. It's not one- but two-directional. It's a sense of collaboration and teamwork. I wonder if the people who are attracted to service-learning have those characteristics themselves, and consequently the community that we have is thus very attractive, a place for finding support under siege. We may not always need that support, yet we keep coming back.

There is that ever-self-effacing, very honest quality, and yet you know there is so much wealth and richness. That enables me to value it even more. If you constantly stay in a very egocentric environment, like most colleges and universities are, you begin to wonder. Everybody else is like that, so shouldn't you be too?

## Sharon Rubin:

The difference between the meeting of the American Psychological Association and going to NSEE is that they talk about new theories and what they teach. People who get together in this field talk about new theories and *how* they teach, *how* learning is undertaken. This is a group that deals with the concept of how students learn and how students change, and that's very different from what a lot of people in discipline-based organizations do.

Garry Hesser:

I think there's one other distinction, and that is that nobody is afraid to give it away, because you won't have less of it. I know that when I go to a disciplinary meeting, it's as if your knowledge and your expertise have a copyright. If you share it, somehow you're not getting your royalties. I've never felt in any NSEE gathering that anybody would fail to help me in any way I needed or share whatever expertise they had, because that would not diminish them in any way. So the concept of empowerment that we talk about, we actually behave that way. We're behaving the way we expect experiential learning to work.

Sharon Rubin:

Jane Kendall was a great mentor. She never made me feel like an idiot, but it's clear that she helped bring my thinking along enormously. I did not start out with a very high level of conceptualization about any of these things. But through our conversations, things she gave me to read, and her trusting me, I had a chance to grow and to learn.

All the NSEE consultants were like that in their own way. We were from different universes, but that was intentional on Jane's part, I have no doubt. We had to learn to negotiate different languages, different backgrounds, and different concepts of what we were doing and why we were doing it. They were great teachers. We'd get together once a year and teach each other. We would share ideas. Sometimes we'd do conceptual papers on cutting-edge issues. We'd share different ways of thinking about our issues, because we were continually challenging each other—and not in the way that academics sometimes challenge each other, which is to say, "My idea is great and yours is . . . " We would be supportive but intellectually challenging. We were not satisfied with just knowing what we knew. We had to know more; we had to think more deeply, be more careful and more articulate.

Greg Ricks:

The very selfish thing about it is that service-learning has been an incredible support system for me, because so many people who are in it are professional colleagues or personal friends. The reality is that my funeral will look like a service-learning conference. It truly will.

Julian Bond said that some of his best friends are those he met in the civil rights movement and sustained over the years.[2] I can't think of a more fun party than one of NSEE people or Campus Outreach Opportunity League [COOL] people coming together who really care.

Some pioneers were not connected with this vibrant, supportive network. And as we shall learn in the next chapter, this supportive community had its shortcomings. Nevertheless, those who connected through this association point to the quality of their interaction, as well as the interaction itself, as being a critical resource for sustaining their commitment and ability to pioneer service-learning pedagogy.

## Reflective Practice and Theoretical Mentors

A final sustaining resource identified by the service-learning pioneers was their orientation to experiential learning itself. As Jane Permaul noted, this group of people tended to practice what they preached, constantly tinkering with their pedagogy and learning from that experience. Permaul raised the question of whether she was drawn to service-learning as a result of its values or whether her values, and similar ones in other pioneers, shaped the values of service-learning, suggesting it was probably an interactive process. Regardless of how that came about, the value and discipline of reflection—of stepping back from intense social engagement to learn from it in order to be more effective the next time, and the connecting of these reflections with existing theoretical knowledge—not only distinguishes service-learning pedagogy; it was a practice that sustained the pioneers themselves.

Bob Sigmon:

Those evening reflection discussions in Pakistan helped me a lot. And so did having nine months in Bangalore to study, think, and reflect. I had time away to think about that experience. I have my own private meditation discipline.

When I worked for the American Friends Service Committee, twelve of us came together every two months for two or three days. We would have deep discussions. When I was at the Southern

Regional Education Board, there were the corporate communities that we associated with and the black community. That was a lot of support. We had a sense of mission and excitement. That was supportive, just to realize you were in these conversations with hundreds of people around things that mattered. It was people talking about their lives and what was important.

Although most pioneers shared Sigmon's proclivity and commitment to a reflective practice, some were resistant to connecting their work, much less their reflections, to empirically based knowledge. These pioneers considered themselves primarily as activists. They focused largely on organizing action on behalf of community and social justice goals. A few, like Hasegawa, had an "anti-intellectual" approach to theory. He explains: "I've never been a theory person. I haven't thought about my work in that way."

Most pioneers, however, felt a need both to theorize about their work and connect it to larger theories related to human, organization, and community development. They identified numerous public leaders and theoretical mentors as helping to show them the way in service-learning.

The largest number of these theoretical mentors were progressive activists and scholars in education and human development. They include DeWitt Baldwin, John Dewey, Paulo Freire, George Klemp, David Kolb, and Mary Conway Kohler. Other social science researchers identified as important were Robert Coles, Robert Greenleaf, Herb Kohl, Jonathan Kozol, Joan Lipsitz, Margaret Mead, Donald Schön, Studs Terkel, and William F. Whyte.

Another large group of activist-scholars viewed as mentors or role models by the pioneers could be classified as political leaders and organizers. They include Saul Alinsky, the Berrigan brothers, Gandhi, Myles Horton, Ivan Illich, John and Robert Kennedy, Martin Luther King, Jr., and Peace Corps officials and volunteers.

Several pioneers pointed to the importance of philosophical and spiritual mentors, such as Dietrich Bonhoeffer and Reinhold Niebuhr, as influencing and sustaining their paths. The significant place of spirituality in many of the pioneers echoes that found by Colby and Damon (1994) in their "moral exemplars." There is a strong moral, values-oriented cast to the way the pioneers describe their work, which may have played an important role in sustaining them as they confronted the challenges and frustrations inherent in institutional and social change.

From the pioneers' stories, it appears that John Dewey and the progressive educators of the first part of the twentieth century broke ground for service-learning pedagogy by connecting education with democracy and conceptualizing the importance of experiential learning in citizenship development.

Rob Shumer:

John Dewey's work was a big influence on me. The more I read Dewey and other philosophers who talked about the role of experiential learning, the more I became convinced that I was on the right path. The premise of Dewey is the notion of engagement. Dewey talks about the aim of education as self-control. I don't think you gain control over your life unless you can be a player. One of the essential elements of service-learning and experiential education is the notion of participation. What I'm about is people participating in whatever culture and whatever unit of society they name. The more people participate, the better the buy-in.

Dwight Giles:

When I read Dewey, it was as if it was my voice that I was reading. He gave voice to what I was thinking. He is the ultimate voice on connecting doing with knowing.

With this foundation the pioneers then embedded much of their work in the alternative education and social change work of the 1960s and 1970s. For example, Paulo Freire's "pedagogy of the oppressed" (1970) and Illich's concepts of deschooling (1972) clearly inspired many, as noted by Whitham. Duley drew on the research of Kolb (1984) and Klemp (1977) to help practitioners both describe and advocate their work. Sharon Rubin describes how scholarly work helped her conceptualize, describe, and advance her goals for undergraduate education:

David Kolb gave us a foundation for thinking about how you connect experience and learning. His work is still the best shorthand for describing experiential teaching and learning I can imagine. But the work of Lee Knefelkamp [1980], which I came in contact with early on in my career at the University of Maryland, gave me a

notion that there was such a thing as student intellectual development. In looking back, it seems sort of screwy that I didn't know
about Lee's work. But when you're being prepared to teach in
college, nobody talks about how students develop intellectually
over the course of their college years. Lee did some workshops for
me on William Perry [1970] in connection with a grant I had. That
was the light bulb. I said, "Oh my God! This is why freshmen are
different from seniors." Suddenly the notion of connecting experiential learning and student intellectual development became a
compelling idea. Perry dealt with moral development as well as
intellectual development, which is particularly compelling with
regard to service-learning.

A small number of pioneers held strong theories about the ills
of society and the limitations of the academy, and their service-
learning work was a means of testing, refining, and applying these
theories in the real world. For example, Harkavy noted, "I have a
theory that higher education is broken. I base my whole professional orientation on that fact."

Most pioneers, however, appear to have been experiential
learners themselves—learning-by-doing practitioners who were
motivated by educational and social commitments and used theory to understand, strengthen, and legitimize their work. Perhaps
Tim Stanton's description of his experiential approach to empirical knowledge best describes the pioneers' posture toward scholarship: "I had a gut sense of where I wanted to go, and I looked for
theories to help me get there."

## Restraining Forces: Hazards and Roadblocks Along the Way

In spite of their considerable sustaining resources, the service-
learning pioneers encountered many challenges. These can be
organized in terms of personal characteristics of the pioneers
themselves, institutional roles and culture, race and ethnicity, and
work and family.

### Personal Challenges

Pioneers are always tested personally. Regardless of how much or
little support they have from colleagues, mentors, or funders, there

is always an intrapersonal struggle to maintain optimism in the face of conflict and lack of recognition. For example, even with her "long haul" philosophy, Helen Lewis at times became disillusioned and embittered:

My conflicts with the colleges were very demoralizing. What was so upsetting was the number of friends on the faculty who wouldn't speak to me, wouldn't even be caught on the street with me. They were so protective of their jobs. I thought, What a privileged position faculty are in. Who else has tenure? These coal miners who lost their jobs—hundreds of coal miners, who were forty, fifty, and sixty years old—had to go to Dayton and Detroit to get jobs. Here were these people with fourth-grade educations who were doing that. And here were these other people with great educations who were so afraid of losing their jobs and who would not speak up.

There was also a personal challenge to maintain and live up to the high standards and principles that the pioneers set for themselves or that they thought others expected of them.

Ira Harkavy:

One of the things I hope to give students is a sense of optimism that you can change things. But I think we are deeply guilty at universities as faculty and as administrators of building in a learned pessimism. Students learn helplessness. Left faculty are at least as guilty of this as anybody else, and I don't mean that as a red-baiting statement. They'll attribute social problems to capitalist control of things, and that lets us off the hook. We don't teach responsibility. So part of this is a personal challenge: how do you remain true to the things that you believe in within a system that has been so unreceptive to that value of personal responsibility?

Dick Couto:

There was the obstacle of people coming to our program in search of a lever to change the world. They had such high expectations of the center, and insofar as I came to embody the center, when things didn't work out and it wasn't the utopia or the ideal they wanted, a lot of criticism focused on me. It was like that in the 1960s. We wanted direct participation; we wanted full participation, full representation. We had a lot of confusion as to authority and student autonomy. All those things fed into every other conflict.

## Up Against the Wall of Institutional Culture

The challenges most often cited by the pioneers related to their marginal positions within or outside institutions and to the culture of those institutions. We have learned much about these challenges already. Campus-based pioneers were often the only ones in their institutions working to establish service-learning, and therefore the only ones concerned with campus-community relationships. They lacked the status and influence of regular faculty. Program and budgetary support was difficult to obtain and maintain.

Community-based pioneers experienced the problems of marginal status as well. Those like Marty Tillman found academic institutions difficult to access:

> The academy will always be the academy. It will always have high walls, and students will always have to jump very high to get across those walls. And people like me, working on the outside, will always have to jump high to get inside. I found it very, very difficult to find points of entry or easy access into the university community, to find people who would support the kind of learning experiences Lisle represented. It was an incredibly demoralizing experience on particular campuses.

Because some community-based pioneers were focused on educational institutions, they often were not mainstream in the community either. Dwight Giles describes this sense of not belonging in either world:

> "Marginal" means that you're not accepted in either community. For instance, when I was a volunteer firefighter, people were sure that someone with a Ph.D. could not get a twenty-ton fire truck to a scene with hoses laid and get into a burning building and do something. At the same time, when I went to Vanderbilt, one of the deans who interviewed me talked about people who had done service-learning and internships, people who had done it as the first stage of their career and then moved on to their "real job." He said, not meaning anything disparaging, in true amazement, "I've never met anybody who's made a career out of experiential learning." Sometimes you're suspect in both camps.

## "The Dead Hand of Tradition"

The seemingly intractable academic culture of institutions was perhaps the most formidable hazard for the pioneers. It affected their ability to sustain their jobs and programs and establish service-learning as a legitimate form of instruction and academic inquiry. One barrier was the traditional concept of pedagogy articulated by Jane Permaul in Chapter Eight: that all knowledge is conceived on campus, and faculty are the ones to dispense it. Service-learning was immediately suspect in such a culture that valued traditional, hierarchical knowledge concepts. Jon Wagner notes, "In some disciplines there's a strong tradition of going out into the field. I'm fortunate in a sense that those disciplines are ones that I have my intellectual training in. When I try to go a little further afield, it's harder to find faculty members who think it makes sense to do that." Rob Shumer adds:

> The downside is feeling that after twenty years, the notion of using the community as the central place for learning still isn't understood, by either higher education or K–12 education. I discovered in the dictionary that the word *academic* means "theoretical, not practical." By definition, service-learning, vocational education, and anything else that has a practical orientation isn't academic. Experiential education is still considered second class. We don't recognize what people learn from their own lives, and we don't give credit for it.

Sharon Rubin:

> Although experiential and service-learning have more legitimacy within higher education, we're a long way from being able to talk about institutionalization. This is still sort of on the fringe. And vice presidents aren't supposed to be on the fringe. I always have to balance my talk. This is where my commitments are, but how do I talk about this stuff in a way that doesn't get faculty saying, "Well, she's finally gone off the deep end. Why is she talking about this funny stuff?" It's really difficult in my role, and in many other people's roles, to explain these ideas in a way that they are taken as legitimate. They *are* legitimate. I know that in my heart. I know that they've been around for generations. I know that they have made a tremendous difference in the quality of education students

have received. Still, they're not accepted in the same way that lab science is. It takes a long time for ideas to get legitimacy in higher education.

Ira Harkavy:

It's the dead hand of tradition, and pedagogy is part of that—the whole notion of separation of theory and applied learning. There is a self-satisfied orientation that academics often have. Like lemmings, we all try to imitate Harvard, as if it's the thing to do. Habits are difficult to change. It's harder to overthrow Plato and institute Dewey than it is to cause the state to wither away. It really is.

Gib Robinson attributes this pedagogical resistance to a more general organizational aspect of institutional culture:

I don't think my departmental colleagues saw the making of deep connections with students as important, and I don't quite under-stand why. When I first got to San Francisco State, the first question I had was basically, "Why are we doing this? Doesn't this feel diffi-cult?" I remember saying, "I don't think if we set out to design a system that kept people on a limited piece of landscape, in ways that separated them from themselves so they were twenty-four thousand mutually repellent particles, that we could have done a more effective job than we did then at the university!"
     It's particularly difficult for an urban university to develop community. But to me, not having a community meant that people were isolated. And the academic and bureaucratic structures that kept them isolated didn't help with getting them together. It put tremendous pressure on teachers, both because we were teaching a lot of classes and because we had tremendous responsibilities for people's lives. I didn't understand why my own faculty didn't see this structure as a primary fault that made their lives much more difficult than they needed to be, and then address it. But for what-ever reason, they didn't. And for whatever reason, I was much more sensitive to that than they were. That meant I was trying to do things that they saw no apparent need to do.

Nadinne Cruz identifies institutional perceptions of academic mission as determining whether service-learning is viewed as cen-tral to that mission, as a distraction, or even as a threat:

There's been a narrowing of the definition of what constitutes the central academic mission at Stanford. That's a threat. It's not as if we are in imminent danger of being kicked out, but when the definition and public rhetoric about the central core mission of Stanford are narrowing rather than expanding what counts as academic, then we have to watch out. The president talks about "main tent" and "sideshows"—that there are distractions that we need to pare down to focus on the central core. That focus on central core means that you don't put too much money into the distractions. We could be one of the distractions.

A major expression of this traditional institutional culture and structure is tenure. Some service-learning pioneers experienced tenure as a roadblock personally. Many viewed it as a critical element in why it was so difficult to get faculty members to change their views on teaching and on the larger academic mission of their institutions. Garry Hesser was one of the pioneers who ran head-first into the tenure roadblock:

> This is hard to articulate, because I don't want to come down hard on the College of Wooster. They had this rather phenomenal urban service-learning program and have it to this day. But where my inclination was to work with those students when they came back to campus, the college wanted me and my colleagues to put our time into much more traditional academic matters. They wanted me to write and do research. When my tenure came up, my colleagues in urban studies were absolutely amazed that there was not a single evaluation given of my interdisciplinary urban studies work, much less living with students in the [community service] house and trying to promote it. The barrier still seemed to be that the college wanted my kind of involvement with students, but they didn't have a way to value and support people who gave that kind of energy and involvement.
>
> I don't think it's fair to point to the college and say, "That's what cost me tenure," but that would be part of it. The college during that time was still trying to become a small Princeton of the Midwest. It had image goals. When I got to Augsburg College in Minneapolis, a much more modest and humble place in both its history and its resources, the faculty had thought through and affirmed the value of the external community as a resource for learning. At Wooster, there was still a very classic, traditional view of education.

Ken Reardon experienced tenure pressures as well:

The conflict is age old, and it seems like a sore that won't heal. But if you want to institutionalize service-learning, it can't be done in student affairs. It has to be done in academic affairs. And with cuts, at least on our campus, tenure criteria are getting more conservative. Fewer people are getting approved for this kind of work. Regardless of the rhetorical commitments of Campus Compact presidents, in places like Illinois, that just doesn't count. I still can't get tenure except on most traditional criteria. That's a big issue. How do you provide support for folks to do this work without burning out?

Dwight Giles observes tenure as separating faculty from other classes of people, thus making it difficult for them to value students as capable of learning on their own, and communities as places where knowledge exists of its own accord:

Tenure's not a roadblock; it is a wall. I think it's hard to defend. I had teachers who were harassed during the McCarthy era. I understand the importance of academic freedom, and I understand why we have tenure. And it's not a problem for me personally.

I just have fundamental moral and intellectual problems with tenure. Maybe that's because part of the way I paid my way through college was working in factories and working with people in unions. It's a class thing. It's hard to justify tenure for a class of people in our society when we don't have it for other people. There are other ways to protect academic freedom.

Many traditional academics see themselves as very liberal, very progressive, and very engaged on social issues. Yet tenure is one reason the academy is one of the most conservative institutions in society. I was debating a colleague at Cornell on the issue of what students should be doing in fieldwork. This was someone who showed up at some of the same meetings I did. But he said, when we were talking about field study, "That's okay, but let them do it on their own time." That idea that faculty own students' time and then this other stuff they do is on their own time infuriates me.

Lacking status and clout, the pioneers often were under continuous attack just to maintain their institutional base. Indeed, most of the pioneers were ousted or resigned from a service-learning-oriented position at one time in their career. Tim Stanton describes how the Cornell pioneers experienced these cultural and structural roadblocks as they tried to institutionalize service-learning there:

> We had three strikes against us with that program. One was that we were committed and mandated to 100 percent teaching, but we were in a research institution. Another was that we had developed an experienced-based curriculum, and that was a major problem with a lot of faculty. Another was that our curriculum was interdisciplinary in a discipline-based structure. We were an interdisciplinary, extradepartmental program under a dean always fighting for budget dollars with the departments.
>
> Another problem was that we were successful. Students wanted to take our courses more than other courses in the departments. That was a threat. And another was that we program faculty were strongly connected, clearly liked and respected each other, and worked as a team. I came to learn after much pain and insult that perhaps that was our biggest problem. As a trusted Cornell mentor said to me once when I was most frustrated, "You all are a family, and they resent it."
>
> Then there were the status issues, because we were not tenure-track faculty, and only Dwight in our group had a traditional academic credential. We were always getting hassled about that. It was constant hassles. What finally turned me off was when the same battles that we had fought off five or six years earlier started coming up all over again.

## Politics, Funding, and Logistics

In a traditional academic culture that viewed education as value neutral, politics became yet another barrier to service-learning, especially when it was designed with overt social justice goals.

Dick Couto:

> Where we were working to bring services to where there were none, generally everybody applauded that. But where we were working to deal with a problem that required either a redistribution of resources or for somebody to stop doing something that they were doing, there was hell to pay. For example, if you moved into a community that was concerned about the quality of its air, then you can bet that the person running the plant had some tie to Vanderbilt.

And the minute you provided support for those local communities and Vanderbilt's name was invoked, Vanderbilt people heard about it.

Tennessee's largest employer is in upper east Tennessee. The vice president had to make a special trip and asked me to go along to meet with the officials up there. There was lunch, and then there was a clear signal that they wanted my program to stop its work in their community. The other clear signal was that this company wasn't going to make its $50,000 contribution that year until the matter of Vanderbilt's relationship to these air pollution protests was made clear.

The incessant need for funds and for attention to logistics required to operate programs was another set of hazards the pioneers experienced. These hazards took their toll not from their complexity, but from the sheer magnitude of effort needed to overcome them and the fact they never seemed to go away. Couto comments further:

> I was director of the Center for Health Services at Vanderbilt for about thirteen years. After about eight of them, I had burned out. Fundraising at the rate of a quarter of a million dollars a year was just exhausting. I got to the point where I was telling foundation people off—stuff like that. You don't do that and stay around and keep that money coming in. The soft money barrier wore me out.

Jon Wagner speaks to the logistical challenges:

> We were always asking faculty and students to be in two quite different places, so we needed ways to support the logistics of that. How do they get from one place to the other? Who else is in both places that knows what they're doing? Whether it's field research or student volunteers, how do you teach people the skills needed to communicate in both places? There are all those logistical barriers.
>
> There are also the barriers simply related to time. If I want to be as thoughtful with my students about their internships as I am about their papers, it takes a lot more time. I know what they're reading; I know what they're adding to it and what they're taking away in what they do. But in field internships, I want to do that same thing. That means I also have to be familiar with the internship settings.

## Race and Ethnicity

Another challenge related to race and ethnicity, of service-learning practitioners and their students. The pioneers identified a lack of diversity in service-learning students that reflected the lack of diversity in the student population generally in the 1960s and 1970s. They wondered as well if this lack of diversity in service-learning students was due to a similar lack in the population of service-learning practitioners. John Duley recounts how the Society for Field Experience Education "almost capsized on the rocks of racism in its early days":

> Bernard Charles, a faculty member in Livingston College at Rutgers University, and, as far as I know, the only black officer the society had during my time of active involvement, succeeded Jim Feeney as president at the Michigan State University conference in 1973. (We did not attract many blacks into our membership. Those who were in the university were steering clear of fringe operations.) Dr. Charles, pretty much on his own, selected the University of Massachusetts at Amherst as the site for the third conference and was well on the way to shaping the agenda by the time the SFEE board met. Mike Hart, who was then on the board and on the governor of Georgia's staff for the Legislative Internship Program, thought that holding the conference in such an out-of-the-way place would kill the society. Although on the surface that did not look like a racist remark, it sure felt like it. The board rejected Charles's plans, which were pretty far along, and went with Hart, who hosted the conference in Atlanta. As I recall, that was the last we saw of Charles.

In addition to the problems Duley identified, some pioneers of color described other race and ethnicity problems as creating barriers and challenges not encountered by white pioneers.

Jack Hasegawa:

> There's a barrier of racial expectation. Because I have this Asian American face, it's expected that I'm going to be careful, analytical, precise, inscrutable. In fact, I'm very emotional, and impulsive, though not compulsive. So there's a lot of sloppy stuff in me. I don't mind that. I actually don't mind that my desk is a mess and

that it takes me a while to find things, or that scheduling sometimes gets messed up. I find that interesting. The thought process is interesting. But I think it's somehow connected to race that there are expectations of who I am and how I will be. When I emerge differently from that, it creates barriers.

Greg Ricks:

Being an outspoken African American is difficult and also an advantage. It is difficult from the standpoint that I find myself forced into playing a role, boxed in a lot with my own ideas, as much by my own people as by white people. A lot of it is that I'm the only one at the table, the only one to represent.

The advantage is that I feel an incredible sense of responsibility to black people. I went to the Million Man March. I agree with 70 percent of Farrakhan, and 30 percent I violently oppose. But the idea of bringing in a million blacks together who are dying— dying right in front of me—was an incredible concept. I just couldn't stay home and say it didn't happen. I had to be there. So for me there is an incredible responsibility to live a life I owe to my elders.

## Impact on Family

Finally, a few individuals, echoing Colby and Damon's "moral exemplars," identified the fatigue, loneliness, and negative impact on family life that comes with being a pioneer.

Tim Stanton:

Trying to do this work and have a family is a major challenge. Trying to do it and have a life is a challenge. Trying to do the important work and not get bogged down by administrivia. Trying to develop and sustain a humane organization that will sustain me and sustain the work. It all turns out to be incredibly hard work.

Marty Tillman:

I was continually struggling to find a place for myself in an institution. But at the same time I was struggling to establish a family too, getting my personal life in order. After flying around and traveling enormously over the years, I found that service had its costs. It became a burden. I would not have an even temper all the time and felt that imbalance. So when I got married, I decided to commit to becoming a father.

The demands on people who lead very committed lives have grown. I say that thinking back to bringing my daughter on a little back-to-the-roots trip to New York, thinking about my childhood in the 1950s in New York City. It was incredibly easy. My mother was home all the time. I had a wonderful life growing up. Being a parent now, being a committed parent and a committed professional at this point in time, is definitely more difficult. For example, child care issues prevent you from fully forgetting about what's going on at home and leading your own organizational life, or staying home and not worrying about what's happening outside in the real world. You're at school for your kid, being called out of your office to deal with a school-based problem, let's say. All of these potential conflicts are there, and they lead to problems.

**Notes**

1. Goodwin Liu graduated from Stanford University in 1991 with a degree in biology and honors in education. As an undergraduate, he was student body co-president and served in the Haas Center for Public Service as newsletter editor and co-director of the 1990 You Can Make a Difference Conference on education. Liu received the Dean's Award for Service and the Dinkelspiel Award for Outstanding Service to Undergraduate Education. After graduation, he went to Oxford University on a Rhodes scholarship to study philosophy and physiology. He then joined the Corporation for National Service as senior program officer for higher education. He is a graduate of Yale Law School and is contemplating a career in legal academia.

2. Julian Bond is a former civil rights leader and anti–Vietnam War activist. In 1967 he was expelled from the Georgia House of Representatives for opposing the war. He is currently a professor at the University of Virginia.

# Chapter Ten

# Passing the Torch

## Advice to Today's Practitioners and Students

Service-learning has grown tremendously since the pioneers began their work. Courses and programs exist on most campuses, with numerous staff and faculty involved. Campus Compact has made its Integrating Service with Academic Study project a high and visible priority since 1990, helping to support these staff and faculty and expand their numbers.[1] There is a growing literature, including a national journal, a national clearinghouse of service-learning-related information, an Internet listserv,[2] and new professional organizations and national conferences entirely focused on service-learning. The Corporation for National Service Learn and Serve America program, focused on establishing service-learning in both K–12 and postsecondary education, has given a major boost to the field. The new territory staked out by these and other pioneers has surely been settled. Although it does not yet have statehood within postsecondary education, it is on the map.

We wondered what the pioneers thought about this "settling." Having toiled in the wilderness for so long, with scars to show for it, how do they feel about a field that now seems closer to mainstream than margin? And what now should be on the agenda regarding current practice and efforts to institutionalize service-learning? Here are their answers.

## Clarify and Debate the Multiple Definitions and Purposes of Service-Learning

"People actually have a lot in common. But because they use different language, it's very hard for them to talk to each other."

Although these pioneers have much in common, they developed varied approaches to the practice of service-learning that represented varied expressions of the degree to which their commitments and purposes focused on change in students, communities, and institutions. For example, Mary Edens's story is one of commitment to the academic, personal, and career development of students. She intends to accomplish this through service to off-campus communities, but she does not expect to have significant impact there. Dick Couto, on the other hand, was primarily concerned with community change while he was at Vanderbilt. Students and their development were means to that end. Thus, when Mary and Dick talk about service-learning, they do not necessarily refer to the same practice or purpose.

The definition of service-learning is problematic because it must express the joining of two different, complex processes: service and learning. It is complicated further because those who use the term and practice the pedagogy often have different and conflicting goals. The pioneers are concerned that neither they, nor those who have followed, have adequately articulated and debated these disparate goals.

### Centrifugal Forces: Conflicting Conceptions of Service and Learning

We have learned throughout this book of the complications contained in service. Blake, Shumer, and others expressed serious reservations about the term *service-learning* itself, and the implications of noblesse oblige, and power and control, that it contains. Nadinne Cruz elaborates:

I started out despising service. I come from a society, the Philippines, which I feel has been undone by service providers. I wrote an essay on this years ago for *Experiential Education* [1990].

Bob Sigmon wrote me back saying, "Nadinne, you despise the stuff which is an integral part of my life!" I was taken by his response. It began many years of dialogue between us.

I've realized there is a thing called service. It's not the same as doing community development or social change. But service has a life and a place of its own that should be valued. It is an expression of certain values, a way of giving witness to a way of life and orientation to the world.

But service can be a disservice to communities. What does it mean to do service out of a missionary narcissism or at least a narrowly defined rescue effort? Charity and philanthropy have a place in the world. But to conflate charity and philanthropy with solving social issues is not the same. It is a disservice to both students and community. I don't despise service, but I despise using service in a glib and superficial way.

Rob Shumer suggests that focus on service in service-learning obscures the important learning that should result:

In our research on Americorps, we have testimony from people who believe that the work they do, like working in a child care center for eight hours a day, is valuable. But they didn't consider it service. They thought it was work. Service was something they did when they volunteered on weekends. So one of the problems we face is to separate service-learning from volunteerism and community service. I'm not against the word *service*, but I think service and volunteerism take the emphasis away from learning. The reason educational institutions should do service-learning is because it's good learning. The focus needs to be on the learning, not on the service. Service is a by-product.

If you do good learning, then service will happen. The major issue is that we focus so much on service that we're not always concerned about whether good learning has happened. When colleges and schools support service-learning, they have an obligation to make sure that whatever the experience is, it helps students learn.

Nadinne Cruz counters that what is to be learned is not always easy to define or agree on:

For me, the most important part is for students to have intimate encounters with questions that arise from seeing for themselves that there are people who have inadequate means to live a digni-

fied life and engaging people in the academy in discussion about
why we have to talk about social change and whether academic
knowledge is complicit in the social problems that we're now trying
to address. It can't just be, "Let's apply what we know and the
talents we have in the academy to address these intractable issues."
What's fallen somewhere in the cracks is how what we know has
contributed to those issues.

Must it be voluntary? Further problematizing service-learning's
definition language, Mike Goldstein raises a critical question about
the nature of volunteerism itself:

What troubles me in the semantic war is the issue of compensation—that the giving of service is the reward. That students learn
that going out and giving service, doing something to improve the
community, is adequate reward in and of itself. That's a wonderful
idea. It's a goal to which we should all aspire. But most students
today can't afford to do that.

Number one, we're limiting the degree to which any student
becomes involved, because they have to make a choice between
earning money and being socially useful, so we're causing a tension
between, if you will, the materialistic and the spiritual. That is the
last thing an institution ought to do. Number two, we are implicitly
discriminating. The less affluent students, who by the nature of
society are disproportionally students of color, are limited in their
ability to participate.

There was an argument in the late 1960s that a student should
not be allowed to receive academic credit and Work-Study. It was
somehow a violation of law to do that. Work-Study was treated
pristinely as a financial aid program. But there was absolutely
nothing in the statute, nothing in the regulations, that even
remotely forbade linking credit and aid.

We're looking at two different things here. Academic credit
goes to the intrinsic value of the experience in terms of the intellectual growth and learning process of the student. Compensation
should go to the value of the work to the recipient organization.
They measure two very different things.

Volunteerism is wonderful, but it has to be a real-world idea.
In an ideal society, everybody should give of their time. But there
are so many people who can't. At Urban Corps we were certainly
not ideologues or theoreticians or, for that matter, social activists.
But it was an absolute article of faith that students were going to

be compensated, because otherwise it was going to look like all the other volunteer programs: a lily-white, middle-class, nice thing to do. This notion that if you get paid, you're less worthy than a volunteer is nonsense. It's overtly discriminatory.

## The Danger of Definitions

Other pioneers worry about efforts to develop a sharper definition for service-learning, thinking such a move could be counter-productive.

Jack Hasegawa:

The main flag these debates on definition raise for me is the temptation to make it too precious. This is our little thing. We have to be professional about it; we have to make it a subject for academic study. Sometimes when you analyze and polish something so carefully, you lose the edges of it.

Dick Couto agrees, feeling that the definitions arrived at will eliminate service-learning's political edge:

There's been a deliberate effort to say that community service does not include policy and advocacy in the recent service-learning initiatives, including the Corporation for National Service. I think community service has to be viewed as a spectrum all the way from noblesse oblige, and that's one expression of it, to policy and advocacy.

Mike Goldstein believes that previous efforts to gain consensus on service-learning terminology result in people and programs being left out. There is a language problem:

The concept of service-learning is broad. It's dynamic, and it's seen by different people in different ways, all of which are perfectly valid. What I'm worried about in terms of how we progress is that we not engage in another effort to define what this is in ways that suddenly people find themselves thinking, "They're not talking about me. I'm doing something different." If you look at the service-learning history timeline [see Appendix B], you could put little red splotches on the wall at points where the wars were fought between different factions: the internship folks and the experiential education folks. The reason for the separation of the National Center for Public Service Internships (NCPSI) and the Society for Field Experience Education (SFEE) had almost nothing to do with substance. It had a great deal to do with the fact that we were calling things differently. Until we could get over the notion of, gosh, 90 percent of what we do overlaps and 10 percent of things we do ought to be looked at, people wouldn't talk to each other.

What's happening in the 1990s is better in many respects than what happened in the 1960s. But we've got to be very careful with the ease with which we fall into "them" and "us" semantics, because lives have been lost, and the blades are sharp. I'm not saying that we label everything where there's student involvement as service-learning and ignore the semantics. There are experiences that are valid and do the things we think are important, and there are ones that do not. My concern is that we constrain service-learning by the words we use.

Bill Ramsay has similar concerns:

Everything tends to be overdefined. I was in Denmark last spring and stopped to visit what they call a folk school. That's a free school. The school is not part of the state system. They gave me a little publication on the school, and it said, "When you try to define this kind of institution, you violate one of its principles"—that is, by defining it, you immediately start to constrict it. I feel somewhat that way about service-learning now that it has become a national phenomenon that has to be legislated, funded. You have to define it. But then the definition begins to limit it. Service-learning was never intended to be limited in that kind of way, yet that happens. It shouldn't be restricted by volunteerism; it shouldn't be restricted by the site of the service.

## Centripetal Values and Principles: Is There a Main Tent?

This pioneer group contains strong and sometimes conflicting views of the purposes of service-learning and of efforts to institutionalize it. Some want to change postsecondary education institutions as a means to social change. Others seek simply to institutionalize service-learning within institutions. Some want to help students come to know the world, while others seek to help students change the world. It is apparent here that some pioneers hold conflicting views as to the value of sharpening service-learning's definition as well. Concerned with these divergent cross-winds blowing through service-learning, Garry Hesser attempts to identify common values, principles, and language that diversely committed practitioners might agree on:

> I think of it as a continuum. At one end, experience-based learning enables one to work on very personal agendas. At the other end, there are agendas that strengthen the community. The question is, How do you keep that teeter-totter balanced so that it's feeding us as individuals yet not making us self-centered, reminding us of the community that's enabled us to be here?
>
> I've been working on something that pulls this together around themes of collaboration. Is everyone at the table being listened to? Are they all trying to share resources and empower one another? Is that what's happening? If it is, then we might want to call it service-learning. So collaboration is one theme that informs everything I do. The other is reciprocity. Is everyone gaining? Is there reciprocity between service and learning? Is there reciprocity between servers and served? Is there reciprocity among student, faculty, and community? Is there give and take in which everyone engaged is feeling genuinely strengthened and empowered, and not taken advantage of?
>
> The third factor is diversity. Are we honoring the multiple gifts of everyone involved? Are we genuinely trying to learn from each other and celebrate those gifts, while at the same time trying to build some kind of cohesive community in the midst of all of that diversity?
>
> Whether it's cooperative education, internships, urban field experiences—whatever it is, I can call it service-learning if it's struggling with and trying to move closer to these three things. They create a tension to hold us accountable. If we address them, then we may legitimately call it service-learning.

Echoing Pollack's service-learning triangle, Dick Couto draws a contextual map to help practitioners pull together in spite of their conflicting, centrifugal purposes:

> Dwight Giles said something that got me thinking: "We service-learning people are not about all higher education reform, and we're not about all social change, and we're not about all community service." If that's true, are we dealing with all three of them?

One way to illustrate that is a three-ring Venn diagram [see Figure 10.1].

When we speak about Highlander-type service-learning, I think we're talking about the basic relationship between education reform and social action. When we talk about volunteerism or community service in higher education reform, I think Campus Compact has embodied that and expressed it for a lot of us. When we talk about volunteerism and social action, I think that the Campus Outreach Opportunity League (COOL) expressed that. There's a tension among us and our organizations, but there's also a sense in which everybody can fit under one tent at the same time as we recognize what is at the core of those things that keep us together.

Jane Kendall describes how she sought to have the National Society for Experiential Education (NSEE) become the kind of tent Couto envisioned:

Even though people come to service-learning from different values, whether it's civic participation or social justice, academic learning or career development, international or cross-cultural learning— all the different parts—the principles are still the same. People actually have a lot in common. But because they use different

**Figure 10.1.  Contextual Map for Service-Learning.**

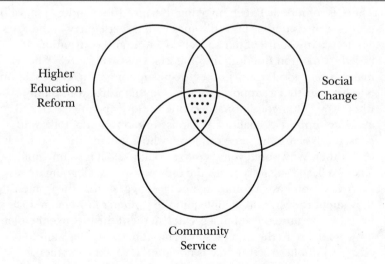

Higher Education Reform

Social Change

Community Service

language, it's very hard for them to talk to each other. I think the loose network that NSEE has with its special interest groups gave people their little home communities, but it also gave them a larger one that tried to articulate broader language. That's important to bridge some of those gaps.

## Support Group or Coalition?

Within this pioneer group, we have observed pushes and pulls regarding purposes, about whether and how to institutionalize service-learning, and now even about language and whether efforts should be made to establish a sharper definition. Several pioneers saw more precise language as necessary to advocate successfully for this pedagogy, to strengthen its practice, and to provide a foundation on which to build a larger movement for education and social change. Others, however, as they reflected on their past, felt that these tensions and conflicting purposes, and the language with which they were expressed, had not been fully explored, much less mapped out. Perhaps, they wondered, because of their collegial desires to give and get support needed to establish and maintain service-learning in its lonely, early days, these differences had been set aside too often. Perhaps, as Nadinne Cruz suggests, the pioneers and, by extension, the field have functioned more as a support group than a coalition:

> There is somebody I keep invoking, Bernice Johnson Reagon, who is one of the founders and still sings with Sweet Honey in the Rock. There is a transcript of her speech to a women's convention. It's called, "Coalition Building into the 21st Century" [1983]. She makes a very good distinction between support group and coalition. She suggests that a support group is one that is like your family, where you get unconditional acceptance, love and affection, and absolute support. A coalition is a loose organization of folks who consciously share the same room but who could in other settings kill each other. Why would you go into a coalition if it is so uncomfortable? Well, she suggests, that's the only way we are all going to survive: so you have a commonality. She suggests that the women's movement reflects that. People join the women's movement, for example, because they want a greater share of the pie, like the men. Or women are in the women's movement because they want to change a whole structure that is not good for men or women.

Those support group and coalition concepts are fundamentally different. As I look at the service-learning groupings that we may call a movement, I observe in our behavior a sense of celebration, a gathering together of friends. And the question that comes up in my mind is, Are the places where service-learning people gather looked on as support groups, or are they places to coalesce? That is important, because it sets the terms of behavior or conditions under which people who are outside this group, the people who are not yet here, the people whose stories have yet to be told, can tell their stories. Why should they want to tell their stories? I suggest that they may want to tell their stories if they see a potential for coalition, understanding that this is not their support group. We are faced with the question of how we widen our scope so that it becomes more coalition than support-like.

I will refer to my own behavior. I must confess that over the years I have primarily respected the ambiance of support. Therefore, I have chosen deliberately to be very gentle with my criticism, with my profound disagreements with some service-learning pioneers for whom I have a great deal of affection. That means I have respected the implicit ethos of support-like behavior even as I have, in terms of my practice, done things other than what a lot of people advocate. I now have to push myself to a different level of maturity. I need to raise these questions respectfully, but with authenticity. I fear that if we stay at a set level of support-like ambiance, we cannot include other people who would not want to be included in a situation where they feel they have to respect a support-like environment, while at the same time raise questions that are potentially critical. I fear that if we can't let loose tensions within service, within our pedagogy—should we even use the word *service?* If we cannot let loose those profound disagreements, we cannot further develop and deepen our thinking on any of our issues.

How do we move to a space where individuals decide as an act of will to become a "we" rather than a collection of "I's"? It's a political choice that people can make. But what are the conditions under which collections of individuals can make that choice? I think that the only way to do that is to tell stories, so that those stories are revealed to each other. Then as a consequence of that, possibly people can decide to become, first, a "we," and second, the nature of the "we" will include others who are not yet here.

Adding to Cruz's analysis, other pioneers wondered if service-learning practitioners' reluctance to articulate and debate conflicting purposes reflects similar reticence on the part of academics to confront difference across disciplines. How can we meet our ultimate goal of engaging the academy in the community, they assert, if we will not engage each other? Does the field, as noted by Joan Schine, have enough strength now to turn toward this needed debate?

> We have a context today that is unique and opens us up to being much more honest than we've been. One of the things that struck me about Nadinne's idea of support group versus coalition is that we have been so self-protected, so beleaguered in a way, feeling isolated in what we've been doing over the past forty years, that we failed to confront warts, never mind failures, because somebody else may pick them up and destroy the movement as a result. I think we're at a stage now where we can afford to be honest about those warts. We know the only way we can move forward is to take a very hard look at service-learning and where it is in society. We still have to do that. The strength of the field now gives us an opportunity to be critically honest with ourselves and not lose optimism because something good has been happening in spite of what I see as warts and possible failures.

There is strong sentiment among this group of pioneers that service-learning will not meet its transformational potential unless practitioners, and interested policymakers and scholars, begin to identify, explore, illuminate, and debate the diverse pedagogical and social change purposes that cross service-learning's multiple strands of practice.

## Strengthen the Practice

> "We really haven't spent much time talking about how you actually do this well."

The pioneers noted that service-learning practice itself varies widely in terms of quality of impact on students and communities. How much variety is too much? some asked. Is all service-learning positive? For example, do students who enter communities of color with racist attitudes return with their attitudes challenged or reinforced? Do we know? Do we know how to challenge constructively such attitudes through service-learning?

Tim Stanton worries that the challenge is not just insufficient debate about the multiple purposes of service-learning. We need substantive discussion on practice as well:

> I see a continuum of practice. On one end is a deep transformational pedagogy that I try to practice and others do. At the other end is what I call "parallel play." Students do service and then some learning, but never the twain shall connect. We have the full spectrum in service-learning courses. We have good ones and bad ones.
>
>   My larger concern is that there's not a deep discussion of what makes practice good. More often we talk about infrastructure or numbers of students. It's been a first-level discussion of getting service-learning in place, regardless of the quality. We aren't getting to deep discussion of how you actually connect the action of service, wherever you are on that continuum, and the action of learning.

Other pioneers agree, suggesting that one key to effective practice is critical reflection on the part of students *and* practitioners.

Dwight Giles:

> One of my colleagues quit this work, and we asked her why. She said, "My job is not to prepare the next generation of greedy capitalists." There's some possibility we do that. But I think the safeguard is to be as critical as you can in your own thinking and try to impart that sense of critical work to students. Critical reflection causes people to bump up against things and consider them. Without it, I worry for myself, but also for this movement that I am part of.

Herman Blake:

> One of the biggest mistakes I made in my early work was not developing a reflective, analytical approach. Everybody wanted to act, but nobody wanted to reflect. This was most clear when we put white students in a poor white community. They couldn't handle it. They were living in homes of people who looked like them— maybe six or eight years' difference between a student and a very poor woman who had four, five, or six children. It was too close. Students couldn't accept the fact that they might have been her. We could never put black students in poor white communities, because then the community couldn't handle it, to say nothing of the students. But we could put white students in low-income black

communities. What I'm trying to suggest is that nobody thought about what was really going on with these dynamics.

Dick Couto:

Reflection: that's the absolute key—especially group reflection to get people to talk out loud about what they're doing in the presence of their peers. When they do that, a lot of their biases appear for the first time. I remember this very well because we were dealing with kids from suburban Philadelphia. For them, the world came in shapes they knew from the suburbs. They met a young woman and her daughter who were both homeless. The daughter had been born addicted to crack. These were people they had read about, but all of a sudden it was a smiling little girl, a human being, and it took on a whole new meaning for them. For students in highly selective schools like Yale and Richmond, who are of traditional age, come from affluent backgrounds, and live on a residential campus, the best thing we can do is to introduce them to new settings, to give them a sense of the human dimension of problems they read about. The problems are not abstract. Get them out of what they know, what they're comfortable with. Get them into a structured disequilibrium—something that unsettles them. But make sure there's a structure so they can reflect and learn from it.

Judy Sorum Brown suggests that critical reflection should be group based:

The leverage is in the dialogue, not in the action. It's not what the individual student does for the client; it's in the conversation that the relationship makes possible. If you bring students into dialogue on what they observe and what questions that raises for them, and make that a community conversation within the academy, that would have remarkable transformative power. That's a piece of it we never did. We moved as far as getting students to reflect on their own experience, but we never moved beyond that to a dialogue among a community of colleagues, meaning the students, about what they were seeing and how they could paint a picture of it.

Rob Shumer reinforces Brown, suggesting that what students learn from each other—cohort learning—must be considered subject matter to be analyzed:

The educational value isn't just in faculty and books we require. It's in the knowledge of the cohort. Higher education needs to acknowledge that even seventeen- and eighteen-year-old college students come with an enormous amount of experience. But they never have an opportunity to share that and begin to see that those experiences can be built upon.

Normal residential life in the university, dealing with parents, and all the things college students learn informally could be subject matter for sociology classes, anthropology classes, and others. Part of what I've learned is that we need to do a better job of allowing the knowledge base of our students to become part of the curriculum. That's a challenge for faculty, because then they're no longer the experts.

John Duley, reflecting the approach he took to institutionalizing experiential education at Michigan State, advocates a more theoretical approach to strengthening service-learning pedagogy:

My fear and joy is that service-learning is riding the crest of a wave. We're at tidal wave height right now. But unless we continue the work we started long ago and never fully completed—making the case for the legitimacy of service-learning as a coin of the realm in higher education, how it can generate credit hours—we're not going to be here very long. The whole business of dealing with the theory of how people learn is critical. We need a holistic approach that includes the hard work of learning. I don't think we've dealt with that. There's a lot of theoretical work that needs to be done as to why service-learning is an important dimension of higher education.

## Service-Learning Content

Not only must service-learning practice be deepened in terms of pedagogical practice. Many pioneers suggest there is a content need in the field. Service-learning requires acquisition of and reflection on knowledge not readily found in the academy.

### Philanthropy and Civil Engagement

Mary Edens:

If we're really serious about validating free association and civic participation, then we need to reexamine what we're doing to help students integrate civic participation in curricular ways. We've been looking at graduate programs that emphasize nonprofit organization, but they emphasize organization and administrative management models. They don't focus much on the community, on what I would call community development civic participation. As much as we proclaim that citizenship is important, I see a long way to go before our institutions fully develop ways for students to study civic involvement. David Cooper, a faculty member in American thought and language at Michigan State, organized a course on the history of philanthropy with a service-learning project. But few institutions really study philanthropy.

### The Action of Service, or Community Development

John Duley:

When you think about Gandhi and Martin Luther King, Jr., it's absolutely necessary to understand what those people were up against: the pain, agony, and suffering they went through. If you're going to work for change, you've got to suffer. But I don't think we've found a way to convey that understanding. We talk glibly about wanting social change agents out of service-learning, but we're not very good at making clear what the cost is to perform these prophetic roles in society—not just from the outside but from within the movements themselves. I don't know how many of you read *Parting the Waters* [Taylor, 1988]. If you want a picture of agony from your potential allies, it's just heartbreaking to see the agony and the infighting that went on in the civil rights movement in addition to the stuff coming down on them from the outside. We don't do a very good job of helping people understand and be prepared for that.

### Issues of Race, Class, and Gender

Ken Reardon:

Race, class, and gender have not been addressed in this business. A lot of what we have are individuals from predominantly white, male-run, middle-class, academic institutions going into lower-income communities of color. The dynamics of reciprocity and partnership need real attention, because of our unconscious replication of oppressive ways of working with communities.

East St. Louis leaders have helped me learn the history of university-community partnerships from their point of view. It's one in which we are viewed often as intellectual carpetbaggers, not dependable partners. There's no intellectual commitment. We work through model cities, the war on poverty, block grants, and so forth. Universities have gotten a lot of money to do that work. But when the going gets tough, where are they? Class and gender issues need to be explicitly addressed, because they're critical to what we're doing.

## How Does Society Really Work?

Michele Whitham:

One thing I'm impressed with from my time outside the academy is how little we understood, and therefore how little we were able to communicate about, how society works. We were so critical of some of our central social institutions: the economy; capitalists; big, bad environmental pollution. We understood how to critique those institutions. We understood what was wrong with them, why they were not serving people. But I don't think we focused very effectively on why they persist. What functions do they carry out? They're there for a reason, or they wouldn't be there and have the power they do. One thing that's impressed me in the last ten years is how 99 percent of the people are out there just trying to live their lives: trying to make their families work, make their jobs work, put food on the table, get education for their children. Be good to their neighbors.

If I were to go back and teach those same courses today, I'd do a lot on what's functional about those institutions and on how our society works the way it does. A lot of it works. It's the unequal distribution and the unfairness from the parts that don't work that we then need to address. I'd bring people together more, and I'd probably have a less confrontational view than I had twenty years ago.

## Community Infrastructure and the Politics of Service

Mel King:

Service is institution building, so people need to understand why it is needed. You have to deal with the politics of why service is needed as part of the learning. Service is not enough. Having

people rake lawns or tutor without having some sense of the political reasons as to why they are having to do that in community A
and not in community B is not enough. That is the scary part of
all of this effort. There's not enough emphasis on building infra-
structure within communities to meet their own needs.

Built into this is an implicit way of saying that people in community A aren't up to dealing with the needs that they have. People
in these areas rarely get money to do the things they need. Some
foundations easily give money to white people to work in black
communities and find it difficult to give money to black people to
work in their own community, and they hardly give any money to
black people to work in white communities. That's just another way
of reinforcing white supremacy that we need to be careful about.

I'm not saying that people who are white can't work in communities of color at all. I'm saying that to the extent that there isn't
thinking through of the implications of what you are perpetuating,
there's a problem. A question could be, Why is it that we need
tutoring, and what is the role of this institution in dealing with the
school systems and their responsibilities? It's important for students
and faculty to raise questions about why these things are needed—
to do that kind of critical analysis. Service without critical analysis
and organizing is not service. It's a perpetuation of the dominant
culture.

### The Role of Faith and Spirituality in Service and Social Change

Helen Lewis:

I've seen people move great distances in terms of their analysis of
the economy and then stop short because the preacher said that
women shouldn't be doing this, or they get upset about a religious
something that conflicts with some of their political and economic
ideas. You need to talk about religion. Most of us as activists or
educators are very nervous about that. It's just not something we're
willing to tackle.

I decided it would be neat to do something where you open it
up and say, "Okay, I want to know how your faith relates to your
politics and to your community development work." I worked with
a program called the Appalachian Ministries Education and
Resource Center out of Berea, Kentucky. We brought together
seminarians from the Church of God, Yale Divinity School graduates, Lutherans, Episcopalians, and Benedictine monks for six

weeks. We had a lot of discussion on community development and rural farm issues, economic issues of the region. It was training for doing rural ministry. I pushed doing community development as a ministry.

It has been a transforming educational process for those seminarians. There's classroom work, papers and some research, and field experience in the communities. It was a highly diverse group, with all different theologians. We had a foot-washing ceremony at the end of our service. At one point we had a snake-handling minister. We had some Pentecostal seminarians who were speaking in tongues. We had Benedictine monks in long robes. We had high Episcopalians, and Catholics and Lutherans all together in this service. It was incredible. They learned from that, and learned from each other, because they had to. You learn emotionally as well as cognitively. You have got to experience and develop some way of empathy.

## The Need for Research

Finally, numerous pioneers called for research to identify instructional strategies that ensure that "service combined with learning adds value to each and transforms both" (Honnet and Poulsen, 1989). Many called for impact analysis research on students, communities, and institutions. Jim Keith suggests case studies "to capture the lives of students longitudinally in terms of their commitment." Jon Wagner thinks the need is not just for service-learning-focused research. He recommends attention to research methodologies that express service-learning's values:

We need to think through how to conduct cooperative research. I've been looking at that in schools where there are extraordinary discussions about what the school should do without paying any attention to data of what's actually happening. And then there are other places that have data drive everything, without any discussion of values. How do you develop inquiry that integrates empirical observation with service values?

## Strengthen the Community's Role in Service-Learning

"It would be like the freedom riders writing the history of the civil rights movement without having a chapter by Rosa Parks."

There is consensus in this pioneer group that the community has generally not been a partner in developing service-learning policy and practice. While the field has lofty aspirations and rhetoric around its service objectives, many feel, more often than not, that the community is treated as a laboratory for students to learn from rather than as a partner in education or community development. They call for much greater attention to these issues—attention that is carried out in a participatory manner that reflects service-learning's best principles. Indeed, pioneers like Ken Reardon, whose inspiration and motivation for engaging in service-learning is the community, go further. For them, the community should be the starting place for determining the relationship between town and gown.

## Challenges

Why is it so difficult for educators, and especially service-learning ones, to establish collaborative, partner relationships with communities? For Herman Blake, the problem is in part attitude:

> We don't have positive ways to think about community because we take a deficit approach. What I learned more from Myles Horton than anybody else is that these communities have real strengths. They have very positive qualities that no one's ever looked at, because we don't even think they're there. When we try to solve a community's problems, we don't look at how they've survived over the decades.

Rob Shumer suggests that the effort to integrate service-learning within the existing academic structure creates an additional partnership challenge:

> When we talk about integration of service into the academic community, we're talking about an institutional framework that still suggests that the community is not the center. We're starting with our courses, and then we're going into the community to learn about it, as opposed to starting first with community improvement and community building. When you start in the community, you don't use the framework and language of academic integration because experience, by its very nature, is interdisciplinary.
> The curriculum does not reflect reality. We need to understand better that we're all part of the community. The old notion that uni-

versities should be separate, that the definition of academic is theoretical, not practical, value—we need to challenge those notions. With the community as a central place for learning, when institutions begin to embrace and understand that, we will no longer think about how to put service-learning into the structure of higher education, integrating it into existing courses. Power still resides within institutions. Until they're willing to give up that status, service-learning will have difficulty truly empowering the community.

Bob Sigmon builds on Shumer's diagnosis, suggesting that the intellectual structure of the academy presents a barrier between town and gown:

Several years ago, an English professor named Townsend was teaching small-town novels at Amherst. He said, "Amherst is a small town. Why don't I send the kids out and have them interview a lot of different people about what a small town is like?"

What happened was that the students came back wondering about economic development, about racial issues, about political issues, about agriculture—all those issues that were alive in Amherst. An English professor is not prepared to deal with all that. He needed a lot of other folks to help students reflect on what they were seeing. He writes in an essay [Townsend, 1973] that he would never be so cavalier again. He was only prepared to help students with how they were writing and expressing it.

If we're going to stay organized as a department of economics or a department of social science or a department of this, that, and the other, and that's the way we're sending our students out—from those kind of departmental, narrow-gauge, disciplined perspectives—we're going to do damage to the communities that we send people out to. And we're going to do damage to the students in the way that they're thinking.

I'm not saying faculty are incompetent in their areas, but when three or four areas come together, the way things naturally do when you send students out, that's where the lack of competence is. I've known very few faculty who've had a holistic approach to the community. It's not a faculty competency. It may be strategically right at this moment to have faculty give a little bit of service-learning exposure to a lot of students. But we need to go to the next level, which is how we start thinking about deeper analysis, how we create programs to restructure the college, based on what students are learning and on what needs to be done in the communities.

Regardless of the challenges for community partnership represented by the structure and curriculum of the academy, Mel King feels that all programs should educate students about who benefits from service-learning and how:

> What's missing is the community's perspective. Why is the community asking for service? I understand the importance of somebody coming and showing a person how to use a computer, if that person uses a computer and is able to get employment as a result or simply learns to read. But in my introduction to the volunteers, I want them to know and ask the critical question about where the payoff is: whether it is in them as the volunteer or in the person he or she is working with. We need serious dialogue around these issues.

## Recommendations

In response to these and other potholes on the road to campus-community collaboration, Sharon Rubin calls for a flexible, long-term approach:

> Partnerships are relationships. They take a long time and a lot of hard work. Think of how much time and energy we put into our marriages. If you think about representing the whole institution and its multiple partnerships with many different things that are identified as community, then you understand how complicated and how long-term a business this is.
>
> What I would like to see is more college presidents not just give calls to service, which are very nice, but ask that all the different parts of the college think about what their current relationships are with communities, what they could be, and how each, in different ways, can contribute to a better set of partnerships. That means that physicists don't have to think about it in the same way as literature people, because they won't anyway. You might as well not ask them to. But when you allow people to feel their own empowerment about who those relationships are with, what they mean, and how to improve and fit them into a larger context, then I think you could actually get somewhere.

Mary Edens recalls lessons she learned from a student, suggesting that community partnership values and strategies must be built into student leadership development:

In 1990 we had a young man out of sociology who independently came across the work of Saul Alinsky [1971]. His name was Darin Day, and he said, "Mary, your programs have weak student leadership. There are structured opportunities with community agencies, but there's nothing here that really creates a new paradigm of community development working with grassroots organizations. The program supports things as they are rather than things as they could be." He challenged me, saying, "If you really want to get your student leaders to be creative, to be innovative, you have to move away from where you are." We had settled too comfortably into my notion of volunteer management, integrating service-learning with the career internship programs. Darin Day threw down a challenge to that.

He met with the mayor of Lansing and with the officials of surrounding communities, and he organized student groups to rebuild neighborhood parks. He helped organize a community land trust in Lansing with the food bank that the neighbors could be involved with. He invited high school students to do an environmental cleanup day and similar projects. He organized community cleanup projects with new neighborhood associations and community watches that hadn't happened before. He became very active in COOL. He got six hundred people involved in Into the Streets.

I learned a lot from Darin. He challenged me and taught me two things. One is that we can get stuck in our own pedagogy, our own theory of how to do this work. The other was to continue to be very creative, continue to be open to new ways that people can associate, especially students—to continually ask the question, How do we work with students in a way that reflects the kind of partnership they and we need to have with community agencies?

Recalling experiences with faculty, Bill Ramsay recommends clarifying their roles in service-learning in a way that ensures that the community controls and owns the service delivered and its consequences:

> I remember once one of our Georgia district people suggested, "We can do this thing without the colleges," and he was right. But our response was, "Yes, but we wouldn't be accomplishing one of our goals, which is to have influence on what goes on in those institutions. That's done through this relationship."
>
> I used to argue with professors because they wanted to get in on the service end. For example, an intern in Memphis did a

manpower study, and the faculty member felt his placement organization used a faulty instrument. Finally he said, "I can't align myself with this program if they're not going to use a proper instrument for the survey." The agency had spent money and adapted this instrument for its purposes, and we ended up saying, "Your job, Mr. Faculty Member, is to do the best you can to give them your best advice. But it's their decision to make. They own it. You help the student interpret why you think it's faulty, and how it might be improved even if they don't accept it. Furthermore, you might want to examine the question, 'Why do people insist on using things that are faulty?' That's your role."

I would argue that you should never credit experience. You only credit what you learn from experience. That's an important distinction. Credit for work experience essentially hands control of the work over to faculty—those who are trained to be academic. People out in the field, in the agencies, have to deal with imperfections. They have to make decisions without complete information. They have to act in the dirty world. They don't have the privilege of saying, "This isn't perfect, therefore I won't use it."

To Bob Sigmon, the important decision is where you start:

I'd start exclusively with community-based organizations and public agencies and put all my effort into helping them think about what's in their self-interest in having this exchange of university resources, students coming in. What role do they want in educating the young? I would put all my marbles on that side of the coin. They would control the agenda, educationally and work-wise. I would start there, because that's where the creativity is; that's where the new knowledge is being created. That's where real learning, experiential learning or service-based learning, occurs. Not in school. It's out where the rubber meets the road. I'd redesign that way. If the community's in control of naming what it is that's to be worked on, hopefully they're getting resources and extra help to do whatever it is they want to do. If! There's a big "if" there.

For Tim Stanton, structuring campus community partnerships for service-learning and community development is, in fact, a root toward postsecondary institutional change:

There's a political element in our work that we often fail to consider. That is that the ultimate power of learning is its epistemological implication. When we suggest that important learning comes from thinking about community experience, that's a political matter as well as a philosophical and pedagogical one. It tells us where knowledge resides and from where it can be derived. So if we change our assumptions about how and where we learn, we'll then change our behavior to align with these new assumptions.

The academy will change when we transform our epistemological paradigms. I see service-learning as a root to that—not *the* root, because it's happening in the sciences, for example, but *a* root. Because of that, I'm much concerned with community partnership—the relationship my program, or anybody else's program, has with the community. Community partnership is critical to the epistemology of service-learning. You can't separate them.

Building on Stanton's remarks, Gib Robinson reflects on his shift of focus from serving individuals to assisting whole communities, and how partnership with those communities is necessary for the "renovation" of both individuals and education institutions:

What I'm doing now is an extension of service-learning. It's not as focused, but it has to do with creating a larger context for a university to continue its service-learning mission. And that has to do largely with a shift in my life—from working with individuals to working with communities and neighborhoods directly. I'm hoping that in the next round of what we call service-learning, there will be more emphasis on becoming allies with those communities: working on community development, community empowerment, economic development, employment training, issues of whole communities in the same way we educate the whole person.

Whenever we go out to the community, the only way we can go safely is to be completely open to self-renovation. And that means institutional renovation and personal renovation by the experience that we go out and seek. If that's true, then our teachers are out there. The resources that we need are simply not on campus.

## Diversify the Field; Make It Inclusive

"When we look at the people who are in the field and look at our institutions, there isn't broad representation."

The pioneers are concerned that service-learning's community partners have largely been absent from the field's development, and thus from their stories. They are concerned as well that service-learning's history is largely lacking in practitioners and students of color. They acknowledge that perhaps this absence reflects the population of faculty, staff, and students in postsecondary education in the 1960s, 1970s, and early 1980s, which itself reflected deep economic and racial stratification in society. Some wondered, however, whether an additional explanation was the "problematic definition of service" (noblesse oblige, deficit-focused, helping) inherent in service-learning, one that alienates faculty and students from poor and minority backgrounds.

Perhaps these definitions, and the stereotypes they convey, present an additional reason for promoting discussion and debate on what service-learning is all about. Clarification of and deeper debate on goals and purposes of service-learning, and the hoped-for expansion of the tent under which practitioners and students may assemble, will bring conflicts and difference to the surface. But failure to address these differences directly inhibits the field from becoming fully representative of our multicultural society in its practitioner, student, and community-based partner populations, and thus achieving its transformative potential.

Rob Shumer:

I think part of the movement has been sustained not only by being on the margin but by being somewhat isolated—a community among ourselves. But if we listen to Greg Ricks and other people, there are folks out there who aren't supportive of service-learning because it's very, very exclusive. When we look at the people who are in the field and look at our institutions, there isn't broad representation.

As a movement, we have to become more inclusive. How do we reach out to community colleges, where we know there is a larger portion of students of color? There are people doing vocational, hands-on things who don't feel connected to service-learning, because we haven't addressed some of their issues. Maybe being a little bit insular as we developed was healthy and needed for survival. If we got too self-critical, we might have fallen apart. But now we need to be exposed to criticism that is real, even while we think what we're doing is worthwhile.

In addition to diversifying the field and making it more inclusive, some pioneers view service-learning as having powerful potential for narrowing America's racial divide. Greg Ricks, who has given his professional life to this cause, wants the field to "mix it up" on race:

> Service-learning can be the most powerful common ground to deal with race. One of my frustrations has been that just as presidents were afraid to mix up service-learning with curriculum issues, people in the service-learning movement have been afraid to mix it up on race relations. That's problematic for me, because that's a hat I've chosen to wear. I wasn't forced to wear it, but I've chosen to wear it, because I see it as a powerful way for people to get to know each other.

Jim Keith, who has followed a similar path, uses service-learning for cross-racial education with adults:

> A group of us in Greensboro have started a leadership school. It's an ecumenical program of classes to bring together members of different communities to become aware of community needs and work together to meet those needs. It's a model from an ecumenical church in Washington, which has been a dynamic force in reclaiming neighborhoods for forty years. I've been responsible for taking groups of church people up there for weekends, and then we began our servant leadership school here a little over three years ago. We've had over three hundred people go through it and have seen powerful effects. It's proven to be level ground for African American and affluent white people to talk to each other and learn together.

## To Be or Not to Be Institutionalized

> "There's a difference between the institution's making the students available—making that part of the program, part of the construct of learning—and the institution itself becoming that engine of change."

This pioneer group does not share a coherent, collective view of whether and how to institutionalize service-learning. On this topic perhaps what they share is a Hamlet-like ambivalence caused by their ability to see both sides of a thorny dilemma. Many pioneers acknowledge that institutionalization is essential to sustaining the pedagogy within colleges and universities. A few are convinced that institutionalization, which will help bring about transformed institutions, is the way to achieve their social goals. But others worry about what can be lost when an innovative, marginal practice becomes part of a mainstream, which they view as highly resistant to change and not supportive of their social goals. Finally, however, two pioneers suggest that too narrow a focus on institutionalizing service-learning perhaps distracts us from larger, more important questions, the answers to which would help illuminate a path for the next generation of pioneers.

## To the Mainstreams

Ira Harkavy views changing higher education as both crucial and inevitable:

> There will be resistance, kicking, and screaming, but when there's violence on the doorstep, when students don't come because of crime, when faculty and staff leave, when students feel afraid, and when budgets start getting cut for their own self-interest, long and short term, plus the mission they have, universities must deal with their communities. Transformation is crucial. It is no longer excusable for universities not to be engaged in the their localities.
>
> Derek Bok, in his wonderful book, *Universities and the Future of America* [1990], said, "If we're so good, why is society so bad?" I believe there is a profound interest now in higher education to make this shift. Pressure is coming from faculty, from students, and from outside, and it's growing.

Ken Reardon concurs, adding that service-learning can help institutions respond to these new demands:

> The walls are being dismantled quickly. There is tremendous pressure on the university. Structural changes in the world economy and technological changes are creating great uncertainty on the part of local civic leaders and students. They're demanding that universities be different.
>
> There's a great article by Bowles [1982] that talks about changes in American work. It is about the breakdown of labor-capital accords in which there had been a structured set of relationships created between labor and management that regularized activity. People could be clear about their roles in a growing

economy. Change forced both sides to sit down and reestablish that relationship.

I think the university and the community had a similar kind of deal, in which, basically, after *Sputnik,* we were given a lot of cash to prepare and create a new generation of thinkers, new knowledge to help compete in a cold war setting. That dynamic has changed. The deal we had in which the university could be behind high walls and not feel accountable no longer holds.

In Illinois, we have articles every week bashing universities. Our new president, who is an engineer, a discipline not often represented in our efforts (although I may not have my engineering history down), is sounding more and more like John Duley twenty-five years ago. He's not alone. New presidents coming on board at both the publics and privates talk our talk. There's a space in which service-learning people could step forward and help the university save itself from its lost mission by listening to voices in the community. We can reconnect the university to the commons. We can help universities understand their role as not only seeking to know how society works, but helping to transform it around the pressing, critical, day-to-day issues in communities, both urban and rural. I'm very optimistic.

John Duley suggests that this rising tide of interest presents the opportunity, and obligation, to make service-learning's theoretical case as central to education:

We're at a point in the history of this movement where service-learning has become a favored child. The question now is, How can we take this opportunity and incorporate this understanding of service-learning into the ongoing life of the institution? I'm encouraged that younger faculty are eager to incorporate service-learning into their courses. I think that's attributable to the fact that many of them were in programs that we facilitated back in the 1960s and the 1970s. We're bearing the fruit of that involvement. They're now saying, "We want to incorporate that into our teaching." If that's true, they will welcome the kind of help we can give, making a case for service-learning's value and importance.

One interesting thing about this is the whole left brain–right brain problem. The university focuses almost exclusively on the left brain, which is the analytical, abstract, conceptualizing part of the learning process. But experiential education has a holistic

approach to pattern thinking, to intuitive understanding. We
need to bring these together, not bifurcate them. It's possible that
service-learning has a significant contribution to make to the full-
ness of higher education.

Joan Schine has a simpler answer. Expressing frustration with
service-learning's theoretical cross-winds, she says, "Just require it":

> I don't know whether it's a function of my age, but I don't think
> we've got much time. We're talking about citizenship, moral devel-
> opment, and other things that are not fashionable, like being your
> brother's keeper. I don't think we have time to waste worrying
> about vocabulary. My argument is that you need to give a lot more
> attention to developing humane people who can systematically and
> not hysterically act out the principles that service-learning embod-
> ies. We don't hesitate to require kids to read Shakespeare. Unless
> you try something, how do you know? I heard a youngster talk
> about having to spend a weekend at a shelter in New York. She
> said, "I was scared to go the first time. I never would have done it
> if they hadn't made me. Now I volunteer all the time." That's a
> powerful argument.

## "Marginal" Concerns

Many pioneers do not share this sanguine picture of institutional
mainstreams. Institutionalizing service-learning, they feel, is something to be approached with caution, both because the institutions
within which we seek to insert service-learning are so impervious to
change and because mainstreaming could dilute service-learning's
transformative potential.

Recalling his experience at the University of California at
Berkeley, Jon Wagner opposes Schine's requirement proposal:

> Maybe it's better to have everybody do service-learning. But if you
> do so, you won't get a vital program like Berkeley Field Studies.
> We had twelve courses serving a couple of hundred students a year.
> These were very intense. Students were interning ten to twelve
> hours a week for two quarters, being strongly challenged. We hired
> our own staff to arrange the field placements and teach the semi-
> nars. You can't do that kind of intense program for a whole
> campus. If you go to a service-learning requirement and then
> have fifty different ways to satisfy it, there'll be no need for a

program like that. If you institutionalize the expectation, you dilute the intensity.

I see broad-brush requirements as a threat to small, intensive programs. You make it more difficult for them to exist. That's what happened at Berkeley. They said, "We don't want an individual program. We want students in all departments to do this stuff."

Some people say a requirement makes people cynical. I'm saying, yeah, you make them cynical in the same way students are cynical about writing papers, or reading books, or going to class. It's not the requirement that makes them cynical. It's how well or poorly it's done. When you move to everyone adopting it, you get the lowest common denominator.

Nadinne Cruz worries that an expanded, more mature field has already lost its political edge:

In the past five years, and especially since the Corporation for National Service, I've not felt that the service-learning community is a community of social change. In NSEE in the earlier years, I found a cohort group, a sense of kinship; we were all figuring out our niches to do social change work within the academy. Now I see professionalization, career tracks of running volunteer programs, and so forth. I meet more people who understand the work in ways that are very different from where I'm coming from. Now we're reintroducing a whole new caucus within NSEE to articulate and give voice to "service for social justice." But I found myself arguing for this track at a recent meeting with people asking it why was needed.

For Jack Hasegawa, service-learning has been "hijacked":

I used to talk constantly about process over content. The most important thing was to get ourselves as people empowered and get the young people with whom we worked out doing, so they would have some reason to reflect, some materials on which to build theory, some experience on which they could derive learning. You couldn't set up a structure for that first. It had to be the other way around. We started working with students under the rubric of experiential education, global education, empowered learning, education for change, reformation of school and society. Those titles were very important, but they always focused on getting people out.

Now I find myself frightened, because I see a hijacking of that process by political forces with an ideology I can't believe in. I'm afraid of my own twenty-five-year history saying that process is more important than content. When we have something like service-learning and we say that all that's important is to provide opportunities for all comers and allow them to draw their own conclusions, or worse, allow them to derive something that is not there, then I think we have a problem. I look at what I've been thinking and saying for twenty-five years, and find myself pushed up against an extremity that I may not be ready to defend. I'm not clear what the next step is.

Bob Sigmon wonders whether the faculty really understand:

The major problem I have now is this frantic rush to have every professor build a ten-hour component of service time into the course. It's such tokenism, and it's missing the mark of what the wholeness of this thing can be. It's a sham. It's not even close to the original vision that we used to work on in those old Oak Ridge Institute of Nuclear Studies (ORINS) days. It's so foreign to that approach; that was in our initial minds. It's as if they're saying, "I'm going to tack this on because it's the in thing to do."

The pioneers' feelings of unease with service-learning's proliferation and increased support from education policymakers may in part be expected from people who have given much of their professional lives to making a toehold for the practice in largely hostile institutional settings. These bruised and in some cases battle-weary warriors wonder, naturally enough, how this once-suspect, marginal pedagogy, on behalf of which many lost their jobs, could now be promoted by college and university presidents and in federal legislation. Do these new advocates fully understand the radical nature of what they promote? They are suspicious of cooptation by inertia-ridden institutions impervious to change.

## Practical Worries

Other pioneers have more practical worries about this expanding field. Jim Keith is concerned about the impact of expanded, but ultimately short-lived, federal funding:

We all know that most federal money is there to feed something at the start with the assumption that the institution will take it on. But I haven't seen that happen much, particularly in service-learning.

We're not doing ourselves or our communities justice by introducing programs that die when the money runs out.

Dick Cone has additional worries about expanded funding and the accountability pressures that come with it:

Service-learning is really about building relationships. But the more we have this rush to get numbers means that we have certain people who are setting the agenda, setting the objectives, going out and measuring those objectives, which is the antithesis of building communities, being responsive to communities, building relationships among people on and off campus. It's the notion that there has to be a model that we're working toward. As long as we have that notion that we've got to have these results, we've got to measure them, and we've got to do it quickly, it's really hard to look at what happens to individuals, at how we support one another, and at how we develop relationships. It's hard to take the time that's needed for this enterprise.

Mike Goldstein assumes that postsecondary education institutions are not likely to be engines of change or change much themselves in the near future. Echoing the motivations he expressed for the founding of Urban Corps, he suggests that the practical route to change is through students:

If you look at service-learning as an engine for significant change, it has to be either marginal to the institution or outside the institution. To the extent that these programs become institutionalized, they're not engines of change because the institutions are not making change by their very nature. We're asking institutions to do something that they're not designed to do.

However, students can be instruments of change. Colleges and universities are not going to change K–12 education except in training for teachers. They're not going to change crime on the streets; they're not going to change health care. But students can be vehicles that help do that. There's enormous power in service-learning's service component, in the power of students properly engaged to make change. The mistake we make is to say that in order for that to happen, the institution itself has to become the engine of that change. That's unrealistic.

When we did Urban Corps in 1965, we weren't changing the world. It was the students. The change is what they did. So if we look at outcomes, what we ought to be looking at is how students become part of change. There's a difference between the institution's making the students available—making that part of the program, part of the construct of learning—and the institution itself becoming that engine of change.

Recalling the support she received from colleagues, Sharon Rubin reminds us that the field's vitality must be sustained by its practitioner community, and that community does not happen by accident:

> I've thought a lot about both the maintenance and the sustenance of this movement. The maintenance is out of our control in a sense. I think we happened to be in the right place at the right time, and there was an opening for doing some things differently than we had done them before. Or we were just in an environment that allowed us to take it one step further. Before we knew it, we were down the path.
>
> But sustenance is not accidental. I've been working on experiential learning issues for twenty years. We're not the bleached bones in the desert; we're the people who are still here. It's interesting to try to figure out what inner qualities and relationships have sustained us over this time. I need to think very deeply about that and to work very cautiously to sustain the people we want to have with us and come after us—whether they're faculty or other administrators, students or folks in the community. Somehow this sustenance can't be an accident. That's a big challenge.

## Promote and Elaborate Debate: Reframe the Questions

Some pioneers feel we are at the crest of a wave, and now is the time to make the academic case for service-learning. Others question whether postsecondary education is in fact a viable base from which to make social or educational change. However, the fact that these issues arise echoes the pioneers' call for clarity and debate of service-learning's goals and purposes. To that debate list should be added the whys and hows of institutionalization.

While service-learning can be found in "Swiss-cheese-like holes" of many institutions, it is rarely articulated in mission statements or as an educational priority. If mainstreaming service-learning is the goal, either to sustain the practice or as a means to institutional and social change, then advocates must be clear about what and for what reasons they advocate. Service-learning has been marginal not just because it is new. Deeper reasons for this marginalization lie in service-learning's purposes and epistemological assumptions, both of which run counter to intellectual and curricular traditions in postsecondary education. Colleges and universities have not traditionally sought to "empower students to change the world," as one pioneer put it. Traditional concepts of knowledge development do not embrace the value of subjective, raw experience. Most academics assume that answers to society's problems will be found in classrooms, laboratories, and libraries as opposed to communities off-campus.

Focusing on understanding and debating service-learning's goals and assumptions inevitably will highlight how these goals and assumptions differ from those that have been valued in the academic mainstream. Identifying these differences may conflict with efforts to legitimize and institutionalize service-learning within that same mainstream. Thus, efforts to legitimize a pedagogy aimed at transforming knowledge, students, faculty, communities, and institutions may conflict with efforts to deepen its impact. While these tensions may not be resolvable, for service-learning to move forward, in terms of both strengthened practice and institutionalization, its transformative potential will need to be elaborated and debated, and clarity provided as to what goals will be served should it become part of the academic mainstream.

Given the complexity of service-learning's institutionalization issues, two pioneers suggest that we reframe the questions. Jon Wagner calls for shifting the focus of debate from service-learning and its institutionalization to broader issues of teaching, learning, and research:

> The boundaries of the field are a little too comfortable. It used to be that we suffered tremendously, because nobody knew about service-learning. There was this tremendous need in the 1970s to take whatever truths we were finding in service-learning and see how they could be communicated within other traditions. What does it mean for liberal arts? You had to find arguments there for doing service-learning. Or you would take social science or field research and try to find arguments there for doing this, or vocational education, citizenship development—a variety of things.

One of my concerns is that we have not intellectually developed the people involved with this as much as we need to, and the current mandate almost makes it more difficult for that to happen. We shouldn't be looking at service-learning all by itself. We should be looking at undergraduate education, asking what happens to kids who are undergraduates today. We ought to be investigating that and seeing where action, field experience, and political expression fit within it.

How do you take research and design it so that it represents a service that you're investigating and reporting about? How do you take graduate training and organize it in such a way that graduate students take advantage of their field experience as part of their research? How do you take teacher credential programs and prepare teachers to give these kinds of opportunities to students?

So few service-learning people talk about how to reform the field of education. How to reform undergraduate teaching in sociology, in history, is the discussion we need to have.

Building on Wagner's comments, Nadinne Cruz suggests that we go beyond how we teach to what is taught. We need to focus on the nature of the knowledge areas in which we seek to institutionalize service-learning and their relationship to the community problems we wish to address:

Is the problem out in the community, or is it really on campus? Is the problem poverty? Is the problem poor schooling? Is the problem hunger? Are we going to change that by any amount of direct-service? Or is the problem the very holders of power, the university being one of the biggest? If we can't change the university, do we have any hope of changing anything at all? My contention is that what we're really trying to do is change educational institutions. They are part of the larger system that's creating problems in the community. We can go do direct service as a way of ameliorating a bad situation, but we're not going to remedy it.

What part of the institution are we trying to change? Is it trying to change the way departments run, or is it, as I would argue, flawed knowledge? The knowledge foundation of the academy is inadequate to address, even if every student learned it very well and went off and applied it, the problems in our communities. What do I mean by flawed knowledge? Well, look at what happens when we impose notions of modernity and economic development on societies all over the world and it doesn't work. It doesn't distribute resources in an equitable way. In countless countries where students come from, the best and the brightest in India, Pakistan, Philippines, go to MIT, Harvard, Yale, and other prestigious institutions, and they learn the same old economic development theories over and over and over again, with disastrous results, from my biased perspective. That's what I mean.

## Conclusions

This book has identified and analyzed the early history of service-learning in postsecondary education. It looks back seeking to learn where and how service-learning pedagogy originated, and at who were its early pioneers. What motivated them? How did they conceptualize their work? What barriers did they encounter, and what sustained them? This chapter looks forward, hoping to examine service-learning's theoretical dimensions and policy implications recommending steps for strengthening the field in its current expression and future development.

From research by Seth Pollack (1996) and others, it is evident that service-learning has roots in a number of antecedent movements, such as land grant colleges and universities, settlement house education, Progressive educators, work programs in the 1930s, the Peace Corps and VISTA, and the civil rights movement.

From the makeup of the pioneers and their stories, we have learned that early practitioners of service-learning were activist in nature, with many of them approaching their work in education from a community base. They were motivated by early family and community experience, by deep philosophical and spiritual values, and especially by political events and social movements of the 1960s. Although they articulate varying priorities in terms of seeking impact on students, communities, and postsecondary education missions and curricula, they share a deep commitment to connecting the academy (especially students) with issues, people, and suffering in off-campus communities.

The outcomes of the work of the pioneers are considerable. They can take credit for a substantial part of the development and establishment of service-learning as an identifiable pedagogy in postsecondary and K–12 education. Their work is represented in numerous and varied service-learning courses and curricula, publications, and campus- and community-based programs across the

United States. Although some of the pioneers have moved out of service-learning and even out of postsecondary education, others are now recognized as leaders of the field.

The pioneer group identified numerous and diverse public leaders and theoretical mentors as inspiring and assisting them to find their way into service-learning and strengthen their practice and advocacy of it. These were scholars in education and human development, progressive political leaders, community organizers, and religious and spiritual philosophers. Many pioneers drew on theory to understand and advocate for their work, while others worked out of a strongly held theoretical stance, which they then expressed through service-learning. There is tension in the group around its theoretical orientation, which may be related to the broader field's long and sometimes frustrating effort to become part of the mainstream of postsecondary education reform.

The roadblocks and challenges the pioneers identified were substantial, and related to each individual's position and role, organizational and institutional context, support within and demographics of the larger field, community impact issues, and work and personal relationships. To sustain themselves in the face of these challenges, the pioneers drew on their deep social and political commitments, fiercely independent and self-reliant self-concepts, and strong political, administrative, organizing, and teaching skills. They repeatedly credited supportive, collaborative, collegial networks maintained by national organizations as critical to their development as professionals, and their survival as change agents in communities and institutions.

In many ways the pioneers are warriors in a long, sometimes harrowing story of social change in the latter half of this century. While their stories focus mostly on change within colleges and universities, they share traits and frustrations with other social change cohorts. They are motivated by deep moral and political convictions. Their gains are hard fought. They have many wounds and have made many personal sacrifices.

## Pioneers' Recommendations

Like other change agents, these pioneers care deeply about their new "land." Tending to see their glasses as half-empty as opposed to half-full, they express serious concerns about it in spite of its apparent proliferation in the past decade. In considering the present and future for service-learning, they recommend increases in the following areas:

- Attention to clarification and debate of varied purposes and definitions that exist in service-learning. This is needed to strengthen the field and connect it more effectively with related efforts to reform postsecondary education.
- Attention toward strengthening service-learning practice. We need to know much more about which pedagogical strategies most effectively combine service experience, critical reflection, and subject matter knowledge in ways that increase learners' knowledge, learning skills, impact on communities, and democratic commitment to social justice.
- Focus on the role of community partners and their knowledge in service-learning practice, policymaking, and advocacy.
- Efforts to make the service-learning community more inclusive and representative of society as a whole.
- Understanding of and debate on the relationship between the varied outcomes sought through and practices contained in service-learning and efforts to institutionalize it within mainstream postsecondary education.

## Pioneering Characteristics

In addition to characteristics of this pioneer group listed above, we wish to note a few additional traits that may still be necessary for current practitioners in an expanded but not fully institutionalized field.

### Movement Consciousness

Although only Couto states this directly, most pioneers acted with a sense of being part of something larger than themselves—larger than their individual calling, their communities, or their institutions. Some identified this feeling as "movement consciousness": being part of social and political struggles of their time, particularly civil rights. For some it was a historical consciousness. One lesson learned from this history is that this larger consciousness provided motivation, sustenance, and direction to the pioneers in the face of considerable cross-winds. Although service-learning has advanced considerably, these cross-winds still blow. What larger consciousness or social movement, some pioneers asked, drives current practitioners?

### Visionary Passions and Commitment

A second characteristic is that the passions and commitment of this group were much more strongly connected to a vision, or a set of morals and values, than to a pedagogical method. The method was and is important, but it is a means to an end, which is deeply connected to the political, moral, and spiritual values held by the pioneers.

Pioneers are visionaries. You do not set off on what to others looks like an impossible task without some vision of what you will find and passion for finding it. The lesson here for service-learning now is perhaps that pioneering passion is generated by social, moral, spiritual, and political commitments. In order for the field to remain vital and attractive to the next generation of pioneers, it must remain connected to some vital vision, or sets of values, that are larger and deeper than the pedagogical processes of service-learning by themselves.

### Independent Self-Direction

A third characteristic was amply noted and described by the pioneers and we simply highlight it here: the attitude that closed doors are there to be opened or, as Herman Blake described Page Smith's philosophy, "Damn the rules: full speed ahead." Pioneers of service-learning, and we suspect in other arenas, are self-directed, independent souls, able and willing to choose or create their own paths, find their own guides and mentors, through uncharted and often treacherous waters. Surely these traits are still needed.

### Encouraging of Mutual Support

Finally, a fourth characteristic is one that Jane Permaul identified when she reflected on whether this pioneer group was attracted to service-learning because of its collaborative, reciprocal values or whether the pioneers brought these values to service-learning. Like Permaul, we suspect both processes were at work. What is clear, however, is that these pioneers had and shared these values with students, colleagues, communities, and, for which we are most grateful, us, as the collectors of their stories. They continually point to the collegiality and mutual support they gave and received through their networks and associations as critical to their ability to sustain their efforts, often in the face of considerable challenges. As Rubin noted, these networks need continuing care and attention.

The pioneers' consciousness, vision and commitment, and courageous or just naive independence surely enabled them to contribute to the establishment of service-learning as a field, a legacy that the field can draw on as it evolves to its next stage. This evolution surely requires the deep questioning and debate called for by the pioneers on goals, purposes, and institutionalization. These debates are likely to illuminate conflict, and they have the potential to fragment a still-nascent field. However, if they can be carried out in a spirit of collaboration, reciprocity, and diversity called for by Garry Hesser, they can be fruitful and rewarding for those who participate, and ultimately for the transformative purposes that brought service-learning into being in the first place.

## Combining Wisdom and Compassion

The last words in this story belong to Gib Robinson:

> This gets us back to this business of wisdom and compassion. If we are willing to say that what we would most like, whether we can ever get there or not, is to help people become wiser than they are and more compassionate than they tend to be—and for those who are more compassionate, let them express that—then let's not keep them so bottled up on campus that that's the last thing they get a chance to do. If we can do all that, then I see service-learning as a very efficient vehicle. Service-learning is perhaps the most important tool for the renovation and experimentation that is necessary in higher education.

**Notes**
1. Campus Compact's Project on Integrating Service with Academic Study provides training, advice on strategy, and technical assistance to colleges, universities, and communities that are working together to build

community service projects that enrich teaching and research and meet the needs of communities.

2. *Michigan Journal of Community Service Learning,* Office of Community Service Learning, Division of Student Affairs, University of Michigan, 2205 Michigan Union, Ann Arbor, Michigan 48109–1349.

National Service-Learning Clearinghouse, University of Minnesota, Department of Work, Community, and Family, 1954 Buford Avenue, Room R–460, St. Paul, Minnesota 55108. phone: 1–800–808–SERVe (7378); fax: (612) 625–6277.

To subscribe to the Internet listserv housed at the University of Colorado, Boulder, send the following message: subscribe service-learning Firstname Lastname to LISTPROC@csf.colorado.edu

# Appendix A: Strands of Service-Learning

The following strands of service-learning practice were articulated as a preliminary step to identifying and selecting a representative group of practitioners to interview for this book.

*Service-Learning Strands*

Action research, community studies

Campus ministry

Career development

Civil rights movement

Community development (as represented by the Community Development Society)

Community organization (or organizers; not campus based)

Community psychology

Cooperative education

Education reform

Education research

Ethnic studies

Experiential education

Field study, field education

International and cross-cultural education

Internship education

National service (for example, VISTA and the Peace Corps)

Peace and justice work (off campus) and studies (on campus)

Service corps

Service-learning (person's first and primary affiliation)

Volunteerism/student activism

Work experience

Youth development, leadership, participation

*Suggested New Strands*

Citizenship education

Clinical training

Environmental action

Intergenerational learning

Urban Corps

# Appendix B:
# An Organizational Journey to Service-Learning

*Robert L. Sigmon*

*A Work in Progress. Add your individual and institutional journeys, and let us know what other important milestones we should add.*

## CIC
*Council of*
*Independent Colleges*

**Governmental Initiatives**

MORRILL AND HOMESTEAD ACT INITIATIVES (land grant colleges) focus on rural development, education

COOPERATIVE EDUCATION MOVEMENT—founded at University of Cincinnati (1903)

**Higher Education and Secondary Education**

Historically Black Colleges and Universities established, based on principles of combining work, service, and learning

Some Folk Schools in Appalachia become two- and four-year colleges with work, service, and learning connected

**Nineteenth and Early Twentieth Centuries**

**Business and Philanthropy**

Prominent businessmen build great wealth, create family foundations now funding many service and learning projects

**Education Associations and Religious Groups**

Missionaries send thousands abroad to help others

Voluntary associations with service focus (for example, YWCA, YMCA) prosper

**Intellectual Markers**

William James, John Dewey developing intellectual foundations of service-based learning

CIVILIAN
CONSERVATION
CORPS—required
ten hours learning
per week

NATIONAL YOUTH
ADMINISTRATION

WORK PROJECTS
ADMINISTRATION
(needed public work for
people who needed jobs)

GI BILL

1930s          1940s          1950s

EXPERIMENT IN
INTERNATIONAL
LIVING (1932)

LISLE FELLOWSHIPS
(Early 1930s)

AMERICAN
FRIENDS
SERVICE
COMMITTEE
(work camps in
United States
and other
countries)

Religious
denominations in
youth service programs
in the United States
and abroad
(post WWII)

Dewey continues writing
about linking experience
and education

**Governmental Initiatives**

PEACE CORPS

VISTA

WHITE HOUSE FELLOWS initiated

URBAN CORPS emerged, funded with federal work-study dollars (1966)

COLLEGE WORK-STUDY (1965)

**Higher Education and Secondary Education**

COMMUNITY COLLEGES ON THE SCENE with experiential learning and connections to practice settings

Political science departments sponsor legislative and public service programs

"Service-learning" phrase used to describe a TVA-funded project in East Tennessee with Oak Ridge Associated Universities—linking students and faculty with tributary area development organizations (1966–1967)

Experimental colleges emerge

**1960s**

**Business and Philanthropy**

FORD FOUNDATION support for National Urban Fellows and Urban Corps

**Education Associations and Religious Groups**

SCHOOL FOR INTERNATIONAL TRAINING founded by Experiment in International Living (1964)

NATIONAL SERVICE SECRETARIAT CONFERENCE ON NATIONAL SERVICE in Washington, D.C. (1968)

**Intellectual Markers**

James Coleman—exponent of alternating experience with schooling; Harrison and Hopkins article (1967); Phillips Roupp, *The Educational Use of the World,* Peace Corps publication

State government internship
programs in New Jersey,
North Carolina, Georgia,
and Massachusetts

ACTION
AGENCY
FORMED
(1971)

1971 WHITE
HOUSE
CONFERENCE ON
YOUTH report full
of calls for linking
service and learning

Professional
clinical training
involved in
linking learning
with service

UNIVERSITY
YEAR OF ACTION
(yearlong service
tied to academic
performance)

January terms popular,
with many experiments
linking learning and
service

URBAN SEMESTER
PROGRAMS
EMERGE

**1970s**

ATLANTA SERVICE LEARNING
CONFERENCES (1968, 1969)—
sponsors include Southern Regional
Education Board, U.S. Department of
Health, Education and Welfare, City
of Atlanta, Atlanta Urban Corps,
Peace Corps, and VISTA. (The 1968
conference focused on service;
the 1969 conference linked service
and learning as a policy thrust for
the future.)

*Associations begin:*
NATIONAL CENTER FOR PUBLIC
SERVICE INTERNSHIPS (1971),
SOCIETY FOR FIELD EXPERIENCE
EDUCATION (1971) (these two
merged in 1978 as National Society
for Internships and Experiential
Education)
ASSOCIATION FOR EXPERIENTIAL
EDUCATION (1972) (initial
conference in North Carolina in
1968; incorporated in 1972)
COOPERATIVE ASSESSMENT OF
EXPERIENTIAL LEARNING (CAEL)
founded in 1974. Name changes in
1977 to Council for the Advancement
of Experiential Learning and in 1984
to Council for Adult and Experiential
Learning

Civil rights movement strong;
Vietnam War and protests

**Governmental Initiatives**

Funding for AREA HEALTH ED CENTERS extends health manpower training into rural/community settings so students can serve and learn (started 1972)

NATIONAL STUDENT VOLUNTEER PROGRAM (became NATIONAL CENTER FOR SERVICE-LEARNING in 1979). Publishes *Synergist,* a journal promoting linking service and learning

Kettering Foundation publishes 3-volume *Service for Development Study* by Irene Pinkau, a comprehensive review of study-service outside the United States (1979)

**Higher Education and Secondary Education**

PRIVATE COLLEGES CREATE SPECIALIZED SERVICE-LEARNING PROGRAMS

**1970s (continued)**

**Business and Philanthropy**

AEE publishes *Experiential Education* journal; Jossey-Bass publishes series New Directions in Experiential Education; NSIEE newsletter grows and carries more articles

"Three Principles of Service-Learning" published in *Synergist* in 1979

**Education Associations and Religious Groups**

Conrad and Hedin research on value added to learning when service involved

**Intellectual Markers**

David Kolb work on experiential learning theory evolving

NCSL phased out; very little
government attention at
federal and state levels

POINTS OF
LIGHT
FOUNDATION
honors service
providers

NATIONAL
YOUTH
LEADERSHIP
COUNCIL—
preparing
future leaders
(1982)

CAMPUS
COMPACT
formed by
college
presidents
(1985)

Colleges and high schools
continue programs and
affiliations initiated earlier.
Primary meeting places are
NSIEE, AEE, CAEL, and
COOP ED conferences

Secondary school service and
learning programs gain in numbers

**1980s**

NATIONAL CENTER
FOR SERVICE
LEARNING FOR
EARLY
ADOLESCENTS
(1982)

CAMPUS OUTREACH
OPPORTUNITY LEAGUE—
student-led service advocacy (1984)

PARTNERSHIP
FOR SERVICE-
LEARNING—
international
opportunities
(1982)

John McKnight work on dangers in service
work. Donald Schön on reflective practitioners:
how professionals are trained and then work

**Governmental
Initiatives**

SCALE—student-initiated
literacy program (nation-
wide) founded in 1989

**Higher
Education
and Secondary
Education**

Spring and fall breaks create
many service opportunities,
some with learning

Carnegie Unit on
Service created (1987)

**1980s (continued)**

**Business and
Philanthropy**

AMERICAN YOUTH FOUNDATION
begins linking programs that connect
service and learning in 1988

**Education
Associations
and Religious
Groups**

YOUTH SERVICE
AMERICA—
promotes service
for youth (1986)

Wingspread *Principles of Good
Practice in Service-Learning*—
more than 70 organizations
collaborate to produce ten
principles (1989)

**Intellectual
Markers**

National Service Bill passed in 1994
(AmeriCorps and other programs
linking service with learning)

National and Community
Service Act of 1990 passed

Service-learning
network on Internet,
via University of
Colorado Peace
Studies Center

NSEE
develops five-
year High
School
Service
Learning
Initiative
(1991)

Campus Compact
expands (state
organizations,
three national
institutes, publica-
tions; more presi-
dents join)

AAHE Annual
Conference (March
1995), on linking of
service with learning

CIC *Serving
to Serve* project
Service-Learning
Chicago (1995)

Stanford Service-
Learning Institute
(1994)

**1990s**

20 BONNER SCHOLARS PROGRAMS
(19 private, 1 public) initiated, honor-
ing high school students who have
served and expecting four years of service and learning experience as condition of scholarship funds

UNCF/FORD
ten-college
program linking
direct service and
learning begun
(1995)

Dozens of state, regional,
and national conference
workshops on linking
service and learning of
many organizations and
institutions

Association of Supervision and
Curriculum Development endorses
importance of linking service with
learning (1993)

Publications: three-volume *Combining Service and
Learning* published 1990; R. Coles, *The Call of
Service;* Praxis I and II: Campus Coalitions;
COOL publications; Michigan Journal for
Community Service, Vol. 1, 1994; and many more

Strong emergence of civic arts, citizen education focus in higher
education (Barber, Battastoni, Lappé, others)

# References

Alinsky, S. *Rules for Radicals: A Practical Primer for Realistic Radicals.* New York: Random House, 1971.

Anderson, J., Hughes, L., and Permaul, J. S. "Research Agenda for Experiential Education in the 80s." PANEL Resource Paper, no. 14. Raleigh, N.C.: National Society for Internships and Experiential Education, 1984.

Argyris, C., and Schön, D. A. *Organizational Learning: A Theory of Action Perspective.* Menlo Park, Calif.: Addison-Wesley, 1978.

Astin, H., and Leland, C. *Women of Influence, Women of Vision: A Cross-Cultural Study of Leaders and Social Change.* San Francisco: Jossey-Bass, 1991.

Baker, B. E. "Are We Really Providing a Service? Some Guiding Principles of College-Level Service-Learning Programs." Unpublished master's thesis, University of Michigan, 1983.

Bandura, A. *Social Learning Theory.* Englewood Cliffs, N.J.: Prentice Hall, 1977.

Batchelder, D. "Developing Cross-Cultural Learning Skills." In D. Batchelder and E. G. Warner (eds.), *Beyond Experience: The Experiential Approach to Cross-Cultural Education.* Brattleboro, Vt.: Experiment Press, 1977.

Blau, P. *The Dynamics of Bureaucracy: A Study of Interpersonal Relations in Two Government Agencies.* (Rev. ed.) Chicago: University of Chicago Press, 1963.

Bloom, B. S., and others. *Taxonomy of Educational Objectives, Handbook I: Cognitive Domain.* New York: Longman, 1956.

Bok, D. *Higher Learning.* Cambridge, Mass.: Harvard University Press, 1986.

Bok, D. *Universities and the Future of America.* Durham, N.C.: Duke University Press, 1990.

Bowles, S. "The Post-Keynesian Capital-Labor Stalemate." *Socialist Review,* 1982, *65*(12(5)), 45–72.

Boyte, H. C. *CommonWealth: A Return to Citizen Politics.* New York: Free Press, 1989.

Bronfenbrenner, U. *The Ecology of Human Development: Experiments by Nature and Design.* Cambridge, Mass.: Harvard University Press, 1979.

Chisholm, L. A. "The Intersection of Church and College." *Views and News on Education,* 1987, *2*(1).

Colby, A., and Damon, W. *Some Do Care: Contemporary Lives of Moral Commitment.* New York: Free Press, 1994.

Coleman, J. "Differences Between Classroom and Experiential Learning." In M. T. Keeton (ed.), *Experiential Learning: Rationale, Characteristics, and Assessment.* San Francisco: Jossey-Bass, 1977.

Connolly, W. E. *The Terms of Political Discourse.* Princeton, N.J.: Princeton University Press, 1993.

Couto, R. A. *Streams of Idealism and Health Care Innovation: An Assessment of Service and Learning and Community Mobilization.* New York: Teachers College Press, 1982.

Cox, H. G. *The Secular City: Secularization and Urbanization in Theological Perspective.* New York: Macmillan, 1966.

Crosson, P. H. *Public Service in Higher Education: Practices and Priorities.* ASHE-ERIC Higher Education Research Report, no. 7. Washington, D.C.: Association for the Study of Higher Education, 1983.

Cruz, N. "A Challenge to the Notion of Service." In J. Kendall and Associates, *Combining Service and Learning: A Resource Book for Community and Public Service.* Raleigh, N.C.: National Society for Experiential Education, 1990.

Dewey, J. *Experience and Education.* New York: Macmillan, 1951. (Originally published 1938.)

Duley, J. S. (ed.). *Implementing Field Experience Education.* New Directions for Higher Education, no. 6. San Francisco: Jossey-Bass, 1974.

Duley, J. S. "Field Experience Education." In A. W. Chickering (ed.), *The Modern American College.* San Francisco: Jossey-Bass, 1981.

Duley, J. S., and Gordon, S. *College Sponsored Experiential Learning—A CAEL Handbook.* Princeton, N.J.: Council for Adult Experiential Learning, Educational Testing Service, 1977.

Ellis, S. J., and Noyes, K. H. *By the People: A History of Americans as Volunteers: An Evaluation Report on the Student Community Service Program.* Washington, D.C.: ACTION, Office of Policy Research and Evaluation, 1990.

Eskow, S. "Views from the Top." *Synergist,* 1980, *9*(1), 20–21.

Eyler, J., Giles, D. E., Jr., and Schmiede, A. *A Practitioner's Guide to Reflection in Service-Learning: Student Voices and Reflections.* Nashville, Tenn.: Vanderbilt University, 1996.

Faimen, R. N., and Olivier, M. E. *A Question of Partnership: Institutions of Higher Education as a Resource in the Solution of National Problems.*

Report and Recommendations. Washington, D.C.: National Association of State Universities and Land-Grant Colleges, 1972.

Farmer, J. A., Jr., Sheates, P. H., and Deshler, J. D. *Developing Community Service and Continuing Education Programs in California Higher Education Institutions.* Sacramento, Calif.: Coordination Council for Higher Education, 1972.

Flanagan, J. "The Critical Incident Technique." *Psychological Bulletin,* 1954, 5(4), 327–358.

Freire, P. *Pedagogy of the Oppressed.* (M. Bergman Ramos, trans.) New York: Herder and Herder, 1970.

Freire, P. *Education for Critical Consciousness.* New York: Seabury Press, 1973.

Giles, D. E., Jr., and Freed, J. B. "Service Learning Dimensions of Field Study: The Cornell Human Ecology Field Study Program." Paper presented at the National Conference on Service-Learning, Washington, D.C., March 1985.

Goffman, E. *Asylums: Essays on the Social Situation of Mental Patients and Other Inmates.* New York: Doubleday, 1961.

Guralnik, D. B. *Webster's New World Dictionary of the American Language.* New York: Warner Books, 1984.

Harrison, R., and Hopkins, R. "The Design of Cross-Cultural Training: An Alternative to the University Model." *Journal of Applied Behavioral Science,* 1967, 3(4), 431–460.

Harvard University. *The University and the City.* Cambridge, Mass.: Harvard Today Publications, 1969.

Honnet, E. P., and Poulsen, S. J. *Principles of Good Practice for Combining Service and Learning.* Racine, Wis.: The Johnson Foundation, 1989.

Horton, M. *The Long Haul.* New York: Doubleday, 1990.

Illich, I. *Deschooling Society.* New York: HarperCollins, 1972.

Jackson, M. "A Comparative Descriptive Study of Michigan State University Student Volunteers and the Relationship of Their Background and Individual Characteristics to Student Activists and to Non-Volunteer Students." Unpublished doctoral dissertation, Michigan State University, 1972.

Keeton, M. "Experiential Learning." In *Innovation Abstracts.* Austin: University of Texas, 1983.

Kendall, J. C. "Combining Service and Learning: An Introduction." In J. C. Kendall and Associates, *Combining Service and Learning: A Resource Book for Community and Public Service.* Raleigh, N.C.: National Society for Experiential Education, 1990.

Kendall, J. C., and others. *Strengthening Experiential Education Within Your Institution.* Raleigh, N.C.: National Society for Internships and Experiential Education, 1986.

Kesey, K. *One Flew over the Cuckoo's Nest.* New York: Viking Press, 1962.

Klemp, G., Jr. "Three Factors of Success in the World of Work: Implications for Curriculum in Higher Education." In D. W. Vermilye (ed.), *Relating Work and Experience.* San Francisco: Jossey-Bass, 1977.

Knefelkamp, L. *Integrating Adult Development with Higher Education Practice.* Current Issues in Higher Education, no. 5. Washington, D.C.: American Association of Higher Education, 1980.

Knowles, M. S. *Self-Directed Learning: A Guide for Learners and Teachers.* New York: Cambridge Book Company, 1975.

Koepplin, L. W., and Wilson, D. A. (eds.). *The Future of State Universities: Issues in Teaching, Research, and Public Service.* New Brunswick, N.J.: Rutgers University Press, 1985.

Kolb, D. A. *Experiential Learning: Experience as the Source of Learning and Development.* Englewood Cliffs, N.J.: Prentice Hall, 1984.

Kozol, J. *Death at an Early Age.* New York: Bantam Books, 1968.

Lewin, K. *Resolving Social Conflicts: Field Theory in Social Science.* Washington, D.C.: American Psychological Association, 1997.

Liebow, E. *Tally's Corner: A Study of Negro Streetcorner Men.* Boston: Little, Brown, 1967.

Liu, G. "Origins, Evolution, and Progress: Reflections on the Community Service Movement in American Higher Education 1985–1995." In R. Battistoni and K. Morton (eds.), *Community Service in Higher Education: A Decade of Development.* Providence, R.I.: Providence College, 1996.

Luce, J. *Service-Learning: An Annotated Bibliography for Linking Service with the Curriculum.* Raleigh, N.C.: National Society for Internships and Experiential Education, 1988.

Malinowski, B. *A Diary in the Strict Sense of the Term.* (N. Guterman, trans.) New York: Harcourt Brace, 1967.

Mead, M. *Blackberry Winter: My Earlier Years.* New York: Morrow, 1972.

Newton, H. P. *Revolutionary Suicide.* New York: Harcourt Brace, 1973.

Permaul, J. S. "Monitoring and Supporting Experiential Learning." PANEL Resource Paper, no. 5. Raleigh, N.C.: National Society for Internships and Experiential Education, 1981.

Perry, W. *Forms of Intellectual and Ethical Development in the College Years: A Scheme.* New York: Holt, Rinehart and Winston, 1970.

Pollack, S. S. *Higher Education's Contested Service Role: A Framework for Analysis and Historical Survey.* Stanford, Calif.: Haas Center for Public Service, 1996.

Postman, N., and Weingartner, C. *Teaching as a Subversive Activity.* New York: Delacorte Press, 1969.

Postman, N., and Weingartner, C. *The Soft Revolution: Student Handbook for Turning Schools Around.* New York: Delacorte Press, 1971.

Powdermaker, H. *Stranger and Friend: The Way of an Anthropologist.* New York: Norton, 1966.

Reagon, B. "Coalition Politics: Returning the Century." In B. Smith (ed.), *Home Girls: A Black Feminist Anthology.* New York: Kitchen Table: Women of Color Press, 1983.

Resnick, L. "Learning in School and Out." *Educational Researcher,* 1987, *16*(9), 13–20.

Rhoads, R. A. *Community Service and Higher Learning: Explorations of the Caring Self.* Albany: State University of New York Press, 1997.

Rudolph, F. *The American College and University.* Athens: University of Georgia Press, 1962.

Schön, D. A. *The Reflective Practitioner.* New York: Basic Books, 1983.

Schön, D. A. *Educating the Reflective Practitioner.* San Francisco: Jossey-Bass, 1987.

Shumer, R. D. "Learning in the Workplace: An Ethnographic Study of the Relationship Between Schools and Experience-Based Educational Programs." Unpublished doctoral dissertation, School of Education and Information Studies, University of California, Los Angeles, 1987.

Sigmon, R. L. "Service-Learning: Three Principles." *Synergist,* 1979, *9,* 10.

Southern Regional Education Board. *Service-Learning in the South: Higher Education and Public Service.* Atlanta: Southern Regional Education Board, 1969.

Stanton, T. K. *Field Study: Information for Faculty.* Ithaca, N.Y.: Human Ecology Field Study Office, Cornell University, 1983.

Stanton, T. K. "Service-Learning: Groping Toward a Definition." *Experiential Education,* 1987, *12*(1), 4.

Stanton, T. *Integrating Public Service with Academic Study: The Faculty Role.* A Report of Campus Compact: The Project for Public and Community Service. Providence, R.I.: Campus Compact, 1990a.

Stanton, T. "Liberal Arts, Experiential Learning and Public Service: Necessary Ingredients for Socially Responsible Undergraduate Education." In J. C. Kendall (ed.), *Combining Service and Learning: A Resource Book for Community and Public Service.* Raleigh, N.C.: National Society for Internships and Experiential Education, 1990b.

Stanton, T. "Academic Study and Community Service: Making the Connections." Unpublished remarks made at the First Annual Conference of the Washington State Campus Compact, Seattle, Apr. 1992.

Stanton, T. "The Critical Incident Journal." In A. Watters and M. Ford (eds.), *A Guide for Change: Resources for Implementing Community Service Writing.* New York: McGraw-Hill, 1994.

Taylor, B. *Parting the Waters: America in the King Years 1954–63.* New York: Simon & Schuster, 1988.

Townsend, R. C. "The Possibilities of Field Work." *College English,* 1973, *34*(4), 481–499.

Trinh, T. M. *Woman, Native, Other: Writing Postcoloniality and Feminism.* Bloomington: Indiana University Press, 1989.

Veysey, L. R. *The Emergence of the American University.* Chicago: University of Chicago Press, 1965.

Wagner, J. "Academic Excellence and Community Service Through Experiential Learning: Encouraging Students to Teach." In *Proceedings of the Ninth Annual University of California Conference on Experiential Learning,* Santa Barbara, Calif., 1986.

Wax, R. *Doing Fieldwork: Warnings and Advice.* Chicago: University of Chicago Press, 1971.

Whitham, M., and Stanton, T. "Prefield Preparation: What, Why, How." In S. E. Brooks and J. E. Althof (eds.), *Enriching the Liberal Arts Through Experiential Learning.* San Francisco: Jossey-Bass, 1979.

Whyte, W. F. *Street Corner Society: The Social Structure of an Italian Slum.* (4th ed.) Chicago: University of Chicago Press, 1955.

Whyte, W. F. *Participatory Action Research.* Thousand Oaks, Calif.: Sage, 1991.

Wigginton, E. *Sometimes a Shining Moment: The Foxfire Experience.* New York: Anchor Books, 1985.

Wutzdorff, A., and Giles, D. E., Jr. "Service-Learning in Postsecondary Education." In J. Schine (ed.), *96th Yearbook of the National Society for the Study of Education.* Chicago: University of Chicago Press, 1997.

# Index

Work-Study. *See* College Work-Study Program

**Y**

Yablonski, J. A., 69, 78n.6
Yale University, Dwight Hall, 28, 81–82, 93n.1, 120n.2, 170–171
Young, A., 74
Young, C., 182
Youth Service America (YSA), 169, 256